macmost .com
Guide to
Switching
to the Mac

Gary Rosenzweig

800 East 96th Street, Indianapolis, Indiana 46240 USA

MacMost.com Guide to Switching to the Mac

ISBN-13: 978-0-7897-3962-9

ISBN-10: 0-7897-3962-3

Library of Congress Cataloging-in-Publication Data:

Rosenzweig, Gary.
  MacMost.com guide to switching to the Mac / Gary Rosenzweig.—1st ed.
       p. cm.
  Includes index.
  ISBN 978-0-7897-3962-9
  1. Mac OS. 2. Operating systems (Computers) 3. Macintosh (Computer)—Programming. I. CleverMedia, Inc. II. MacMost.com. III. Title. IV. Title: Switching to the Mac.
  QA76.76.O63R6814 2010
  005.265—dc22
                         2009031289

Printed in the United States of America

First Printing: September 2009

Trademarks

All terms mentioned in this book that are known to be trademarks or service marks have been appropriately capitalized. Que Publishing cannot attest to the accuracy of this information. Use of a term in this book should not be regarded as affecting the validity of any trademark or service mark.

Warning and Disclaimer

Every effort has been made to make this book as complete and as accurate as possible, but no warranty or fitness is implied. The information provided is on an "as is" basis. The author and the publisher shall have neither liability nor responsibility to any person or entity with respect to any loss or damages arising from the information contained in this book.

Bulk Sales

Que Publishing offers excellent discounts on this book when ordered in quantity for bulk purchases or special sales. For more information, please contact

> **U.S. Corporate and Government Sales**
> **1-800-382-3419**
> **corpsales@pearsontechgroup.com**

For sales outside of the U.S., please contact

> **International Sales**
> **international@pearson.com**

Associate Publisher
Greg Wiegand

Acquisitions Editor
Laura Norman

Development Editor
Todd Brakke

Managing Editor
Patrick Kanouse

Project Editor
Ken Johnson

Copy Editor
Margaret Berson

Indexer
Ken Johnson

Proofreader
Katherin Ruiz

Technical Editor
Yvonne Johnson

Publishing Coordinator
Cindy Teeters

Book Designer
Anne Jones

Compositor
TnT Design, Inc.

CONTENTS AT A GLANCE

TABLE OF CONTENTS

Prologue

This Book Is Only the Beginning

You hold in your hands the *MacMost.com Guide to Switching to the Mac*. This book will teach you what you need to know about using Macintosh computers and Mac OS X 10.6, or Snow Leopard, as it is more commonly called.

But time marches on. By the time you get this book, chances are that one or more updates to Snow Leopard will have been released. Also, more Mac models will be in stores and old ones will have been updated.

Things will change. So how can you stay up to date?

Fortunately, MacMost.com is much more than just this book. It is a website with hundreds of video tutorials and articles. The library of information dates back a few years and will continue forward.

While the words and images in this book will remain the same, the videos, articles, and information at MacMost.com will constantly be updated, So look at this book as a starting point in your Macintosh journey. That's a journey that will never end, as new OS updates, software, and hardware are released. Then look to MacMost.com as your source for keeping up to date with the latest news, tutorials, reviews, and even commentary about the world of Apple computers.

You can visit **http://macmost.com/book/** for information specific to the pages in this book. Then you can visit the main page, **http://macmost.com**, for your daily dose of Mac know-how.

I'll see you there.

Gary Rosenzweig

About the Author

In 1987, the year Gary Rosenzweig started college, Drexel University in Philadelphia had the foresight to require every student to purchase a computer. Better still, they required that computer be a Macintosh.

From the 1987 Macintosh SE with two floppy disk drives and a little monochrome screen, to his current 2009 Mac Pro with two four-core Xeon processors, Gary has always owned a Mac.

His Mac was his primary tool used in creating games and websites from 1994 to the present day. But it wasn't until 2007 that he took his love of Macs to the professional level with the launch of the MacMost site and video podcast.

At first, MacMost covered Apple news each week. But soon it evolved into a more frequent show with tutorials, tips, news, and reviews. The website grew as well, featuring iPhone games, ringtones, a weekly newsletter, and other features.

Gary has also written many books, most on programming using Macromedia/Adobe software like Director and Flash. He lives in Denver, Colorado, with his wife, Debby, and daughter, Luna. Also a dog and too many cats.

The home page for this book is http://macmost.com/book/, but if you are interested in more information about the author, you can also visit Gary's website at http://garyrosenzweig.com and follow Gary on Twitter at http://twitter.com/rosenz.

Dedication

I'd like to dedicate this book to my grandfather, Herbert Pitt. He passed away when I was very young, but I think he would have been proud of what I've accomplished. I wish I could have shared my success with him.

Acknowledgments

Thanks, as always, to my wife, Debby and my daughter, Luna. Also thanks to the rest of my family: Jacqueline Rosenzweig, Jerry Rosenzweig, Larry Rosenzweig, Tara Rosenzweig, Rebecca Jacob, Barbara Shifrin, Richard Shifrin, Barbara H. Shifrin, Tage Thomsen, Anne Thomsen, Andrea Thomsen, and Sami Balestri.

Thanks to the people who helped get the MacMost video podcast started: Jay Shaffer, Molly Lynn, Layle McFatridge, Eve Park, William Follett, David Feldman, and Kevin Frutiger.

Special thanks to all the people who watch the show and participate at the MacMost website.

Thanks to the podcasters and web video makers who inspired me: Leo Laporte, Cali Lewis, Anji Bee, Victor Cajiao, and many others.

Thanks to Apple, iTunes, Blip.tv, YouTube, Google AdSense, the folks at the Cherry Creek Apple Store in Denver, The Captain, Arlen Britton, and "The Cabal of Which We Do Not Speak."

Thanks also to everyone at Que and Pearson Education for their hard work on this book.

We Want to Hear from You!

As the reader of this book, *you* are our most important critic and commentator. We value your opinion and want to know what we're doing right, what we could do better, what areas you'd like to see us publish in, and any other words of wisdom you're willing to pass our way.

As an associate publisher for Que Publishing, I welcome your comments. You can email or write me directly to let me know what you did or didn't like about this book—as well as what we can do to make our books better.

Please note that I cannot help you with technical problems related to the topic of this book. We do have a User Services group, however, where I will forward specific technical questions related to the book.

When you write, please be sure to include this book's title and author as well as your name, email address, and phone number. I will carefully review your comments and share them with the author and editors who worked on the book.

Email: feedback@quepublishing.com

Mail: Greg Wiegand
                Associate Publisher
                Que Publishing
                800 East 96th Street
                Indianapolis, IN 46240 USA

Reader Services

Visit our website and register this book at informit.com/register for convenient access to any updates, downloads, or errata that might be available for this book.

Introduction

You could be switching to Mac for many reasons. Perhaps you were impressed with the clean interface or sharp design. Maybe you were tired of common problems with Windows like dealing with virus protection or frequent crashes.

You could be switching to Mac from Windows XP or Vista, or perhaps an older version of Windows or another operating system. Or, this could be your first computer, or your first personal computer after only using one at work.

Whatever your reason for buying your first Mac, you can now start enjoying the best computing experience available.

A Mac is a combination of hardware—the physical computer—and software—the program that reacts to what you type and click and displays information on your screen.

The hardware is your MacBook, iMac, Mac Pro, or Mac Mini. The software is Mac OS X, the Macintosh operating system. You get both when you buy a Mac.

But you don't really care about that. You want to get things done, create art, and write stories. You want to connect to the Internet and learn, shop, and explore. You want to organize your photos, make videos, and compose music.

Mac OS X's greatest strength is that it doesn't get in your way when trying to do these things. Instead it enables you. And, at times, it can even inspire you.

> **NOTE**
>
> It's true. Your Mac can inspire you, just as a fine set of brushes can inspire a painter, a beautiful landscape can inspire a photographer, or new lab equipment can inspire a scientist. Your new Mac can help you reach your creative potential. Or, it can simply help you get your work done.

But Mac OS X is a tool, and as with any tool, it is important to know how to use it. This book looks at all of the different aspects of Mac OS X and how to use it well. We'll also look at the Mac hardware, products that work with your Mac, other software that comes with your Mac, and common problems and questions people have when switching to Mac.

Who Should Read This Book

This book is targeted toward anyone who has just bought their first Mac. You could be a switcher, having previously used Windows, or you could have been a Mac user a long time ago, but are unfamiliar with the way that modern Macs work. Mac OS X is quite an advancement over the older Mac operating systems of the 80s and 90s. And with every version, it keeps getting better and better.

Or, perhaps you have been using a Mac for a while now, but feel that you really haven't explored its full power. Have you created a movie in iMovie? Composed a song in Garage Band? Organized your week with iCal?

This book takes you deeper into Mac OS X and tells you what you need to know to get started with the most frequently used aspects of your computer and the applications that come with it.

> **NOTE**
>
> Macs come with software to help you write, communicate, organize your life, edit video, manage your photos, and even compose music. But you can find even more free and inexpensive software to do almost anything on your computer.

Although it is fun to explore the features of your new Mac, it can also be useful to have a guide show you around. Let me help you get the most from your Mac!

What You Need to Know

This is a book for switchers, so a basic understanding of computers is assumed. That said, even if this is your first computer, you may have picked up that basic understanding at work or school.

You should know how to use a mouse and keyboard. You should know what a file is and that files are stored in folders on your hard drive.

After all, Mac and Windows are essentially the same. The difference is in the details. So if you know how to manipulate icons on the screen by dragging and dropping them, and you know how to click on a menu and select a menu item, you are all set to start using this book.

At the beginning of each chapter is a brief statement about "Who Should Read This Chapter." You might not need every chapter in this book. Some chapters may be about things you already know. Other chapters may be about subjects that you are not interested in.

The first few chapters of this book cover the basics and build on each other, and later chapters are about specific applications and topics. You may want to read the first eight chapters to get the basics. Then, decide on the next chapters on a subject-by-subject basis. The last four chapters are perhaps the most important and should be read by all.

Who Am I, and What Is MacMost?

Hello. I'm Gary and I'm a Mac.

I bought my first Mac in 1987. It was a little Mac SE with two disk drives, a monochrome screen, and no way to connect to anything.

Since then I've used PowerBooks, various Mac towers and desktops, iMacs, and MacBooks. I've used Macs working in desktop publishing, programming, multimedia, game development, web development, and writing. But I also use Macs to organize my photos, video, and social networking.

I've always been a Mac guy. At one point, in the mid-1990s, I was forced to use a Windows computer. I got by with that at work, and a Mac at home. But when deadlines approached and I was asked to put in extra hours, I replied: "OK, but if you really want me to get things done fast, I'm bringing in my Mac!"

Two years ago I was running a small company making websites and games for the Web when web video started to take off. We had the talent to make our own web videos, so we started a variety of shows. But most of our efforts failed because we lacked the passion behind the topics they covered.

Then I realized that the number one topic in the office was always Apple. We all used Macs and had iPods. We followed the Apple culture. We talked about it constantly.

So, why not do a show about Apple? That's how MacMost was born.

Our passion for Apple meant that MacMost soon took over all of our video efforts. Soon, it became our most important website, overshadowing even the game sites that we had for more than 10 years.

MacMost is a website, a video podcast, and a community. Every week brings several more episodes of the video show. Each episode features a new tip, tutorial, review, or news summary. They all help you get the most from your Mac.

> **NOTE**
>
> What is a video podcast? A podcast is a regularly updated audio or video show that you can subscribe to using your Mac's iTunes application. They are almost all free and cover a wide variety of topics, from sketch comedy to financial news. They are produced mostly by individuals and small companies. You can find out more in the section "Subscribing to Podcasts" in Chapter 17, "Managing Your Music and Video."

Each week also brings a new edition of our free newsletter. There are recommendations for free and inexpensive software applications you can download, tips, a weekly news summary, and even iPhone app recommendations.

In addition to getting started with your Mac using this book, I invite you to join the community at MacMost.com and learn how to get the most from your Mac!

- The MacMost website—http://macmost.com
- Subscribe to the video podcast—http://macmost.com/itunes
- Subscribe to the email newsletter—http://macmost.com/newsletter
- Updates to this book—http://macmost.com/book
- Follow MacMost on Twitter—http://macmost.com/twitter
- Follow MacMost on Facebook—http://facebook.com/macmost

WHO SHOULD READ THIS CHAPTER:

If you haven't yet bought a Mac, and are not sure which model is the right one for you, you should read this chapter immediately. However, if you already have a Mac, you may skip right ahead to Chapter 2, "Examining Mac Hardware."

1

Buying a Mac

So you've decided to buy a Mac. Congratulations! Macs are great computers and your Mac will soon be a valuable tool for work, recreation, and communication.

Perhaps, however, you're not sure which Mac to buy. You are not alone. There are many choices. Most people who switch to Mac have this same question. Which one?

You've got three major choices in a desktop machine: the Mac mini, the iMac, and the Mac Pro. And you have three choices in a notebook: the MacBook, MacBook Pro, and MacBook Air.

So which one is right for you? In this chapter we'll sort that out.

The Mac Product Line

Let's take a quick look at the Mac product line, without going into specifics. That will be difficult because the current Mac models are always changing. By the time this book gets into your hands, the chances are pretty good that one or more of these products will be updated.

So we'll look at each according to what is available in mid 2009. The spirit of each product is likely to remain the same, even if some of the details change.

First, let's review each model. Then in the next section, "What Do the Options Mean?" we'll look at the specific features, like memory and hard drive space, and what they mean.

The iMac

The flagship Macintosh product is the iMac. This is the descendant of the product that saved and revitalized Apple in 1998. It is an all-in-one machine, which means that the computer and the monitor are in a single body.

The original iMac used a CRT monitor. But in 2002, the iMac G4 moved the line to an attached flat-panel LCD.

> **FYI—MONITORS**
>
> There are two types of computer monitors: CRT and LCD. CRT, which stands for cathode ray tube, is the large bulky monitors that look like picture tube TV sets. They are rarely sold with new computers any more, but you may still have them in your workplace.
>
> The new monitors are all LCD, or liquid crystal display. These are flat panels and are included as the screens on all iMacs and MacBooks sold today. Although they were originally more expensive than CRT monitors, the prices have come down far enough to make CRTs obsolete.

The third incarnation, the iMac G5, put the entire body behind the LCD display. This variation remains more or less how the iMac looks today (see Figure 1.1).

Figure 1.1

The iMac with a dual-core Intel processor, aluminum body, and LCD screen, circa January 2009. Photo Courtesy of Apple, Inc.

The iMac comes with a keyboard and mouse. The optical media drive plays and creates CDs and DVDs. You also get a set of USB2 expansion ports, a port for an external monitor, a speaker jack, and an audio line-in jack.

FYI—OPTICAL DRIVE

An *optical drive* is also called a CD-ROM drive or a DVD drive. CD stands for Compact Disc, and DVD stands for Digital Video Disc. The drive is capable of reading CDs with data on them, called CD-ROMs. It can also read DVDs with data on them, which store about six times as much data as a CD. To the eye, CDs and DVDs look the same.

Your optical drive can also play music CDs through your computer's speakers, and video DVDs on the computer screen.

You can create your own data, music, or video CDs and DVDs with the help of software that comes with all Macs.

The iMac comes in two screen sizes: 20-inch which has a native resolution of 1680×1050 pixels and 24-inch with a native resolution of 1920×1200 pixels. The larger the screen resolution, the more content you can fit on the screen. If you plan on using graphics programs or developing websites, you want as large of a screen as you can get. But if you plan on just visiting websites and writing documents and email, you can use a smaller screen.

You can get up to 8 gigabytes of memory in an iMac, but the base models come with only 2 or 4 gigabytes. For typical users, the memory that comes with your Mac is probably fine, but graphics professionals may want to consider adding more. You can always purchase and add more memory later on.

The Mac Mini

The Mac mini is the headless iMac. There's simply no display. Instead, you get a very compact box that contains the computer and optical drive. To bring costs down further, it comes without a keyboard or mouse. So you can reuse an old USB keyboard and mouse, buy one from Apple, or get a third-party keyboard and mouse.

NOTE

You can buy a USB keyboard from Apple for $49, the same one that comes with an iMac. New iMacs ship with a small keyboard without a numeric keypad, while older ones had the keypad. You can find both from Apple for the same price. Apple also sells wireless Bluetooth keyboards that will work with your Mac mini for $79. You can also get cheap third-party USB keyboards for as little as $10.

Cheap mice also run around $10, or you can buy an Apple Mighty Mouse for $49. If your old PC used a USB mouse, you should be able to use that mouse with your Mac mini. A PC USB keyboard might not work, however, because it is most likely missing the all-important Apple command key.

Figure 1.2 shows the Mac mini, circa January 2009. One of the reasons it can be so small is that the power supply is external, much like the power supply of a laptop. So in addition to the Mac mini itself, you've got an additional piece of hardware sitting on the floor by your power strip.

Figure 1.2
The Mac mini is tiny. Not much bigger than this book, actually. Photo Courtesy of Apple, Inc.

The Mac mini is the smallest and the most often overlooked model. However, it is also the only model to have fan clubs. People who like the mini love it. There are online communities devoted to doing things like installing the Mac mini in home theater systems and cars.

The mini weighs in at less than 3 pounds, and is only 6.5 inches square and 2 inches tall.

The Mac Pro

The king of all Macs is the Mac Pro. Descended from a long line of towers and top-of-the-line professional machines, the Mac Pro takes the shape of a large aluminum box that opens to give access to expansion card slots, disk drive bays, and memory slots. Figure 1.3 shows the Mac Pro, probably the largest and heaviest Mac ever made.

Figure 1.3
The Mac Pro is the one Mac to rule them all. Photo Courtesy of Apple, Inc.

The Pro does share some things in common with the little mini, however. It comes without a monitor, so you have to supply your own. However, you do get a keyboard and mouse.

It also comes with the most powerful of processors—quad-core Intel chips. This makes it ideal for heavy lifting like video editing and high-resolution image editing.

There are two main configurations of Mac Pro: a single quad-core processor or two quad-core processors, for a total of eight cores.

One area the Mac Pro excels in is expandability. The eight-core model can take up to 32GB of memory. The Mac Pro can fit four hard drives inside. It also has some expansion card slots for adding various pieces of hardware.

The MacBook

Apple wasn't the first to make a portable computer, but with its PowerBook series of laptops it really pushed the market forward in the early 90s. Laptops continue to be a major part of Apple's product line today with the MacBook and its variations. The basic MacBook line underwent a thorough shakeup in mid-2009. Most Mac notebooks are now part of the MacBook Pro line, and there is only a single budget MacBook model to stand by itself. It retains the white plastic look used in MacBooks for the past several years (see Figure 1.4).

Figure 1.4
The lone MacBook model is made from white plastic, which brings down the price somewhat.

The MacBook is an all-in-one computer just like the iMac. Actually, it is even more so, as the keyboard and trackpad are built in as well. Also contained in the body is a battery. The only external part is the power cord and power supply.

MacBooks strike a balance between portability and power. The expansion potential for a MacBook is minimal, with just some USB2 ports and a video port as your only options.

The MacBook Pro

The big brother to the MacBook is the MacBook Pro. Visually, the biggest difference is an aluminum case, as you can see in Figure 1.5.

Figure 1.5

The MacBook Pro sports a unibody aluminum case. Photo Courtesy of Apple, Inc.

There are three sizes of MacBook Pro: 13-inch, 15-inch, and 17-inch. The smallest has a 1280×800 screen, the largest a 1920×1200 screen, and the middle child has a 1440×900 screen.

The MacBook Pro adds power and expandability over the MacBook. You've got a FireWire port to match the USB2 ports. This can come in handy for accepting input from digital video cameras. You've also got an SD card slot in the 13- and 15-inch models, and an ExpressCard 34 expansion slot in the 17-inch model. Those SD card slots are great for photographers who use SD cards.

The MacBook Air

The final variation of the Macintosh is the MacBook Air, shown in Figure 1.6. Like the basic MacBook, it is a consumer-level basic laptop, only less. Gone is the internal optical drive. The hard drive is smaller and the processor is slower.

Figure 1.6

The MacBook Air is thin and light. Photo Courtesy of Apple, Inc.

What you get in return is simple: it weighs only three pounds. For frequent travelers and people who carry a laptop around all day, this was enough for them to switch to the Air the day it was released.

Thanks to the video port and single USB2 port, you can still expand your Air to include a larger external monitor, keyboard, and mouse. You can even get a special USB2 Apple optical drive, or share the internal drive of another Mac.

What Do the Options Mean?

Each Mac model varies not only in appearance, but also in specific features. Let's examine the main features you should be looking at when deciding to buy a Mac. This guide will not only help you choose between the current six models, but also any future variations that Apple produces.

CPU

The CPU, or central processing unit, is the "brain" of your Mac. The faster your CPU, the more powerful your computer.

FYI—PROCESSOR SPEED

Gigahertz, or GHz, is used as a measurement of the speed of a microprocessor. It tells you how many cycles per second occur inside the chip. A single hertz means that one cycle occurs per second—so one instruction can be executed every second. One gigahertz means that one billion individual instructions can be executed every second.

For a modern computer to do just about anything, it needs to run millions of tiny instructions. So the faster the processor, the quicker you'll see results when you use your computer.

But speed is not the only measure of a processor. Today we have chips that are multicore. This means that a single computer chip actually holds more than one processor. They can execute two or more instructions simultaneously.

Most Macs come with dual-core processors. The Mac Pro comes with quad-core processors capable of running four instructions at the same time. In addition, one version of the Mac Pro come with two quad-core processors, meaning that they can run eight instructions simultaneously.

System Memory

How much memory your Mac has also affects its speed. Back in the early days of personal computing, memory affected what you could do. A more complex program required more memory. Simple ones required less.

But that is no longer true, as memory is now shared between actual memory chips and the hard drive inside the computer—a technique called "virtual memory." So even a machine with very little memory will have plenty to run whatever program you want.

However, the portions of memory stored on the hard disk take a lot longer to access than the memory stored in chips. So the more memory you have, the faster your applications run.

New Macs come with at least 2GB of memory. A Mac Pro can currently hold up to 32GB. For most users, about 2GB is enough in 2009. If you've got the money and the need to run more intense applications like video editors, 4GB or more may be a good investment.

Graphics Processor

As powerful as modern CPUs are, they still don't do all of the computing inside a modern machine. A lot of work needs to be done to take the data inside the computer and display it in pretty windows on a pretty desktop on your screen.

For this, a second microprocessor and supporting chips perform the graphics processing in your Mac. Just as with the CPU, these chips can be fast or slow. These chips are made by two different rival companies: ATI and Nvidia.

To confuse things even further, graphics processors have their own memory. So you might see one Mac with 256MB of video memory and another with 512MB.

FYI—MEMORY MEASUREMENTS

In 2009, system memory is almost always measured in GB (gigabytes), or just "gigs," but many graphics cards are still measured in MB (megabytes). There are 1,024 megabytes in a gigabyte. So a graphics card with 512MB has half a gig.

Video memory is used to store pieces of the display—like windows, text, backgrounds, and so on. In 3D applications, textures are stored in video memory as well. The more video memory you have, the faster complex screens can be drawn.

If you are wondering what a "complex screen" is, look no further than your desktop. You've got a background, windows, the dock, the menu bar, icons, and so on. So even just displaying your computer's desktop after starting it up is a task that relies heavily on the graphics processor.

The power of a graphics processor also determines the maximum screen size you can use with your Mac. Most models are capable of handling a large 30-inch display with 2,560 pixels across, but even larger screens may be in our future.

Optical Drive

In 2009 almost all Macs come with what is called a Super Drive. It can read and write CDs and DVDs in almost any format. It can even read dual-layer DVDs, which contain twice as much data as a standard DVD.

In addition, a Super Drive can write both kinds of discs as well, including dual-layer DVDs.

With your optical drive, you will be able to import and play music CDs, watch video DVDs, create your own mix CDs, burn your home videos to DVD, and back up or archive your data.

Only the MacBook Air is missing an optical drive, and it comes with the capability to use an external optical drive plugged into the USB port, which Apple sells for $99.

USB2 Ports

All Macs include USB2 ports. USB2 is a type of connection that allows you to hook up almost any peripheral, starting with the keyboard and mouse. You can also plug in external hard drives, printers, image scanners, digital cameras, and so on.

It is nice to have as many USB2 ports as possible. However, all you really need is one, as you can plug a USB2 hub into that one port and turn one into many.

The original USB ports used in the first iMacs were slow and only suitable for the keyboard, mouse, and perhaps a low-end digital camera. USB2 ports are an order of magnitude faster and can be used to connect even live video devices and fast hard drives.

The MacBook Air comes with just one USB port. In contrast, the Mac Pro has five—two on the front and three in the back, as you can see in Figure 1.7.

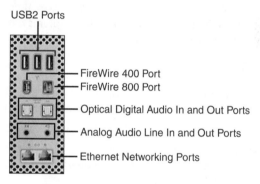

Figure 1.7

A recent configuration of ports found on the back of the Mac Pro. Photo courtesy of Apple, Inc.

FireWire Ports

FireWire is an alternative to USB2, used mostly for external hard drives and video cameras. It is also known as an IEEE 1394 interface and it is called that on some devices.

FireWire comes in two speeds: 400Mbit/sec and 800Mbit/sec. A port that supports the higher speed also supports devices running at the lower speed—which is what we find on the MacBook Pros.

The two speeds have ports that look a little different as well. Adapters can be bought to hook a 400Mbit/sec device into the square 800Mbit/sec port.

All Macs except the MacBook Air and MacBook have a FireWire 800 port. The Mac Pro has two of them. The MacBook Air has none, and the current MacBook is the only model with a FireWire 400 port.

Many cameras use a smaller connection port but usually provide a cable that goes from one size to the other. However, video cameras with IEEE 1394 ports are notorious for not including any FireWire cable at all, requiring excited new video camera owners to rush to the nearest Apple Store to buy one.

Video Ports

Two primary types of video display ports are found on computers and displays: VGA and DVI. The first is the old standard, usually used to drive old CRT monitors. The second is the digital standard, used in most new LCD screens today.

Until October 2008, Apple appeared to be supporting DVI throughout its product line. Some machines included DVI-to-VGA adapters so you could plug into older monitors and presentation projectors. The iMac and MacBook began to use a mini-DVI plug but came with an adapter to make it easy to plug into a standard-sized DVI screen.

However, this all changed in October 2008 when Apple put Mini DisplayPort ports on their MacBooks, MacBook Pros, and MacBook Airs. They promised to put DisplayPort on all of their other machines as well.

This little port requires an adapter to hook up to almost any type of screen. Apple sells one for VGA and one for DVI. A more expensive adapter is required to power a large monitor, if it requires a Dual-Link DVI connection.

Hard Drive

Today's Mac is more than just a computer—it is a media storage device. You store music, photos, and video on it. Well, actually, to be more accurate, you store those things on the hard drive.

This is why having a large hard drive may be important to you. If you plan on collecting a lot of media, you'll need one. For example, if you plan on taking a lot of photos or home video and editing it on your Mac, you'll need a larger hard drive.

However, if you are not concerned about media storage, even the smallest hard drive offered by Apple is probably enough.

On the lower end, some Macs, such as the MacBook and Mac mini, come with 120GB or 160GB hard drives at the low end, but you can get larger drives for both if you think you'll need it. On the other end of the spectrum, the Mac Pro and iMac can come with 1 terabyte (TB) drives; the Pro also comes with multiple drives.

What Type of Mac User Are You?

There is no such thing as a typical Mac user. Everyone is unique in what they want from a computer, what they use it for, and how they use it. That's why Apple has so many choices.

To determine which Mac is right for you, you'll need to examine a number of factors. No one factor will tell you which Mac is right for you, but when combined, they may offer a clue.

Where Will You Use Your Mac?

Will this machine sit on a desk at home or at work? That's the primary question. But there are other places you can use your Mac as well. For instance, if you are a notebook user, you may find yourself on the sofa with the notebook in your lap more often than at a desk. If you are a student, you may find that the classroom or the school library is the most common place to use your Mac. A salesman or marketing professional may need her Mac more on the road more than in the office.

Here are some typical location situations and which Mac models may fit best:

- **Desk at home**—One of the three desktop models
- **Desk at work**—One of the three desktop models
- **Living room at home**—One of the three MacBooks, or possibly a Mac mini hooked into your TV
- **School dorm or around campus**—One of the three MacBooks
- **Traveling for work**—One of the three MacBooks
- **Home office and work**—One of the three MacBooks
- **Seasonal commute**—An iMac, or one of the three MacBooks

In general, you'd want one of the MacBooks if you are going to be changing your location. If you never plan to move your Mac, save the extra money and go for an iMac.

A seasonal commute is an interesting situation. Say you are in school in one location most of the year, but home for the summer. Or, perhaps you travel to a different location for the winter. In this case, you may not need to get a MacBook model, but instead pack up an iMac, take it along, and set it up at the new location.

The Mac mini has a unique application as the best Mac for hooking up to your TV. You could use it for general web surfing and email, as well as viewing video and listening to music.

What's Your Primary Use for Your Mac?

A Mac is a multipurpose tool. But everyone has something in mind that they will be using their Mac for most often. Is it going to be for using a particular business application? For writing? For keeping in touch with friends over the Internet? For web surfing?

Here are some typical uses for a Mac, and what model would work best for that use:

- **Email and social networking**—MacBook, MacBook Air, or iMac
- **Web surfing**—MacBook, MacBook Air, or iMac
- **Writing**—MacBook, MacBook Air, or iMac
- **Composing music**—MacBook Pro, iMac, or Mac Pro
- **Photography**—iMac or MacBook Pro
- **Video editing**—Mac Pro or MacBook Pro
- **Programming**—iMac or MacBook Pro
- **Web or print design**—Mac Pro or MacBook Pro
- **Games**—iMac, Mac Pro, or MacBook Pro

For most tasks that don't require handling heavy graphics or video, a MacBook or iMac is your best bet. If you need something very lightweight, a MacBook Air will do as well.

However, the Mac Pro and MacBook Pro are better at handling media like photos, video, and audio. They have faster processors, better video chipsets, and also come with larger hard drives needed for these applications. An iMac's screen may also be too small for some common photo and video editing tools.

The 17-inch MacBook Pro might be ideal for a media editor who needs to have as much screen real estate as possible to handle programs like Final Cut or Photoshop.

A programmer who does not handle a lot of data can get away with almost any Mac, but a faster processor may be desirable.

If you are a gamer, you'll want to focus on the video chipset and hard drive space, which means staying away from the Mac mini or basic MacBooks.

Must-Haves

Another way to approach finding the right Mac is to figure out what you really must have in a new machine. Here are some typical must-have features and which Mac they would indicate:

- **A Media Center Mac**—Mac mini or Mac Pro
- **Very large screen**—Mac Pro
- **More than two screens**—Mac Pro
- **Portability**—Any MacBook
- **Lightweight**—MacBook Air
- **Limited desk space**—Anything except a Mac Pro
- **Additional hard drives**—Mac Pro
- **Expansion cards and special hardware**—Mac Pro
- **FireWire video**—Anything other than a MacBook Air
- **All-Apple support**—iMac, Any MacBook

The iMac and all MacBooks let you hook up a second monitor, in addition to the built-in screen. MacBooks will operate with the lid closed and a monitor and external keyboard and mouse plugged in. But in that case they will only support one monitor. So if you really need a custom dual-monitor (or more) setup, a Mac Pro is the way to go. Desktop publishing and video editing often require this.

Although all MacBooks are portable by nature, only the MacBook Air carries this to an extreme by weighing in at barely three pounds. So if carrying around the lightest laptop possible is your requirement, the Air was made for you.

The Mac Pro is the only Mac that is truly expandable in every way. All Macs include USB2 ports for the addition of external hard drives. But only the Mac Pro allows additional internal drive bays. It also has expansion slots and by far the most power, with up to eight CPU cores.

If you do go with a Mac Pro or Mac mini, you'll need to supply your own monitor. And in the case of the mini, you'll need to supply a keyboard and mouse. If the ones you choose aren't Apple products, you'll be relying on other stores for support as well as Apple.

Making the Decision

So now that you've learned all about the Mac line-up, you may already know which Mac is right for you. But if you are still undecided, we can work on narrowing it down, step by step.

Desktop or Laptop

Your first decision is perhaps the easiest. Do you want a MacBook or a desktop machine?

In general, there's nothing that a desktop can do that a MacBook cannot. However, many people feel that a desktop machine offers a better experience—with a keyboard that can be easily positioned and a screen that is higher on the desk and with larger pixels that are easier to read.

MacBooks can feel cramped, with the keyboard just an inch from the screen and the trackpad right under that. A setup with an advanced, or perhaps even an ergonomic, keyboard can be more comfortable if you plan to do a lot of typing. An iMac screen or separate display is much easier to view from a distance like sitting back in your chair or looking over someone's shoulder.

A MacBook offers portability, naturally. For instance, a student who wants to use his computer in the dorm, library, classroom, and at home during breaks should really consider a MacBook. A business traveler who likes to work on airplanes and make presentations using her own computer will likewise favor a MacBook.

In fact, it is thought that MacBooks make up roughly half of Mac sales, although Apple doesn't release official numbers. Certainly if you visit an Apple Store you will see as many, if not more, MacBooks than desktops.

Weight or Power

Assuming you do want a laptop, you need to choose between the MacBook Pro, the MacBook, or the MacBook Air. This pretty much is a choice between portability and power.

The MacBook Pro is the heaviest, although at five pounds it makes older laptops seem very heavy. But you do get more processor power, a larger hard drive, and more expandability. If you need the FireWire port or ExpressCard slot, your decision is simple, as the MacBook Pro is the only one with these features. But if you plan on editing video or large images, especially at the professional level, you should also consider a MacBook Pro.

The MacBook Air is on the other side of the spectrum. It is lightest, at three pounds, and very thin. It is so thin that the idea of a laptop case seems silly—it can just be carried in whatever backpack, briefcase, or satchel you already use.

But the Air lacks power and expandability. Its processor is the slowest in the Mac line, and it doesn't even come with a built-in optical drive. So it is ideal for tasks like writing, surfing the net, and email. Students may find this machine to be the best if they have the budget to go above the standard MacBook.

As for the MacBook, there's a lot to be said for compromise. You get a slightly heavier machine than the Air, but have a better processor, larger hard drive, and an optical drive as compensation. You also get a much lower price tag. The MacBook comes in less than $1,000 in price, which might really make it the ideal student machine.

The small price also makes it a good second machine for many people. If you have a Mac Pro for video editing, for instance, you may find a simple MacBook to be a good companion for Internet, email, and travel.

All-In-One or Headless

The three MacBooks are very similar, with slightly different features, but the three desktop machines are very different from each other.

The iMac is different from the other two in that it has an attached screen. The advantages are mostly in design and simplicity. The iMac is pretty. Chances are, if you are reading this book you probably think so too.

One of the primary principles behind the design of the iMac is that, well, it has a design. That's what changed the industry in 1998 when it was introduced. And since then Apple has continued to make sure each generation of iMacs looks better than any other computer on the market.

There's nothing wrong with bringing design into your decision process. The comparison I like to use is why people think so much about color when buying a new car. After all, color is the most superficial decision when buying a new car. But, on the other hand, if you are spending $25,000 on a car, shouldn't you get the color you want?

That's one way to look at it: If you are spending good cash on a Mac, why shouldn't it look good?

The iMac, by combining the computer and the screen, has an impressive design. It looks nice sitting in your den, home office, bedroom desk, or cubicle.

And it also simplifies things. You buy an iMac and you're done. It comes with a keyboard and mouse, so everything you need is in the box. One purchase, one price, no hidden costs. There is a lot to be said for that.

On the other hand, a mini or a Pro comes without a screen. You can buy one of Apple's displays, a third-party display, or use one you already have. This gives you ultimate control over the size, quality, and cost of the display. A video editor or photographer might want to get a screen that meets certain high quality standards—although the iMac display is relatively good.

Mighty or Mini

The Mac mini and Mac Pro are an odd couple. They are both headless Macs that can be hidden away under a desk and drive virtually any screen or keyboard.

But this is an easy decision, usually, because of price. The Mac Pro is about four times the cost of the mini. So if you are a professional who needs power and expandability at any cost, the Pro is for you. If you want a budget machine, the mini is for you.

But the mini can be mighty as well. For typical home use, like surfing the Internet or watching video, the mini works just as well as any Mac.

Take a Test Drive

Before you make your decision, try to visit an Apple Store if one is near you. You'll get to test drive the Macs you are interested in. Because design is such an important part of every Mac, it is important to see the machines physically, instead of relying on the pictures on the websites.

You may be surprised at how small the Mac mini is. It really is "mini"! You might also be surprised at how light the MacBooks are. It is hard to believe that they cram an entire computer into the space the MacBook Air occupies.

You may also find yourself seduced by the design of the iMac. It is so thin and the aluminum and glass make it look so different than what we traditionally have thought of as a computer.

Making the Purchase

Now that you know which Mac is for you, it is time to buy. You've got several choices yet to make, like who to buy your Mac from and whether you should go for an extended warranty, like AppleCare.

Buying in the Store

There are more than 250 Apple Stores in the United States and many more throughout the world. This is probably your best bet for buying a Mac if you live near one.

Macs don't vary much in price, so you typically won't find bargains on new Macs by looking at non-Apple-owned stores. But sometimes other stores will throw in bonuses like more memory, printers, or extended AppleCare.

You can also find Macs in some major U.S. electronics stores like Best Buy. Some Mac sections are larger than others, and they may vary in how much they support Macs after the purchase. You can always go into an Apple Store with questions no matter where you buy your Mac.

There are also some great third-party Mac stores out there as well, some providing both new and used machines and repair services.

Buying Online

You can buy a Mac online from many places, including the online version of the Apple Store. The Apple.com website lets you customize your Mac with different memory, CPU, and hard drive options. However, a custom configuration will always take longer to ship than one of the preconfigured models.

At other online stores, you are usually stuck with the preconfigured Macs. But some offer their own custom upgrades.

Buying a Used Mac

You can also find used and refurbished Macs online and in some stores. There are some online stores that specialize in non-new Macs, but you can also go to the online Apple Store to see if they have any refurbished machines.

A refurbished machine is one that was either used in a store as a display model, or was returned for some reason. Apple will then fix anything that is wrong and offer the machine at a reduced price.

It is usually pretty safe to buy a refurbished Mac from Apple. You get a warranty and support, so if anything isn't quite right you have some recourse.

But buying a used or refurbished machine from somewhere else can be risky. You want to access that risk by planning for the worst—the machine is unusable when it arrives or just after. If you bought over eBay, good luck getting your money back or a new Mac. But if you buy from a local store that has a physical location and a written guarantee, you are somewhat safer.

Should You Buy AppleCare?

A big question for first-time Mac buyers is whether they should get the extra AppleCare. Usually at the time of purchase you are offered two additional years of AppleCare.

AppleCare is basically an extended warranty. It extends the coverage you already get for one year after purchasing your Mac from Apple and extends the 90 days of telephone support. You can read more about AppleCare in Chapter 25 in the section "AppleCare and the Genius Bar."

One thing that many buyers don't understand is that you already get a full year warranty on a new Mac from the Apple Store. The AppleCare package simply extends that warranty for another two years.

Another misconception about AppleCare is that it will cover you if you have an accident—like dropping your MacBook. But AppleCare is a warranty, not an insurance policy. It will cover your Mac if a part is defective or breaks over time when it shouldn't, for instance, if the hard drive fails after 18 months or if the screen stops working.

AppleCare also gets you extended phone support beyond the initial 90 days that comes with your Mac purchase.

But you don't need to decide now. You actually can buy the two years of additional AppleCare any time during the first year of owning your Mac.

Knowing which Mac to buy and whether to get AppleCare is not an easy decision for some people. You also have to look at your budget and how important the computer is compared to other things in your life. But hopefully this guide has helped with that decision.

If you still feel that you need to know more, check out the next chapter, where we'll go into detail about the hardware options that come with each Mac.

WHO SHOULD READ THIS CHAPTER:

If you are curious about the ports and cables attached to your Mac, you can learn more about them here. If you'd rather get right to learning how to use your Mac, you can skip to Chapter 3, "Starting Up and Shutting Down."

2

Examining Mac Hardware

Every computer has two parts: the hardware and the software. The hardware is the physical part, such as the case, screen, keyboard, and so on. The software is the digital part, such as the operating system, programs, and your files.

Most of this book is about how to use the software that makes up Mac OS X and the programs that come with it. But let us also look at the hardware to get a complete understanding of your Mac and how you can use it.

Standard Parts, Fantastic Design

The original Mac launched in 1984 and was an all-in-one machine with a monochrome screen and a floppy disk drive. You can see it in Figure 2.1.

For the first decade, Macs and PCs were very different on the inside and out. From the microprocessors to the ports, there was little compatibility between Macs and PCs.

But in the mid-90s, things started to change. For instance, the special Apple networking cables were replaced with standard ports, connectors, and cables used by all computers. Later in the decade, keyboard and mouse connectors were replaced with the new industry-standard USB connectors.

Figure 2.1

The original Mac launched in 1984. Photo Courtesy of Apple, Inc.

The transition was complete in 2006 when Apple began to use Intel processors for their CPUs. These were the same as used in PCs, making Mac and PC hardware virtually identical—on the inside.

But the outer design is where Apple maintained a lead. The iMac was the beginning of a new era of Apple design. From multiple colors, Apple then moved on to embrace the aluminum and glass used today. The design of the iPod and iPhone follows this lead as well, using the same basic materials and curves as the Mac.

However, at their hearts, the Mac and PC are the same basic machine. They use the same processors, memory, video cards, hard drives, slots, and ports. So if you have any experience with understanding PC hardware, you'll find understanding Mac hardware is pretty simple.

Built-In Devices: Standard Parts and Ports

Although it isn't necessary to understand the uses and history of every part of your Mac, it can come in handy when trying to expand your computer or just trying new things. Let's take a look at all of the parts of your Mac and see what they are used for.

USB2

USB stands for Universal Serial Bus, and it really lives up to its name. Not only do you connect your keyboard and mouse using USB, but you also can connect printers, scanners, external hard drives, game controllers, digital cameras, and much more. Figure 2.2 shows a standard USB cable end.

USB is different than earlier connectors in that it also carries a small amount of power. So you can plug in some devices without needing to also plug them into a power outlet as well. For instance, some web cameras and small hard drives can be powered from the USB port.

You can also chain devices together. For instance, it is common on a Mac to plug the keyboard into the USB port, and then plug the mouse into an extra USB port in the keyboard.

Figure 2.2

All Macs accept the standard USB connector, though other versions exist that plug into printers and digital cameras.

But combining these two features is troublesome. For instance, you can't plug any power-needy devices like a hard drive into the keyboard's USB port without getting a low-power warning.

With the original USB ports you had a very slow connection, only really useful for the keyboard and mouse. Sometimes it was used for digital cameras, but they took a long time to transfer images to your computer.

USB2 is faster than USB by an order of magnitude. It can be used for all sorts of high-speed data transfer, including hard drives and video devices. All new Macs come with USB2. However, USB2 is backward compatible and can handle all USB devices as well.

Even though Macs come with from one (MacBook Air) to five (Mac Pro) USB ports, you can extend each port with a USB hub, like the one in Figure 2.3. These usually cost between $10 and $40 and usually add about four new USB ports. You can actually get up to 127 USB devices connected by chaining together USB hubs.

NOTE

USB hubs come in a few different varieties. Make sure you get one that has its own power supply and is USB2-compatible. Otherwise, you may end up with one that only works at old USB speeds, or does not support devices that need any amount of power.

Figure 2.3
USB hubs come in many shapes and sizes.

FireWire

FireWire is used mostly for external hard drives and video cameras.

FireWire ports come in two flavors on Macs: 400Mbits/sec and 800Mbits/sec. You can see both in Figure 2.4. The first usually has a 6-pin "alpha" connector, which is rectangular with one rounded side, and the second a 9-pin "beta" connector, which is close to square in shape.

Figure 2.4
The FireWire 400 and FireWire 800 ports of an older MacBook Pro.

Most FireWire devices come with a smaller FireWire connector and a cable that converts that small connector to a 6-pin or 9-pin connector.

The newer MacBook Pros only include FireWire 800, which can be used for both types of devices. However, you may need to get a cable adapter to plug a 6-pin cable into a 9-pin port.

Display Ports

The Mac mini and Mac Pro require an external monitor. MacBook owners often look to add an external monitor or plug into a presentation projector on occasion. For this, a display port is needed.

The MacBooks and all desktop Macs come with the new Mini DisplayPort. This little port can be adapted to connect to almost any modern monitor. Other Macs and older Macs come with either DVI, Mini-DVI, or VGA ports. The Mac Pro has a Mini DisplayPort as well as a standard Dual-Like DVI port. And the Mac mini has a Mini-DVI port as well.

DVI connections are higher quality than old VGA connections, as the signal contains the information for each pixel on the screen and lets the monitor display that pixel exactly. There are actually two types of DVI: regular DVI and Dual-Link DVI. They look the same, but the second is needed for large 30-inch monitors.

Mini DisplayPort is similar to Dual-Link DVI. So connecting to anything—VGA, DVI, or Dual-Link DVI—is just a matter of getting the right cable. Only the 24-inch Apple Display allows you to connect a Mini DisplayPort with a DisplayPort cable that does not convert to either VGA or DVI. In the future, Apple will probably use this on their other monitors as well.

Speakers and Speaker Port

All Macs come with some sort of built-in speakers. The Mac mini, MacBook Air, and Mac Pro have a single speaker suitable for hearing system beeps and sound effects, and perhaps spoken audio. The iMac and other MacBooks all come with two built-in stereo speakers. The iMac comes with an additional 24-watt digital amplifier to make the sound carry into a room.

All Macs have a minijack port for audio out. You can plug either headphones or an additional speaker system into this port. This can be as simple as a $10 set of computer desk speakers, or a multi-thousand-dollar stereo system.

You can add more speaker and line-in ports through your USB ports. You'll just need a USB audio device, of which there are many third-party options to choose from.

The new MacBooks come with a single audio port for headphones. But this special port also includes support for the iPod accessory known as the Apple Earphones with Remote and Mic. The mic then works as a microphone in your Mac and you can use it for recording or audio and video chat.

Microphone and Line-In

The iMac and all MacBooks come with a built-in microphone. This simple medium-quality device is meant for audio and video chatting, and perhaps voice memos. It is not good enough for professional audio. In addition, since it is part of the Mac's body, it will pick up a certain amount of noise from the spin of the hard drive and your fingers clicking on the keyboard or trackpad.

The line-in port still available on desktop Macs is for piping audio into your Mac for recording or telecommunications. For instance, you could plug in a headphone cable from your MP3 player or voice recorder.

FYI: MICROPHONE INPUT

A common misconception is that you can plug a microphone into the audio line-in. But a mic port and a line-in port are two different things. A mic port would provide power to a microphone to amplify the signal. A line-in expects a full-powered signal to arrive on its own.

So you cannot plug a microphone into the line-in port. You may get a faint low-quality signal, but that is it.

This seems like one of the cases where PCs have an advantage over Macs. Most PCs have a mic-in port. But there is a huge range of quality involved in circuits that convert mic input to digital audio. Most PCs have a very low-quality circuit behind their mic input. On a Mac, you need to get a USB microphone adapter, and can find ones of varying quality and price.

You can add additional audio inputs into your Mac through USB. In fact, you'll want to do so if you plan on using your Mac for professional audio. But many audio devices, like microphones and headsets, are USB now anyway. So you may find yourself not even needing the line-in port, and just using USB mics.

iSight Camera

The iMac and all MacBooks come with a built-in web camera called an iSight. This is a fairly high-end web camera that is excellent for video conferencing or taking quick pictures of yourself for use with social media sites.

It isn't a good substitute for even a consumer video camera, however, if you want to produce DVD-quality video.

One of the interesting features of the iSight is the autofocus. Most web cameras don't have this, instead making you turn a manual focus ring around the lens of the camera.

Ethernet and WiFi

Every Mac except the MacBook Air comes with a RJ45 jack, also known as an Ethernet port or network connector, shown in Figure 2.5. You can plug this into a cable modem or DSL home Internet connection, or a network cable at the office.

Figure 2.5

The Ethernet jack on a MacBook Pro.

Alternatively, you can connect to a wireless network through the built-in WiFi card that comes with every Mac except the Mac Pro. To do this, your cable or DSL modem needs to have wireless capability. Or, you can extend your network with a separate wireless base station like the AirPort Base Station from Apple.

WiFi will also let you connect to networks at schools, hotels, and hotspots all over town.

There are different versions of WiFi, with names like 802.11b, 802.11g, and 802.11n. Newer Macs come with the latter, but are downward compatible with hardware that uses the earlier versions.

MacBook Air users get an adapter with their Mac that allows them to plug an Ethernet connector into their USB port.

Bluetooth

Your Mac also has another way to wirelessly communicate with other devices. *Bluetooth* is a short-distance, slow communication method that uses radio waves to connect your Mac to things like wireless headsets, mice, keyboards, and even some digital cameras.

Bluetooth is also the standard used by many mobile devices like phones and PDAs.

Keyboard

Much of the design of the Mac is based on usability. The Apple keyboards are no exception. The external keyboards that come with the iMac and the Mac Pro, shown in Figure 2.6, as well as the built-in keyboards of the MacBooks, are all excellent devices, suitable for casual users and serious typers.

Figure 2.6

The Apple keyboard that ships with iMacs and Mac Pros. Photo Courtesy of Apple, Inc.

You can get the external keyboard in two flavors: wired and wireless. The wireless keyboards use the Bluetooth built into your Mac, so no special device needs to be connected to your Mac, unlike many third-party wireless keyboards.

In addition, there are two keyboard configurations: with a numeric keypad and without. The standard is the new smaller keyboard without the keypad. But you can purchase your Mac with the larger keyboard at no additional cost. You can also opt for the wireless keyboard at the time of purchase for an additional $30.

Mouse and Trackpad

The famous one-button mouse is pretty much a thing of the past, as the Mighty Mouse and multitouch trackpad have become standard on Macs. You can see the Mighty Mouse in Figure 2.7.

Figure 2.7
The Apple Mighty Mouse has many buttons that can be configured to do many things. Photo Courtesy of Apple, Inc.

A Mighty Mouse includes different buttons for left and right, hidden under the shell of the mouse. There are also secondary left and right buttons that you can squeeze, and a central mouse ball that can be used to scroll both horizontally and vertically.

The trackpads on the new MacBooks have a hidden button underneath that you press by simply pressing on the whole trackpad. In addition, the trackpad recognizes how many fingers you have on the pad, allowing you to perform different functions depending on how many fingers you use.

If a trackpad just doesn't cut it for you, you can always plug a Mighty Mouse, or any third-party USB mouse, into your MacBook and use that instead.

It is common, in fact, for a MacBook users to work at a desk using an external monitor, external keyboard, and a mouse. You don't even need to have the MacBook open to use it that way. Then you get the best of both worlds: a laptop when traveling and a desktop when at your desk.

You can also get a wireless Mighty Mouse, which uses Bluetooth to connect to your Mac.

Expansion Slots

Two Macs include expansion slots: the Mac Pro and 17-inch MacBook Pro. The first has internal PCI slots that can be used with a variety of professional hardware like a RAID drive array, advanced audio and video inputs, and super-fast optical network connections.

The 17-inch MacBook Pro has an ExpressCard 34 slot. This very new standard for laptop extension cards allows you to add things like digital camera card readers.

SD Card Slots

New MacBook Pros come with an SD card slot. An SD card is a common storage card used in many digital cameras. With this slot, you can pull the card out of your camera and stick it into your MacBook Pro to quickly bring your photos and videos into iPhoto. You can also use SD cards to store data.

Batteries

Every MacBook comes with a battery so that you can use it while on the go and away from a power outlet. The batteries in MacBook Pros and the MacBook Air are fixed inside the case and can't be replaced or swapped. Apple claims that these batteries will last five years. If a replacement is needed, you can get one from Apple.

MacBook users find that batteries last longer if they follow the ritual of *battery conditioning*. This is the practice of occasionally draining the battery until the MacBook shuts down, then immediately and without interruption charging it up fully again.

This helps the circuits in the battery recognize the lower and upper limits of power storage and produce longer battery life and a more accurate battery indicator on your Mac's screen.

More Hardware

You may want to extend your Mac with various pieces of hardware that perform certain tasks. Thanks to a large selection of drivers and the USB2 ports on your Mac, you will most likely be able to plug just about any piece of common equipment into your Mac and have it work instantly.

Here is a summary of some of the devices you may want to get.

Printers

The promise of a paperless office hasn't yet come to pass. There are just too many things that require printing, even if you never intend to print documents simply to read them.

For instance, it is common to print airplane boarding passes at home, or coupons from websites to take to the store, or packing slips and postage for sending items in the mail. Of course, you may also want to print important, interesting, or handy documents.

Printers generally come in two varieties: ink jet or laser. The first variety is the cheapest and uses cartridges of ink and a moving head to print. The second variety uses a toner cartridge. Table 2.1 summarizes the advantages and disadvantages of each.

Table 2.1   Comparing Ink Jet and Laser Printers

	Ink Jet	Laser Printer
Cost	$0–$200	$100–$400
Uses	Ink cartridges	Toner cartridge
Color	Always	Only expensive models
Moving parts	Many	Few
Reliability	Low	High
B&W quality	Low–Medium	High
Ink replacement	Often	Seldom
Noise	Noisy	Quiet
Speed	Slow	Fast

If you print a lot of text documents, you may want to consider buying a laser printer. If you seldom print documents, or if you need color, an ink jet is probably your best bet.

In both cases, you usually get what you pay for. So a cheap or free-with-purchase printer is not something from which you should expect much.

Hard Drives and Backup Drives

Almost every Mac should be accompanied by at least one external hard drive that you can use as a backup device using Mac OS X's Time Machine backup program.

External USB hard drives are easy to come by. You can find them for under $100 at local megastores or electronics stores. Just about any one will be usable as a Time Machine backup drive.

You may also want to have another drive for a variety of reasons. One would be media storage, especially if you have a lot of music or videos. Photographers may also want to have a place to archive large photo collections.

Larger hard drives, and ones with various methods of ensuring data integrity, can also be important for some users.

Scanners

Image scanners allow you to scan in documents and pictures. They come in two varieties: paper feed and flatbed. The first allows you to feed in multiple sheets of paper, and the latter lets you precisely position various forms of media like pictures.

Besides being able to import physical documents and convert them to digital files on your computer, you may use a scanner as a substitute for a fax machine or copier.

You can also get multifunction devices that combine a printer and scanner in one body. Usually, they can also act as a copier even without your Mac being connected.

Headsets

Headsets combine headphones and a microphone. They are common among people who use VOIP (Voice Over Internet Protocol) instead of a telephone, or simply iChat to communicate with others. They are usually USB and can be as cheap as $10 or as much as $100 or even more.

The advantage to a headset is that the microphone is kept at a set distance from your mouth, allowing you to move around somewhat and still maintain the same volume as you talk to someone.

You can get headsets both as wired USB devices and as wireless Bluetooth.

Headsets are also useful if you plan to use dictation software or Mac OS X voice commands.

External Web Cameras

You can buy a variety of external web cameras, but finding one that works on a Mac can be tough. Cameras are one of the few remaining hardware devices that require very specific software plug-ins, called drivers, to work on a computer. Most cameras come with PC drivers, but not Mac drivers.

Even ones that do come with Mac drivers tend to come with bad ones—it almost seems like a tradition in the web camera industry. Sometimes you can only use the cameras with software that comes with it, and not iChat, PhotoBooth, or iMovie.

So you'll need to do research when buying a third-party web camera. Read reviews, particularly ones from Mac users.

The good news is that things are getting better. Standards have been agreed upon, and more and more manufacturers are producing cameras that work without specific drivers on the Mac.

Displays

Whether you are connecting an external display to a MacBook, or a primary display to a Mac Pro or Mac mini, you can choose from three Apple displays or hundreds of third-party displays. Just make sure the display has the same type of connector as your Mac, or that you purchase an adapter cable at the same time.

Almost all new displays are flat-panel LCD screens. There are many levels of quality and size. One of the principal measurements of an LCD screen is the number of horizontal and vertical pixels it can display.

Table 2.2 summarizes the screens that come with the iMacs and MacBooks, as well as Apple's three external displays.

Table 2.2   Available Mac Displays

Display	Pixel Width and Height
iMac 20-inch	1680×1050
iMac 24-inch	1920×1200
MacBook	1280×800
MacBook Pro	1440×900
MacBook Air	1280×800
Apple Display 24-inch	1920×1200
Apple Display 30-inch	2560×1600

The Apple Display 24-inch, shown in Figure 2.8, also contains a microphone, iSight camera, and speakers.

Figure 2.8

The 24-inch Apple Display is kind of like an iMac without the computer. Photo Courtesy of Apple, Inc.

One of the ways a display can vary is in physical screen size. However, this doesn't necessarily correspond to pixels. For instance, a 20-inch display can have the same number of pixels as a 23-inch display. The second will simply have larger pixels. This can be a good thing or a bad thing, depending on your needs.

More Gadgets

Besides the basics like displays, printers, and scanners, you can keep on expanding the network of devices around your Mac. In the realm of cameras, you can get small, compact still cameras or large, professional single-lens reflex cameras. You can get compact video camcorders as well as professional-quality high-definition video cameras.

If you have a MacBook, you may want to look into a cooling pad—usually a USB device that sits under your MacBook and fans air over the bottom.

If your home network hub, usually provided by your broadband modem, is not already wireless, you may want to get your own wireless hub such as an Apple Airport Extreme or Time Capsule. This allows you to use your MacBook anywhere in the house without being hard-wired to your Internet connection. Plus it works with the iPhone and iPod Touch as well. You can get any 802.11g-compatible hub, some of which run under $50.

There are even some ridiculously useless, but fun, USB devices you can get for your Mac, like a snowman with eyes that move like a Cylon from the original Battlestar Galactica, or a small fan or light to illuminate your keyboard if you prefer to type in the dark.

New hardware and gadgets are something you can always add to your Mac. So let's start to look at how to use your Mac and take your first steps into Mac OS X.

3

Starting Up and Shutting Down

Now that you've found the right Mac and have it ready in your home or office, you can get to work… or play. Let's start by looking at how to set up your Mac, and then how to start it up. Before getting too far, we'll look at how to shut off your Mac—and if you even should.

The basics are similar to Windows machines, but some of the terminology is different, and you'll find these commands in different places in the operating system.

Setting Up

Setting up your Mac hardware is relatively quick and easy. In fact, it is probably easier than setting up a television and a DVD player in your living room. There are five main steps. Here is a list, and then we'll go into detail:

- Plug the Mac into a wall outlet or power strip.
- Plug the display into your Mac (Mac Pro and mini).
- Plug your keyboard and mouse into your Mac (not necessary with MacBooks).
- Ready your Internet connection.
- Press the power button.

Figure 3.1 shows what a typical iMac setup might look like as compared to that of a common PC. There are three cords: the power cord, the line to the keyboard, and the line to the mouse.

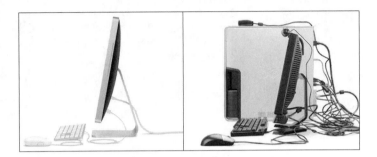

Figure 3.1

This Apple promotional photo compares the simple setup of the iMac with a PC setup. It is a bit over the top, but it gets the point across. Photo Courtesy of Apple, Inc.

The first step in setting up your Mac is to plug it in. The iMac and Mac Pros have simple power cords, whereas the Mac mini and MacBooks have power adapters. There are blocks or "bricks" that convert AC wall power to DC power used inside computers. All computers have them, but the iMac and Mac Pro have them inside the case. Either way, you plug them into the wall socket.

If you have a Mac mini or Mac Pro, you'll next need to connect your display to your Mac. Your display probably came with a cable that may or may not hook directly into the Mac's video port. If it doesn't, you'll need an adapter.

Depending on what Apple is shipping in the box with your Mac at the time, you may have that adapter already. If not, refer to the "Display Ports" section in Chapter 2, "Examining Mac Hardware," to see what you need. Chances are it is a Mini DisplayPort to DVI or VGA adapter. You can get both of these from the Apple store.

Then, of course, you need to plug your display into a power outlet.

POWER STRIPS

You can plug your computer and display directly into a wall power socket, of course. But you can also get a power strip to go between your wall and Mac power cords. Cheap ones will do little more than provide an extension to help you reach a faraway socket. Most will also have an on/off switch, which could come in handy for shutting power completely off to your computer when not using it for a long time.

Slightly more expensive power strips also include a surge protector. This shields your Mac from any power surges or irregularities that could harm it. There are good and bad surge-protection strips, so read up on them if you have an interest.

Even better than a power strip with a surge protector is a UPS—uninterruptible power supply. These larger devices include a battery, so you have anywhere from a few minutes to an hour or so of power remaining when you lose electricity at your location. You could use this time to save your work and gracefully shut down your Mac.

Next, for the Mac mini, iMac, and Mac Pro, you'll plug the keyboard into one of the USB ports. It may be tempting for Mac Pro owners to plug the keyboard into one of the front USB ports, but you are better off leaving those for portable USB thumb drives and digital cameras. Use one of the rear USB ports for your keyboard because you'll almost never need to unplug it again.

The mouse then can be plugged into the left or right side of your keyboard, depending on which hand you use to operate a mouse.

One last thing you may want to do is to ready your Mac to connect to the Internet. If you have a wireless connection, make sure your wireless router is turned on and connected to your broadband modem.

If you have a wired connection, plug it into the Mac. Most broadband modems, whether they support a cable or DSL connection, use RJ45 connectors that you can plug directly into your Mac's Ethernet port. If it is a standard connection and is already set up by your cable or telephone company, you can plug it in now and your Mac will recognize it and use it during the set up process.

Starting Your Mac the First Time

To start your Mac, look for the power button. Press and release and then you should hear the classic Mac bootup sound and see the power light come on.

NOTE

What is that shape that makes up the power button symbol? It is the number 1 wrapped inside the number 0. The numbers 1 and 0 represent "on" and "off" in the digital language of computers. This symbol is now used on other electronic devices and even appliances.

The first thing you should see is a gray screen with an Apple logo in the middle. Under the logo will appear a spinning status wheel. It takes a minute or so for your Mac to get to the next step.

Then you are asked about which language you want to use. When you select that, the welcome animation plays. You can click your mouse or press a key to skip this, but few people do. Why miss out on the welcoming experience?

 TIP

Want to see the opening animation again? Apple doesn't make that easy, but you can find it on your hard drive at /System/Library/CoreServices/. Ctrl-click on Setup Assistant.app and select Show Package Contents. Then look in /Contents/Resources/ for TransitionSection.bundle, select Show Package Contents again, and look in /Contents/Resources/. Here you will find a .mov file with the animation and a .mp3 file with the audio.

Next you may be asked to identify your keyboard if you are not using a standard one from Apple. This ensures that non-U.S. users can properly indicate their keyboards, which sometimes feature keys in slightly different places.

For instance, on a UK keyboard, pressing Shift-2 gives you a double quote instead of the @ symbol on an American keyboard. Keyboards in other countries also have layouts that include letters in non-English alphabets.

You may also be asked to select a wireless network if you haven't plugged in an Ethernet cable and you have a Mac with a wireless card inside it. You'll be shown a list of wireless networks that the Mac detected around it. If one of them is yours, you can select it. If the network requires a password, you'll need to enter it.

Then you will be asked to register your new Mac. Doing so now is certainly the easiest way to register, so consider not skipping this step. Otherwise, you can go to http://register.apple.com at a later time.

Another option you are presented with is the ability to import data from an old Mac. Let's assume for now, that you are not going to do that. If you are moving from a Windows computer, check out Chapter 8, "Moving from Windows to Mac," for various ways to bring over your data to your new Mac.

Finally, you will also be asked to establish your user account on your new Mac. Let's take a closer look at user accounts.

Creating Your User Account

A Mac can support one or more people using it. For instance, a shared family Mac may be used by mom, dad, several children, and even grandma. A married couple may share a Mac. Or, the Mac could be yours and yours alone. But you might later want to allow your no-good brother-in-law to use it to hunt for a job on the net. What a deadbeat.

You could certainly decide to let everyone use a single account on the Mac. But a better way would be to establish individual accounts for each person. Accounts may differ in simple ways, like using a different desktop background. Every account has a different set of user preferences. Plus, each account also gives each person a space on the hard drive to put his own personal files. Here is a summary of some of the things that differ per account:

- Each account has its own Documents folder.
- Each account also has its own Music, Movies, and Pictures folders.
- Application preferences can be set per user.
- Applications remember different data per user, like web bookmarks.
- Mail accesses different email accounts for each user.
- Mac OS preferences, like desktop backgrounds, languages, sleep timers, and so on, can all be set per user.
- Unless a user is an administrator, she can only see her own documents.
- Parental controls can be set on a user, restricting what they can do.
- Individual users access different calendars, address books, and email.

So for now, let's create the main account for the computer. In most cases you will want to make this your account. You can enter your name, plus a nickname to use.

Think carefully about what nickname you want to use because you'll use it when logging in to your account and in other ways. You may want to stick with something simple like your first name. Or, you might have a nickname that you commonly use for social networks or email addresses, like "fuzzybunny22."

You are also asked to include a password for this account. Whatever password you use, be sure to write it down. You may need to know this password later to perform critical tasks with your Macintosh.

> **CAUTION**
>
> Take the selection of your password seriously. If your Mac is connected to the Internet, your password can be used to access files on your Mac from anywhere. So choose something that you will never forget, but don't use a dictionary word or a date. Such passwords are too easy to guess. A combination of letters and numbers is always best.

Later on we'll look at how to create new user accounts on your Mac. But for now all you need to continue is this one account.

After a short period of time, the Mac OS X interface loads up and you'll see your Desktop, menu bar, and Dock filled with applications at the bottom. But before we go any further, let's think about what to do when you are finished using your computer at the end of the day.

To Sleep or To Shut Down

So it is the end of the day, and you're finished working with your new Mac. The only thing left to do is to turn it off, right?

Don't be too sure. Shutting down your Mac may not be the best option. You may just want to let it sleep, instead. There are advantages to both options.

Shutting Down

Shutting down your Mac doesn't require you to touch a special button or switch. Instead use your mouse to navigate your cursor to the Apple menu at the very upper left of your screen, as in Figure 3.2. Select that menu and look for the Shut Down menu item.

This will gracefully shut down your Mac and turn off the power. It may take a minute, as your Mac needs to quit all running applications and shut down the operating system, perhaps saving some user preferences and other data. Some of your applications may prompt you to save your work, if you haven't already done so.

Shutting down your system at the end of the day will certainly save some amount of power. But putting your machine to sleep, or letting it go to sleep on its own, has its advantages as well.

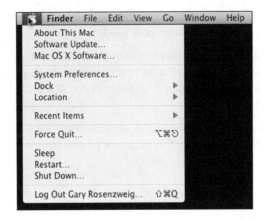

Figure 3.2

You can use the Apple menu to shut down your Mac or put it to sleep.

Sleep

In the same Apple menu, you will find a menu item called Sleep. This puts your Mac in a low power mode by turning off the screen and shutting down many other systems as well.

Your Mac uses very little power while sleeping. But a huge advantage of putting your Mac to sleep rather than shutting it down is that you can wake it fairly quickly, rather than having to go through the bootup sequence.

Another advantage of sleeping is that you can leave applications running, and even documents open, while the computer is asleep. You can be writing a document, reading a web page, listening to music, and doing many other things when you put your machine to sleep. When you wake it up, all of those things will still be on the screen and you can resume immediately.

Another advantage of simply letting your computer go to sleep is that the operating system performs many maintenance tasks in the middle of the night, or when it recognizes that you're not using it. If you shut your machine down every night and start it up every morning, your Mac never gets to perform these maintenance tasks.

NOTE

Sleep is like the standby function in Windows, but it uses almost no power or resources. Older Windows machines also had a hibernate mode, that shuts down the computer but saves every detail of what you were doing first. Sleep works well enough that hibernate mode isn't really an option on Macs, or newer Windows machines for that matter.

Energy Saver Preferences

Back in the Apple menu, you will see an item called System Preferences, which, when selected, opens a window with many different icons. Look for the one called Energy Saver. This set of system preferences, shown in Figure 3.3, allows you to specify how long your Mac will wait before going to sleep.

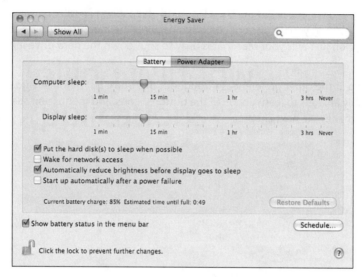

Figure 3.3

The Energy Saver preference panel allows you to specify how quickly your Mac goes to sleep.

If you are using a MacBook, then you'll see both Battery and Power Adapter as choices at the top of the window. You can set different values for each, and your Mac will use those values depending on where it is getting its power. If you are using a desktop Mac, then you will only have one set of values.

The main setting on the screen determines how much time is allowed to pass from when you stop using your computer to when it goes to sleep. For instance, if you set your computer to sleep when it is inactive for 15 minutes, it will enter sleep mode 15 minutes after you last type on the keyboard or move the mouse. This means you can walk away from your computer to go to lunch, or for the rest of the day, knowing that it will go to sleep fairly soon.

> Even if you don't touch the mouse or keyboard, your Mac may not go to sleep. Things that will keep it awake include playing a DVD movie, listening to music in iTunes, running a Time Machine backup or downloading large files with your web browser. In these cases, your Mac waits until these actions are complete before sleeping.

You can also specify an amount of time for the display to go to sleep. The display uses a lot of power, but it is quick to turn on or off. So you may want to set a shorter period of time for display sleep. For instance, you may set the display to sleep after only five minutes.

When the display is asleep, the computer is actually still completely on and a tap on the keyboard or movement of the mouse will snap the display on pretty much in an instant.

Another option you will see is Put the Hard Disk(s) to Sleep When Possible. This is checked by default. Not everything you do on your computer requires the hard drives to be constantly spinning, so this option just tells your Mac that is okay to shut down the hard drive if it isn't using it at the moment.

We'll be looking at the other preferences throughout this book. But before we go any further, you are probably anxious to learn about all the buttons, icons, and menus you see on the screen. We'll dive into that in the next chapter.

WHO SHOULD READ THIS CHAPTER:

If you are unfamiliar with the Mac interface and things like the
Desktop, folders, windows, the menu bar, and the Dock, this is
the chapter for you. You will learn what these things are and how
to use them. These are fundamental for getting around in Mac
OS X and knowing where your files are and how to access them.

4

Getting Around

At the center of your Macintosh experience is the Desktop. From the
pretty-looking customizable background to the menu bar at top and
the dock below, the Desktop is where you start any project and is the
hub for all your computing activities.

Let's take a look at each element on your Desktop, which you can see
in Figure 4.1: the menu bar, the Dock, the icons on the screen, and
how to use and customize each. But first, let's look at the Finder.

Finder Windows

Notice in Figure 4.1 that the word "Finder" appears on the menu bar
at the upper-left corner of the screen. This is the space where the
name of the application you are using appears. Right now, it shows
that the application called Finder is running.

The Finder works by showing you files in windows. For instance if
you double-click on the only icon on the screen, named Macintosh
HD, it will open a window that shows you the files on your hard drive,
as in Figure 4.2.

Figure 4.1

The screen shows your Desktop, with the menu bar at the top, one icon in the upper right, and the Dock at the bottom.

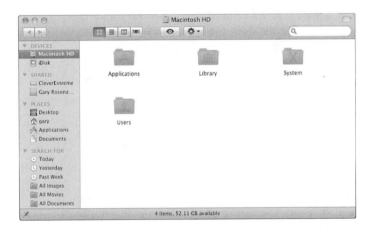

Figure 4.2

A Finder window shows you files and folders inside a folder on your hard drive.

In this case, the top level of the hard drive contains four other folders: Applications, Library, System, and Users. You can drill down into one of these by double-clicking on the folder icon representing each folder.

NOTE

You can have as many Finder windows open at a time as you like. This makes it easy to do things like copying or moving a file from one folder to another.

If you double-click on the Users folder, and then again on the folder with the icon that looks like a house, you will find yourself in your User folder, also known as your *home folder*. We'll be taking a closer look at these folders and what they are used for in Chapter 5, "Working with Files and Folders."

The windows in the Finder have their own set of controls. At the top you will see a set of buttons and a search field. On the left, you will see the sidebar with a list of locations and preset searches. At the bottom you will see more information about the folder you are looking at.

The very top of a Finder window shows the name of the folder you are looking at. Clicking and dragging on the top allows you to reposition the window. Holding down the Command key and clicking on the title of the window shows you a menu with a list of folders—from the one this folder is contained in, all the way back up to the top level of the hard drive . You can select one of these to open a new Finder window.

Window Controls

The buttons all the way at the upper left of a window are round little bubbles colored red, yellow, and green. When you roll your mouse over them, they light up with symbols in them: X, -, and +. Here is what they do:

 Close button—Closes the window and removes it from your screen. Closing a window, or even all windows, of an application will usually leave that application running, just with no documents open.

 Minimize button—Shrinks the window down to an icon and puts it in your Dock. You can click on that icon to open the window back up again.

 Maximize button—Expands the window to a maximum reasonable size. This is usually enough to view all the items in the window, if possible, and not necessarily the entire size of your screen.

Below these three colored buttons are left and right arrow buttons. Like the back and forward buttons in a web browser, these let you return to the previous folder you were looking at in the window, and let you advance forward again after going back.

In the example earlier in this chapter where you double-clicked to get down to your home folder, you could use the back button to then back out to the Users folder and then the Macintosh HD folder.

View Buttons

The next set of buttons gives you four choices of how you can view files in Finder windows: icons, list, columns, or cover flow.

The view in Figure 4.2 is the icon view. But if you click on the second button in the group, the one that looks like four lines, you get the list view, shown in Figure 4.3.

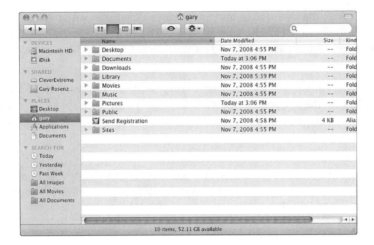

Figure 4.3

The list view of the Finder shows you more details about each item.

In this case, the view shows mostly other folders. You'll notice a little triangle next to each folder name. When you click on one of these triangles, it expands the contents of a folder and shows them in the same window, indented under that folder. This way, you can navigate to almost any file in a single Finder window.

> By selecting View, Show View Options (Command+J), you can change some things about the list view. You can include other columns of information such as date created, size, kind, version, comments, and label. You can also choose to have the sizes of folders calculated, and whether to use relative date descriptions like "yesterday."

Another way to do the same thing is to use the column view. Click on the third button in the group, the one that looks like three rectangles. You'll get the column view, as shown in Figure 4.4.

The column view is the power user view. You can quickly dive down into folders while still seeing the folders and their contents above. In addition, you'll see a preview of files you select. For instance, if you select a picture file, you will see a small preview of that picture in the rightmost column.

> **TIP**
>
> By selecting View, Show View Options (Command+J), you can change some things about column view. You can select whether to show icons and the preview column. You can also choose to sort by something other than name, such as date, size, kind, or label.

Figure 4.4

Column view puts each folder into its own column and lets you navigate around your hard drive quickly.

The fourth view type is cover flow. This is a view type similar to how an iPod or iTunes presents music. You can see it in Figure 4.5.

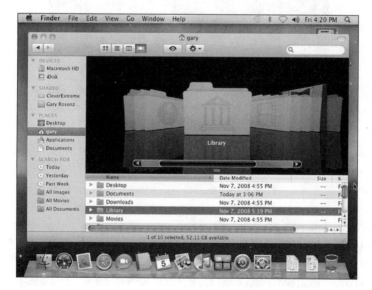

Figure 4.5

The cover flow view shows you icons or previews in a 3D space at the top of the Finder window.

Cover flow is actually a modification of the list view. You can see the list view, in fact, at the bottom of the window. But at the top you get a 3D view of the icons, which you can flip through using the scrolling bar under them. Often the icons are previews of the documents, especially in the case of images.

Although cover flow may not really add any extra functionality over list view, it does provide you with a great way to visually examine a folder full of images.

Quick Look

Icons have been around on computers for decades now. They are little graphical representations of a file. The icon for a word processing document may look like a piece of paper, and the icon for a sound file may look like a waveform or speaker.

As you use OS X you'll find that some icons go even further than simple representations. Some will actually look like miniature versions of the contents of the files. For instance, an image file may look like a tiny picture of that image.

But sometimes even that is not enough to get an idea of what the file contains. You could open the file up in the program it was created with. Or, you could use what is called Quick Look.

Select a file in the Finder and simply press the spacebar or press the Quick Look button at the top of the Finder window. It looks like an eye. A semitransparent window will appear with either a larger icon of the item, or a larger preview of its contents. In Figure 4.6 you will see a larger folder icon, because it was a folder that was selected at the time.

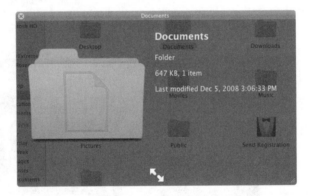

Figure 4.6
The Quick Look window gives you more information about an item in the Finder.

You'll notice that in Figure 4.6 you can see the name, description, size, and number of items in the folder. You can also see the modification date. Other item types show different things. For instance, images will simply show a large preview of the image and no additional information.

However, if you select multiple images, the Quick Look window turns into a slideshow presentation tool. Figure 4.7 shows the arrows that appear at the bottom of the window in this case.

If you click on the icon at the bottom that looks like four boxes, you will see all of the images selected laid out in a grid. This lets you quickly select an image from a group.

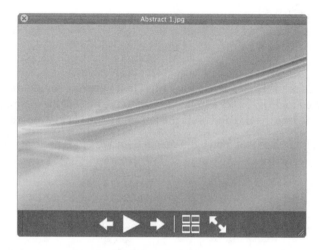

Figure 4.7
The Quick Look window can also be used to view images as a slideshow or an index sheet.

Action Button

Back to the main Finder window, the button next to the Quick Look button is the Action button. It looks like a gear or a cog.

Clicking on this button presents you with a menu of options. You can see this in Figure 4.8.

Figure 4.8
The Action button gives you access to many commands concerning the selected items in the Finder.

Many of these commands are also available in the menu bar at the top of your screen, or by a keyboard shortcut. For instance, the first item is New Folder. That same task can be done by using the menu item File, New Folder or the keyboard shortcut Command+Shift+N.

We'll look more at the Finder's functions like the ones in this menu later on in this chapter and in Chapter 5.

Search Field

At the very right side of the Finder window is a small text field. You can use this to start a search for a file. All you need to do is to click in this field, just to the right of the magnifying glass icon. Then type something into the box and press the Return key on your keyboard.

The result will be a list of files that match the search term. We'll look more at this in Chapter 5 in the section "Searching for Files."

The Sidebar

The left side of the Finder window is a list of locations you may want to access frequently. They are broken into sections such as Devices, Shared, Places, and Search For.

The Places list simply shows folders on your hard drive, like the Application folder or your personal Documents folder. If you click on any of these, the window shows the contents of that folder.

Likewise, the Devices are physical hard drives, CD-ROMs, DVDs, or some other sort of media directly connected to your computer. Click on one of these and you will see the contents of the top level of the device. In addition, the Shared section shows other computers or networked disk drives that your Mac sees.

The Search For section is a little different. It performs a predefined search for you and shows the results in the Finder window. For instance, the Today search shows you files modified today.

You can add folders to the Places section by simply dragging them from a Finder window to the Places area in the sidebar. This won't move or copy the folder at all; it just adds the folder to the list for easy access.

Status Bar

At the very bottom of a Finder window you will see some text. For instance in Figure 4.5 it reads "1 of 10 selected, 52.11 GB available."

This is the status bar and it gives you some simple information about the contents of the Finder window. In this case, you have one item selected, and there are 10 total items in the folder. You also know that there are 52.11 gigabytes of free space available on the hard drive.

Resizing and Modifying the Finder Window

There are two other active places on the Finder window that we should look at before moving on. The first is the flat button at the upper right. Clicking this removes the toolbar, sidebar, and status bar of the Finder window, making it as simple as possible. Click it again to get those features back.

Also, in the bottom right is a set of three diagonal lines. You can grab these with the cursor and drag them to resize the window.

The Menu Bar

At the top of the screen you will find the menu bar. This gray line starts on the left with the Apple symbol and continues with a series of words, each of which represents a different menu.

The contents of the menu bar vary from application to application, but in the Finder it will usually look like in Figure 4.9. Let's take a look at each Finder menu and examine the functions of each menu item.

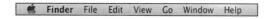

Figure 4.9

The Finder's menu bar contains some basic menu items and some that are specific to performing file and folder functions.

In most cases the menu bar is present; it just changes to adapt to the current applications. But in some cases, most commonly in large games, the menu bar may be removed to allow the game to fill the entire screen. The same is true when you play a DVD movie on your Mac in full screen mode.

The Apple Menu

The Apple menu is so-called because the Apple symbol is used as its title, rather than a word. It is always the leftmost menu, as you can see in Figure 4.10 and it always contains the same items, no matter which application you are running.

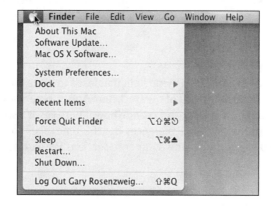

Figure 4.10

The Apple menu allows you to perform some system maintenance functions and access preferences.

ABOUT THIS MAC

The first item in the Apple menu is About This Mac. When you select this item, you get a window that contains information about your computer and the OS installed on it. It will tell you the processor in your machine and how much memory is installed. You can also see which version of OS X is running, such as 10.6.

> The About This Mac window also gives you a More Info button that, when clicked, launches the System Profiler application. This tells you almost every detail of your computer, from serial number to the amount of video memory on the video card.

SOFTWARE UPDATE

Next is the Software Update item. This launches a utility that checks in with Apple and sees if you are running the latest version of Mac OS X, other components like the QuickTime video playback engine, and Apple software like iTunes and iPhoto. You'll learn more about it in Chapter 23, "Keeping Your Mac Up to Date."

MAC OS X SOFTWARE

The Mac OS X Software item is simply a shortcut to open your web browser and go to http://www.apple.com/downloads/ where you can learn about and download Mac software. It features both software from Apple and from third-party software makers.

SYSTEM PREFERENCES

The System Preferences menu item launches the system preferences utility. This is what gives you access to choices you can make about how your Mac looks and operates. Throughout this book we'll be looking at various parts of System Preferences. In particular, Chapter 22, "Customizing Your Mac," focuses on it.

DOCK

Next is the Dock. This is an example of a menu item that leads to more menu items. You can tell by the right-pointing triangle at the end of the Dock item. This submenu leads to menu items that let you quickly reposition the Dock and change how it behaves. It also includes a Dock Preferences item that launches System Preferences, but this time takes you right to the Dock preferences instead of displaying all of the preference sections. We'll explore the Dock options in a section later in this chapter.

RECENT ITEMS

The Recent Items menu is a list of shortcuts to allow you to open the most recently used applications and documents. So, for instance, if you were working on a Pages document yesterday, you may find it listed here. You can select it and your Mac will run Pages and open the document.

FORCE QUIT FINDER

Next is Force Quit Finder, an item that launches a list of currently running applications and allow you to force a troublesome one to quit. This is similar to hitting Ctrl+Alt+Delete on a Windows machine and forcing an application closed through the Task Manager. You can also bring up this menu by pressing Command+Option+Esc on your keyboard.

SLEEP, RESTART, SHUT DOWN

The next three menu items are ones that you learned about in Chapter 3, "Starting Up and Shutting Down." They allow you to put your computer to sleep, restart it, or shut it down.

Likewise, the last item in the Apple menu is similar to shutting down, but it doesn't turn off your computer. Instead, you are logged out as a user and returned to the login screen. This is what you would do if you are on a computer used by many people and you wanted to log off so the next person to use the computer does not have access to your documents and media.

The Application Menu

If you look back at Figure 4.9, you will see that there is no menu named Application—this is because the menu changes names to match the currently running program. So it is not only a menu, but an indicator of which application is currently being used.

Figure 4.11 shows the Finder's application menu. It shows you tasks specific to the Finder.

Figure 4.11

The Finder's application menu includes some functions that you will find in any application's menu.

In Figure 4.11 you will see some items that are written in gray letters, rather than in black. These "grayed-out" menu items are inactive. They currently cannot be used because of some other factor.

For instance, the Empty Trash menu choice can't be used because in this case the trash is already empty. The Hide Finder choice is grayed out because the Finder is the only program running, so if it is hidden, there would be nothing else to show.

ABOUT

The first item in almost any application's menu is the About item. Usually if you choose this a small window appears, telling you the name of the application and what version. Sometimes there is a link to the software maker's website, or a list of credits and other information.

PREFERENCES

Also common in the Application menu is Preferences. This usually brings up a window with preferences specific to the application. In the case of the Finder, you get Finder Preferences. This is the topic of the last section of this chapter.

EMPTY TRASH

In Chapter 5 we'll deal with deleting files. That is what Empty Trash and Secure Empty Trash are used for.

SERVICES

In addition, the Services menu is a long submenu that allows you to pass information along from one application to the next. For instance, you could select a file, then choose Finder, Services, Mail, Send File. This would run the application Mail and start a new message that contains the file as an attachment.

HIDE FINDER, HIDE OTHERS, AND SHOW ALL

The last set of items in the application menu is usually found here for all applications. The first, Hide Finder, allows you to hide the current application, making it and all of its windows invisible, but still running in the background. Likewise, Hide Others would do that for everything except the currently running application. The Show All option would make any hidden applications visible again.

Command+H is the keyboard shortcut for hiding the current application, and Mac pros use it often. For instance, when you are done writing an email, you would hit the Send button and then immediately press Command+H to hide Mail and return to the application you were working on previously. Mail works in the background to connect to the server and send your mail, and may even continue to work to retrieve new mail, which will be waiting for you the next time you switch back to Mail again.

The File Menu

The File menu is usually the place you will find commands like Save and Open. But since we are examining the Finder, which is all about files, the File menu has some of the main functionality of the Finder.

Figure 4.12 shows a long list of file functions, most of which we will examine in Chapter 5.

NEW

The first four menu items under File give you the ability to create new things. You can open a new Finder window, create a new empty folder, or create something called a *smart folder*. You can also create a *burn folder* for gathering together items to burn onto a CD or DVD.

Figure 4.12

The File menu contains most of the powerful functions of the Finder.

OPEN, OPEN WITH

The Open menu item is the usual way you would open files in the application you are running. For instance, if you are running Pages, you could open Pages documents with this menu choice.

In the Finder, however, the Open menu item allows you to open any file with the application that is associated with that file. So if you selected a Pages file and chose File, Open, the Pages application would launch and then open the file.

Likewise, the Open With menu choice lists all of the applications that could possibly open the file. So a text document might allow itself to be opened with Pages, TextEdit, Microsoft Word, and anything else that you have installed that works with text documents. The applications will be listed in the submenu.

> **NOTE**
>
> If you hold down the Option key and select the File menu, the Open With option will change to Always Open With. This gives you a chance to tell the Finder to open a document with a specific application and remember that choice for next time. This way you can double-click on that document later on and know that it will open in the correct application.
>
> This is useful when you have more than one application that can open a type of document, like a word processing document, and the Finder seems to want to choose the wrong one each time.

PRINT

The Print menu item is similar to Open, but it should trigger the application it runs to immediately print the document. This is true for most applications and document types, although a few do not follow the Finder's instructions.

CLOSE WINDOW

You can close a selected Finder window by clicking on the red button at the upper-right corner of the window, or by choosing this menu item. You can also use the keyboard shortcut Command+W.

GET INFO

The Get Info menu item and the keyboard shortcut Command+I bring up a small window giving you various pieces of information about the file or files selected. Figure 4.13 shows one such window.

Figure 4.13

The Info window in the Finder will tell you the kind, size, dates, and other information about a file or group of files.

You can also press Option+Command+I to bring up the Inspector window. The difference between the Info window and the Inspector is that the Inspector is a floating palette that remains above all other Finder windows and its contents change to reflect whatever file or files are selected.

COMPRESS

The Compress menu item takes the file or files selected and creates a .zip archive file that contains them all. You can then email this compressed file, or simply use the .zip archive to compact a large file that you may not need in the near future.

DUPLICATE

Duplicate, or Command+D, creates a copy of the selected file. It appends the word "copy" to the end of the new file's name. This is useful when you want to make changes to a document but want to keep a copy of the document as it stands now as well.

MAKE ALIAS

Aliases, called shortcuts in Windows, are pointers to a file or a folder. When you create an alias with the Make Alias menu item, it appends the word "alias" to the filename so that it is not confused with the original.

The point to an alias is to stick the alias in a place where you may look for the file, while the real file stays in the place that makes the most organizational sense.

For instance, you may want to keep an important document in your user Documents folder. But for easy access, you may create an alias and place that alias on the Desktop. Then you can open the file by double-clicking on this alias without going to the Documents folder.

You can do this in one step by holding down Command+Option and dragging the file. Instead of moving the file to a new Finder window or the desktop, you will create an alias in the new location. Chapter 5 explains more about dragging, dropping, and moving files.

QUICK LOOK

The Quick Look function brings up a preview window showing the contents of the file. This works best for things like text documents and images. Quick Look is also accessed by pressing Command+Y or simply pressing the spacebar while a file is selected.

SHOW ORIGINAL

When you select an alias, the Show Original menu item activates and allows you to find the file that the alias links to.

ADD TO SIDEBAR

In the section about the Sidebar earlier in this chapter, I mentioned that you can drag a file or folder to it to add it to the Sidebar. You can also select an item and use this menu choice to put it there.

MOVE TO TRASH

To delete files, you need to go through a two-step process. The first is to select the file and use this menu choice to move it to the Trash. The Trash is a temporary holding place for unwanted files. You can always choose to retrieve an item from the trash and rescue it, or to empty the trash using the menu choice from the Finder menu.

You'll learn more about the Trash when we look at it as part of the Dock later in this chapter.

EJECT

If you have selected an item in the Finder that represents removable media, like a CD-ROM or a USB thumb drive, you can select the Eject option to have it removed from the Finder.

In the case of a CD or DVD, this also physically ejects the disk. In the case of something like a USB thumb drive or other external drive, you have to complete the physical part yourself by unplugging the device.

Using the Eject menu choice first ensures that the Finder checks to make sure the media is not in use. If it is in use, Finder takes care of any unfinished business, such as closing files.

BURN

One way to create a CD-ROM or DVD-ROM is to simply select a file or folder, and then choose File, Burn. You will then be prompted to insert a writeable disk into the optical drive and the files are burned on to the disk. We'll be taking a closer look at burning disks in Chapter 24, "Backing Up and Archiving Your Files."

FIND

After you use your Mac for some time, you will begin to accumulate a lot of files. It may be necessary to search for a file by its name or contents when your Document folder gets large enough.

Pressing Command+F or using the File, Find menu item changes the current Finder window, adding a search box and some options at the top. You'll learn more about this in the next chapter, in the section on Spotlight.

LABEL

The File menu also includes a way for you to color-code your files. You can add a color label to any file with the small color blocks under the Label section of the File menu.

Labeling your files in this way may help in future searches. It may also separate the files for you visually.

The Edit Menu

The Edit menu is also present in most applications. It usually contains many of the same choices, like Cut, Copy, Paste, and Undo, as shown in Figure 4.14. However, what those functions mean may differ depending on the application.

In the Finder, of course, these functions all pertain to the selected files or folders, and the actions performed on them.

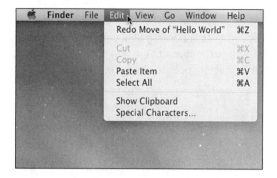

Figure 4.14

The Edit menu is rather simple in the Finder.

UNDO

The Undo function, usually accessed from the keyboard shortcut Command+Z, reverses the last major action you took. For instance, if you moved a file from one place to the next, the menu will look the same as it does in Figure 4.14.

You can continue to use the Undo function to reverse a whole series of actions.

CUT, COPY, PASTE

The standard three edit commands are Cut, Copy, and Paste. Their keyboard equivalents are Command+X, Command+C, and Command+V.

In the Finder, only the Copy and Paste functions work to copy files from one location to another. You can select a file, copy it, and then go to a new folder and Paste it to make a copy.

The Cut function does not work with files, but all three work when you are editing filenames.

SELECT ALL

The Select All function, also accomplished with Command+A, is very useful, but often over-looked. For instance, if you have a Finder window open and want to move or delete all of the files in it, you can use Select All instead of making a grand drag and outline cursor movement to indicate that you want all of the files.

Then you can drag them all as a group, or Move to Trash, or perform most any Finder function.

SHOW CLIPBOARD

When you do use the Copy function, the items you copy are saved to a temporary location called the Clipboard, just like in Windows. You can view the contents of the Clipboard using File, Show Clipboard.

If you have copied a file, you will see the name of that file. If you have copied text, you'll see the actual text.

SPECIAL CHARACTERS

While typing text in text documents or naming files, you may occasionally want to use a character that is not represented on your keyboard. One way to do this is to choose File, Special Characters to bring up the Characters palette, shown in Figure 4.15.

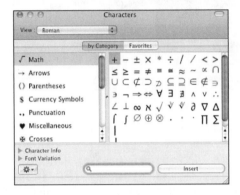

Figure 4.15

The Characters palette lets you search through various symbols and choose one to insert into text that you are working on.

The View Menu

The View menu, shown in Figure 4.16, includes several ways to modify how Finder windows look and behave.

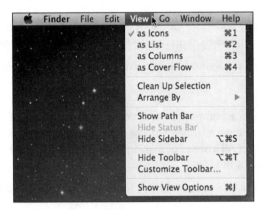

Figure 4.16

The View menu lets you determine how files are listed in a Finder window.

AS ICONS, AS LIST, AS COLUMNS, AS COVER FLOW

Earlier in this chapter we took a look at the four different ways that a Finder window can display files. You saw how to select them using the button at the top of the Finder window. These menu choices are simply another way to do that.

CLEAN UP SELECTION

This function only works in icon view. It will attempt to take the files you've selected a[nd arrange] them in a neat, orderly grid.

ARRANGE BY

There are several options under Arrange By, including Name, Date Modified, Date Creat[ed], Kind, and Label. This will reorder the appearance of the files in the Finder window. It ev[en works] in icon view, rearranging the files on a grid according to the criteria.

SHOW/HIDE PATH BAR

The Path Bar is an optional part of the Finder window that shows each part of the path [leading] to the currently selected file. So it might show Macintosh HD > Users > gary > Documer[nts].

SHOW/HIDE STATUS BAR

The Status Bar is something we looked at earlier in the chapter. You can toggle the visib[ilit]y o[f] just the Status Bar with this menu option.

SHOW/HIDE SIDEBAR

The sidebar, dominating the left side of any Finder window, can be removed and reinstated using this menu option.

SHOW/HIDE TOOLBAR

Likewise, you can toggle the visibility of the top toolbar of a Finder window.

CUSTOMIZE TOOLBAR

If you feel like it, you can customize your Finder window toolbars with this menu command. It shows you a graphical list of all of the buttons currently in the Finder window toolbar, plus some additional ones, like a Delete button and a New Folder button. You can drag these buttons to the toolbar to insert them.

SHOW VIEW OPTIONS

This option allows you to customize the appearance of each type of view (icon, list, columns, Cover Flow) for the Finder window. When you select this menu item, a window opens that displays options that are specific to the current view. So before you select Show View Options, you must change the current view of the Finder window to the view that you want to customize. The icon view has the most options, even letting you set an image as the background for the Finder window.

The Go Menu

The Go menu will change what the current Finder window shows. Some of the commands, which you can see in Figure 4.17, will work even if there is no Finder window, simply opening up a new one to show the location.

Connect to Server... ⌘K

Figure 4.17
The Go menu includes icons next to some of the locations to help you determine what they are.

BACK, FORWARD

The Back and Forward menu items work just like back and forward buttons in a web browser. If you have been using the same Finder window for a while, and want to navigate back to the previous folder you were looking at, just click Back, and likewise for Forward. This works the same as the Back and Forward buttons mentioned earlier in the chapter.

ENCLOSING FOLDER

Sometimes it is necessary to move up to the folder enclosing the folder you are viewing at the moment. For instance, if you are in Documents, you might want to move up to your user home folder.

COMPUTER, HOME, DESKTOP, APPLICATIONS, UTILITIES

Among the next set of options are several that take the Finder window to familiar places. Computer goes to the root level of the hard drive, while Home goes to the user top level. Desktop takes you to the Desktop folder of the user folder, which is another way of looking at the files places on your desktop background.

Likewise, Applications takes you to the folder on the top level of the hard drive where most of the applications are installed. In that folder is another named Utilities that contains some more applications.

NETWORK

Choosing Network takes you to a folder that actually isn't a folder at all. Instead, it is a Finder window that lists all of the other computers and networked storage devices that it sees.

This would be one way to find another computer on your network and begin file sharing with it. You can read more about sharing files with other computers in Chapter 13, "Networking and File Sharing."

IDISK

Another, more distant, file-sharing location is your iDisk. But you will only have an iDisk if you subscribe to the MobileMe service from Apple. One of the benefits of this service is a storage folder called your iDisk that is housed remotely by Apple. Check out the MobileMe section of Chapter 13 for more information about this service.

RECENT FOLDERS

Just as the Apple menu had a Recent Items submenu, the Go menu has a Recent Folders sub-menu. This allows to you quickly go to any folder you may have used recently.

GO TO FOLDER

In Mac OS X there are often many ways to accomplish the same task. The Go to Folder menu command allows you to type in the path of a folder to take the Finder window to it. So, for instance, you can type /users/gary/documents to go to Gary's Documents folder.

CONNECT TO SERVER

There are also many different ways to connect to a networked computer. Instead of using the Network menu command above, you can choose Connect to Server or press the keyboard short-cut Command+K to bring up a window that allows you to type in the location of a networked device.

This option should be left to expert users, unless you have been told to use it by someone else at your organization. Sometimes networked computers will be available to you, but will not show up in the Network list. Using Connect to Server allows you to request that your Mac look for that device anyway. You may be typing a local server name, or a remote Internet IP address.

The Window Menu

The Window menu contains some items that duplicate the functionality of the buttons at the upper left of each window, as well as some other things. As you can see in Figure 4.18, there are only a few functions for the Window menu in the Finder.

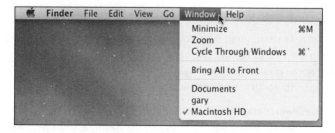

Figure 4.18

The Window menu in the Finder ends with a list of all open Finder windows.

MINIMIZE, ZOOM

These functions get the same result as the Minimize and Zoom buttons at the top of each Finder window. It is worth noting that the keyboard shortcut for Minimize is Command+M. This comes in handy if you want to get the frontmost Finder window out of the way. You can also use Command+Option+M to minimize all Finder windows.

CYCLE THROUGH WINDOWS

If you have many Finder windows open, you can use this command or Command+` to bring each one to the front in succession.

BRING ALL TO FRONT

Finder windows will intermingle with other applications' windows. For instance, if you have the Safari web browser open, you can have one Finder window behind that, then the Safari window, then another Finder window in front of both. Using Bring All to Front ensures that all Finder windows are in front of all other windows.

WINDOW LIST

The end of the Window menu is a list of all open Finder windows. You can select any one to bring it to the front. The name of the frontmost window has a checkmark next to it, as shown in Figure 4.18.

The Help Menu

The Help menu, shown in Figure 4.19, changes quite a bit from application to application. Some applications have special documentation that can be found in this menu.

Figure 4.19

The simple Help menu in the Finder.

In the Finder, it is a simple search text field. You can enter any term and then you will be shown where it is located in the Finder. For instance, enter **Copy** and you will see the menu item appear and a floating blue arrow point it out (see Figure 4.20). In addition, you will see a variety of help topics appear that lead to documentation if you select them.

If you choose the Mac Help menu item shown in Figure 4.19, you will get a small window that invites you to ask a question. Then it will try to match up your question with a page in the Mac OS X documentation.

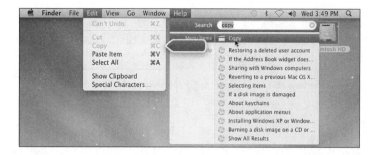

Figure 4.20

*If you type **Copy** into the Help menu search field, you are shown where the Copy menu item is located.*

Menu Bar Status Items

The menu bar's right portion contains some small icons and sometimes text that allow you to access system preferences or simply to tell you the time. Figure 4.21 shows a simple set of icons that may be found when you first run your Mac. The specific icons that appear in the menu bar depend on the particular model of Mac and the equipment or features that are installed on it.

Figure 4.21

The default set of icons at the upper-right corner of the menu bar.

In Figure 4.21, the items represent: Time Machine, Bluetooth, Airport, Volume, the clock, and Spotlight.

These status items have two purposes. The first is to display some information. For instance, if your Mac is connected to a wireless network, the Airport item would show you how strong your signal was. The Volume item shows you generally how high your volume is set, by the number of curves to the right of the speaker.

The other purpose of these status items is to act as a menu to access common functions. For instance, the Airport item gives you a menu of all local wireless networks and allows you to connect to one without having to open the network system preferences.

The Dock

The Dock is a strip of icons at the bottom of your screen that contains applications, folders, files, and a few other things. You can see it in Figure 4.22. It is similar to the Windows taskbar in some ways, but it can do much more.

Figure 4.22

The Dock has a 3D appearance with icons sitting on a shelf at the bottom of your desktop.

Using the Dock

To launch an application, simply click on its icon in the Dock. For instance, clicking on the third icon in Figure 4.22 launches the Mail application.

You can also add more applications to the Dock, rather than just sticking with the default set. If you open your Applications folder, you can drag and drop any application into the Dock. This won't "move" the application there, but rather put a shortcut to it in the Dock. Now you can launch that application by clicking on it in the Dock instead of finding it again in the Applications folder.

You can also drag and drop files and folders into the Dock, but you must put them to the right separator that is shown in Figure 4.23 between the twelfth and thirteenth icons.

Special Dock Items

The leftmost item in the Dock is the Finder. Mac OS X usually treats the Finder like any other application with the exception that the Finder is always running.

If you are using another application and want to switch back to the Finder to look for files or some other Finder function, just click on the Finder icon in the Dock.

Next to the Finder is the Dashboard icon. The Dashboard contains lots of little programs, such as a calculator, clock, weather widget, and mini calendar. You'll learn more about the Dashboard in Chapter 7, "Applications That Come with Your Mac."

With the default setup of the Dock, the last application listed before separator is System Preferences, an icon that gives you an alternate way to launch the System Preferences windows besides using the Apple menu.

To the right of the separator are shortcuts to your Documents and Downloads folders. But if you click on them, you'll find that they don't just open a Finder window. Instead, they spring up with a column of icons that show the files in the folder, as in Figure 4.23.

You'll learn more about Stacks later on in this chapter.

The last item in the Dock is an icon for the Trash. Instead of using File, Move to Trash, you can simply drag any file or folder on to this icon in the Dock to place it in the Trash for later permanent deletion.

Figure 4.23

Folders linked to in the Dock work as Stacks, springing out to show you their contents when you click on them.

Dock Preferences

You can change the appearance of the Dock, and even where it appears on the screen in the Dock preferences. To find this window, shown in Figure 4.24, choose the Apple menu, Dock, Dock Preferences.

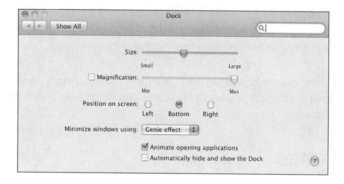

Figure 4.24

The Dock preferences window allows you to change the size and location of the Dock.

You can play around with the settings to see how you would best like your Dock to look. Changing from Genie effect to Scale effect may be a good option on a slower Mac. The same goes for the Animate Opening Applications option.

If you prefer that the Dock not be visible when you don't need it, select the Automatically Hide and Show the Dock option. This makes the Dock disappear. But it reappears when you move your mouse over the area with the Dock.

Stacks

When you place a folder on the right side of the Dock, you will create a Stack. This is simply an expandable part of the Dock that allows you to quickly see and select a file in that folder, just as in Figure 4.23.

You can customize a stack to appear in many ways. If you Ctrl-click on the icon in the Dock, you get a menu that looks like Figure 4.25. This lets you decide how the Stack will appear.

Figure 4.25
Stack options let you choose the sort order and display type of a folder in the Dock.

You can change with these settings to see what you like best. The Display As choices determine how the icon looks in the Dock. If you select Stack, the icon changes to match the most recent item added to the folder.

Finder Preferences

You'll find that most parts of Mac OS X are customizable. You can make choices as to how things look and work. Choose Finder, Finder Preferences to open the window shown in Figure 4.26.

The Finder Preferences stretch over four tabbed portions of the window: General, Labels, Sidebar, and Advanced.

General Finder Preferences

On this tab, you can select which items appear on the Desktop. Typically, hard disks, both internal and external to your computer, and optical media appear. But you can choose not to show them on the Desktop if you want. You will still see them in the Finder window sidebars.

You can also change the behavior of a brand new Finder window, choosing to show your home folder, or something else like the hard drive root folder or your Documents folder.

You can also set a preference in the Finder so that any time you double-click on a folder, it will open that folder in a new window, rather than making the current Finder window change to show that folder.

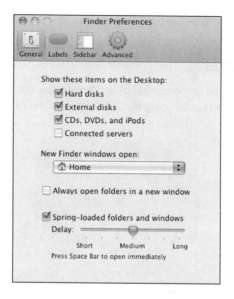

Figure 4.26

The Finder Preferences window showing the General tab.

The last setting refers to spring-loaded folders. This behavior occurs when you are dragging a file in the Finder to copy or move it. When you drag it over a folder, and wait a second, the folder opens to allow you to place the file inside the folder or navigate deeper into subfolders.

Labels Finder Preferences

Earlier in the chapter we looked at file labels. You can choose from one of seven colors to label any file or folder. By default, these labels have names that match their colors, like you can see in Figure 4.27.

Figure 4.27

The Labels tab of the Finder Preferences window.

If you are using labels to help organize your files, you may find it useful to change the names of these seven labels. For instance, you could use one as "Personal" and another as "Business."

Sidebar Finder Preferences

You can add and remove items in the sidebar of any Finder window. One way to specify some of the items you want to see there is by using the Sidebar tab in the Finder Preferences window, shown in Figure 4.28.

Figure 4.28

The Sidebar portion of the Finder Preferences window.

One of the advantages to using the Finder Preferences is that it is easy to remove items directly in the Finder window, but it can be hard to add them back. The check box system here gives you control either way.

Advanced Finder Preferences

The last tab in the Finder Preferences window, shown in Figure 4.29, contains some miscellaneous, yet very powerful, functions.

The first choice, Show All File Extensions, is probably something any power user will want to turn on. This way, a text file named "mydoc.txt" actually appears as "mydoc.txt" in the Finder. Otherwise, it appears simply as "mydoc." Power users like to know the exact filename.

The next two choices are about whether warnings appear when you try to perform specific actions. They are self-explanatory, and probably should be left as-is unless you are a power user who wants these turned off.

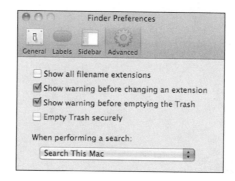

Figure 4.29

The Advanced tab of the Finder Preferences window contains a list of powerful options.

The next option enforces performing a secure delete when you empty the Trash. Normally you have the option of selecting either in the Finder menu. A secure delete overwrites the file's remains on your hard drive, permanently erasing any sensitive data.

The last item is a pop-up menu that lets you customize Finder searches a bit. You can choose to start a search by looking at the whole Mac, the current folder, or remember the scope of the previous search performed. You can find out about more search options in the section "Searching For Files" in Chapter 5.

That wraps up a look at the Finder, but only begins to show us how files and folders are manipulated on your Mac. The next chapter teaches you how to move them around, how to search for them, and how your hard drive is organized.

WHO SHOULD READ THIS CHAPTER:

If you are new to Mac and want to learn the basics of handling files in the Finder, this is the chapter for you. For Windows users, you'll learn the Mac way for handling files.

5

Working with Files and Folders

Now that you know your way around the Finder, you can apply that knowledge to organize your files. In this chapter you'll learn how to move files around, rename them, copy them, and delete them. You'll also learn how to search for files and how to use some advanced forms of search, like Smart Folders.

How Your Hard Drive Is Organized

Even before you move the mouse on your Mac for the first time, there are already thousands of files on your hard drive. These are Mac OS X system files and preinstalled applications.

There is a method to how these files are arranged. It is a relatively simple method, though. Understanding this structure doesn't take much time, and can help you to better use your Mac down the road.

Hard-Drive Level

The top, or root, level of your hard drive is named whatever you like. But chances are it has the default name of Macintosh HD. On a new or clean Mac system, it should have only four subfolders: Applications, Library, System and Users. Figure 5.1 shows the hard drive selected and several columns of folders and subfolders using the Finder window's column view.

Figure 5.1

The first column is the hard-drive level, the second shows the Users folder subfolders, and the third is one user's folders.

The System folder contains Mac OS X and all of its supporting files. A typical user will never need to look in here. In addition, a System folder should contain only the system itself, not any files specific to this one Mac. Those would be in the Library folder.

The Library folder is where your copy of Mac OS X begins to differ from any other copy. Files specific to your computer and choices you have made—and supporting files from applications you have installed—are in this folder. It would start the same as any other Mac's Library folder, but then diverge from there.

> **NOTE**
>
> Of interest in the Library folder is the Fonts folder. If you install any new fonts, you have the choice of making them available to just you or to any user on the machine. If you choose to make them available to anyone on the Mac, they would go in the Fonts folder in the Library folder.

The Applications folder is where all of your programs go. It starts off with the Mac OS X default programs like TextEdit, Safari, Mail, and so on. It also contains iLife and iWork programs if you have those installed.

When you install a new application, this is the default location for the install. In most cases, it might be the only place you are allowed to install the program.

A simple installer for an application may, in fact, ask you simply to drag and drop the application file into your Applications folder. This is because many applications don't need support files at all, making an installer unnecessary.

The Users folder is where individual users each have a folder of their own. In many cases there will just be one folder for one user, as in Figure 5.1. But there is also a Shared folder that is meant to be a place where any user on the machine can place and retrieve files.

User Home Folder

Your home folder is where you should store most of your files. You can see it in Figure 5.2. There are several standard folders in the home folder, as shown in the following list.

Figure 5.2

The user home folder includes standard folders like Documents, Movies, Music, Pictures, and Public.

- **Desktop**—This corresponds to files and folders found on the background of the Finder, also known as the Desktop.

- **Documents**—This folder is the main place you will store things you create, like word processing files, spreadsheets, presentations, and so on.

- **Downloads**—By default, when you download a file from the Internet, it will be placed in this folder for you to find.

- **Library**—Both applications and the system use this folder to store preferences you set and data collected. Most users will never have to look in here.

- **Movies**—This folder is used to store data files made by iMovie and other video-editing programs.

- **Music**—This folder is where iTunes stores your music, videos, and podcasts that you download or create.

- **Pictures**—This folder is where iPhoto stores any digital pictures you load onto your Mac.

- **Public**—Files in the Public folder are available for other users on the Mac or on your network to view and copy. More about that later in this section.

- **Sites**—This folder is where you can create your own local website. It is used mostly by web developers who are testing designs or web programming.

We'll be using these folders throughout the book as you learn to use different parts of Mac OS X and different applications.

The Desktop

The Desktop deserves some special attention. On the one hand it is just a folder inside your user folder. But you also see it represented as the file icons on the background of your screen.

For example, look at Figure 5.3. In a Finder window you can see the contents of the Desktop folder inside the user's folder. There are three sample files.

Figure 5.3

Desktop files appear in both the Desktop folder and the Desktop itself.

At the same time, you can see those three sample files as icons on the background at the right side of the screen.

The Desktop folder and the actual Desktop are one and the same in this respect. Anything placed in the Desktop folder also appears on the Desktop background. Anything placed on the Desktop background appears in the Desktop folder. They are simply two different ways of looking at the same thing.

There is a difference between what you see on the Desktop and what you see in the folder. In Figure 5.3, for instance, you can see an icon representing the Macintosh HD on the Desktop, but not in the folder. So the Desktop shows the contents of the Desktop folder, plus some other icons as well.

Which items appear on the Desktop depends on your Finder preferences. We reviewed the options in Chapter 4, "Getting Around," and you can see them in Figure 4.27.

By default, all hard disks, optical media, and iPods are shown on the desktop as icons. You can also choose to have connected servers shown as well.

Public Folder

Most of the standard user folders like Documents and Pictures are just folders. But, along with the Desktop folder, the Public folder is something special.

Anything put into your Public folder can be seen by other users on your machine. In addition, when you learn how to share files between computers, you'll find that the Public folder is one of those places that is commonly shared.

Other users can see, open, and copy anything put into your Public folder. However, no one else can edit or delete them, nor can anyone place new files in your Public folder.

But there is a folder called your Drop Box that is inside your Public folder. This is a place where any other users can place a file. In a way it is the opposite of the Public folder—they can put files in there, but then they can't view them.

This is all for security, of course, as you don't want one user seeing a file that another user gave to you.

Yet another special folder is the Sites folder. Files put in here are also public, and in fact can be viewed by other users and even other computers as a website. You'll learn more about file sharing and the Sites folder in Chapter 13, "Networking and File Sharing."

Moving, Copying, and Renaming

The Finder is all about manipulating files. Learning how to move them around and rename them is the most basic skill that you will need to keep your hard drive organized.

Moving Files

To move files, simply drag and drop them from one place to another.

Now, by "place" I mean folders. So, for example, you could have two folders represented by two different Finder windows, as in Figure 5.4.

You can create as many Finder windows as you want by choosing File, New Finder Window or by pressing Command+N while in the Finder. Then you can navigate each one to show a separate folder's contents.

Now to move Sample File Two to the Notes and Things folder, you would just use your mouse to drag it from one window to the other. Figure 5.5 shows this in progress, with the cursor "carrying" the file into the second window.

Figure 5.4

Two Finder windows, each one showing the contents of a different folder.

Figure 5.5

The file Sample File Two is being dragged from one folder to another.

To move more than one file at a time, you can drag and select multiple files and move them together. This works only in icon view. Just click in the Finder window away from any files and drag to create a box around one or more icons. Figure 5.6 shows this in progress.

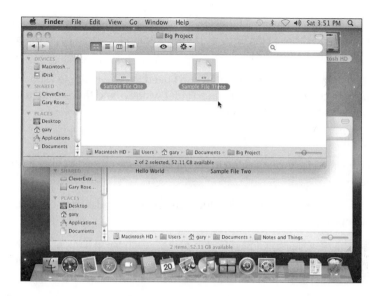

Figure 5.6

By dragging a box around several files, you can select more than one file at a time.

Now you can click and drag any of the selected files and they will all move together. This allows you to move many files at the same time.

Another way to select more than one file at a time is to click on the first file, and then hold down the Shift key and click on other files. This way you can select files that are not adjacent to each other.

Moving files from one Finder window to the other also works for the Desktop. You can move a file from the Desktop to a folder, or the other way around.

Copying a File

Copying a file is essentially just like moving a file. The only difference is that you are leaving the original in place. You end up with two files—one in the original folder and a duplicate in the new folder.

The way to copy a file is pretty much the same as the way you move a file. You just need to hold down the Option key after you start dragging the file. You know that you are doing it right if you see a green + symbol appear next to the file you are dragging.

You can also copy multiple files by selecting them all and dragging them while holding down the Option key.

There are times when you will actually be forced to copy a file rather than move it. For instance, if you are trying to move a file from one disk drive to another, you are technically not moving it at all, but making a copy of the file and deleting the original. The Finder will, in that case, convert your move into a copy, leaving the original in place. You can then delete it yourself if you like.

Another way to copy a file or group of files is to use the Copy and Paste method. You can select a file in one location and choose Edit, Copy or press Command+C. Then go to the other location and choose Edit, Paste or Command+V.

One advantage to doing it this way is that you don't need to have multiple windows open at the same time. You could copy from one folder in a Finder window, and then navigate in that same Finder window to another place and paste.

Duplicating a File

A variation on copying a file is duplicating it. This makes a copy of the file, with both files remaining in the same folder.

To duplicate a file, select it and choose File, Duplicate, or Command+D. You can also do this with a selection of several files.

The result is that the new file is given a different name—each file in a folder must have a unique name, of course. So if you were to duplicate the file "Hello World," you would end up with both "Hello World" and "Hello World copy" in the folder.

If you continue to make duplicates of a file, you get names like "Hello World copy 2" and "Hello World copy 3."

REASONS TO MAKE A DUPLICATE OF A FILE

1. Save a copy of your work as it stands before making new changes, so that you can revert back to it if you need.

2. Use a common starting point for two documents, like several documents that have the same first few paragraphs.

3. Start a new document by using an old document as a starting point, such as writing a letter similar to one you wrote many months ago.

Renaming Files

Changing the name of a file in Mac OS X is easy, but many new Mac users have trouble knowing where to start. The simplest way is to select a file in the Finder by clicking on it once. Then press the Return key on your keyboard.

The filename will now be selected and you can type something new. If you have your Finder set to show extensions, such as .txt or .doc, everything but the extension will be selected so that you can quickly and easily change the main name of the file, leaving the extension as-is.

NOTE

File extensions, like .doc for Word files or .psd for Photoshop files, tell the finder what application to use to open up a document. They can also help you remember what a document is, and help you differentiate between them. For instance, Vacation.doc might be your vacation diary, while Vacation.jpg would be a picture. You don't need to use extensions at all when creating files, as Mac OS X knows the file type of most documents. But some users find it useful, especially when making the transition from Windows, which requires them.

If you want to change the extension, however, you can do so using the arrow keys or the cursor to select the entire filename. You will be presented with a warning about changing the extension, as the Finder may no longer know what type of document the file is without the extension.

You can also change the names of folders you create in this way. However, Apple warns against changing the name of the Home or Applications folder, as Mac OS X relies on these folders having these specific names.

Examining Files and Folders

As you may have gathered, there is a lot more information associated with a file than just the file contents itself. For instance, there is a filename, its size, creation time, and so on.

File Info Window

You can view all information about any file by selecting the file and then choosing File, Get Info, or pressing Command+I. What you get is an Info window like the one in Figure 5.7.

Each section of the Info window contains different information about the file being examined. Much of it is only interesting for advanced users, but there are some pieces that can be used by anyone.

SPOTLIGHT COMMENTS

Spotlight is the program used to search for files in Mac OS X. Spotlight can search the titles and contents of files, and also file comments. So, for instance, if you add a Spotlight Comment of "Taxes" to a text file, it will show up in searches for "taxes" even if the word "taxes" does not appear in the name or content of the document.

To add a Spotlight Comment, just click on the white area under Spotlight Comments and start typing. You may need to click the little triangle to the left of Spotlight Comments to open up the area.

SIZE

In the General area, you'll see the size for the file selected. It is shown in two ways. Figure 5.7, for instance, shows 4 KB and also 328 bytes. The first is the amount of space the file takes up on your hard drive, and the second is the actual size of the file.

Figure 5.7

The Info window for a file is a long narrow window with many sections.

> **NOTE**
>
> Files are stored on your hard drive in blocks—a block is 4K, or 4096 bytes. Think of it like a piece of paper. You can fit 7 words on a piece of paper or 400 words, but you usually wouldn't cut a piece of paper to fit only 7 words—you would just leave the rest of the paper blank.
>
> A block is like that piece of paper. A 328-byte file will take up one block, and so will a 4096-byte file. A 4097-byte file will need to use two blocks of hard drive space, and so would show up as taking up 8K and 4097 bytes.

STATIONERY PAD

There are two ways to lock a file to prevent yourself from making changes to it. The first is to check the Stationery Pad, seen in Figure 5.7. A stationery pad is a locked file that opens as a new document using the original file as a template.

For instance, you could create a TextEdit document that is a sample letter. Save it and change it to a stationery pad. Now when you open it, TextEdit loads the contents of that file, but as a new file. So when you go to save your document you will be prompted to enter a new filename.

LOCKED

The second way to lock a file is simply to check off the Locked option. This allows you to open the file, but not save changes to it or overwrite it. In addition, if you try to delete the file, you will get a warning and have to give permission for the file to go into the trash.

OPEN WITH

This option allows you to specify an application to be used to open the file when you double-click it. You can also choose to change all files of the same type to use this application by clicking the Change All button. However, it is rare that you would need to do this.

Finder List View

Another way to get information about files is to use the List View of a Finder window. You can do this by selecting the List View button at the top of a standard Finder window, or by choosing View, as List from the menu bar. Figure 5.8 shows the list view with some sample files.

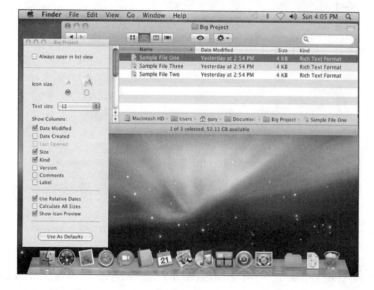

Figure 5.8

The List View can be modified using the View Options panel.

The advantage to using a Finder window in List View is that you can see details about several files at once. You can choose which details you see by choosing View, Show View Options to get the small window you can see in Figure 5.8 that allows you to add new columns like Date Created or Comments.

You can adjust the size of the columns by dragging the line in between the column titles. Clicking on the column titles themselves sorts the files by that column. Click again to reverse the sort order.

Searching for Files

There are several ways to search for files in Mac OS X. At the top-right corner of every Finder window is a search box. Just type something in that box, and the Finder window changes to a Spotlight window.

Spotlight is just the name that Apple gives to the search functionality in the Finder. A Spotlight window is a Finder window that shows search results rather than the contents of one folder.

Spotlight Window

Figure 5.9 shows a Spotlight window with results in the main area, and the search criteria at the top. You can view the results as a set of icons, or select the list view button at the top of the windows to see a list. You can also choose to view them using cover flow.

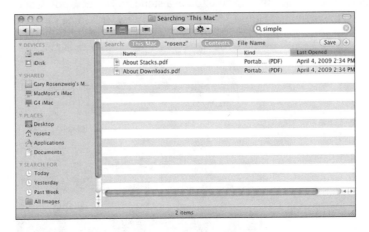

Figure 5.9

The Spotlight window is like a Finder window in icon or list view, but with search results rather than the contents of one folder.

At the top of the Spotlight window, in addition to the search field, is a set of buttons with names next to the label "Search." You can usually choose whether to search "This Mac" or the current folder that was selected when you started typing in the search field.

You can also select "Contents" or "File Name." The default is to search the contents of files. But sometimes this can return too many results. Searching by file name is better if you already know part of the name of the file and don't want results that also include that text as part of the contents of the file.

When you have some results, you can click on one of the columns to sort by that criteria, such as name or kind. At the bottom of the window you can see the path to the file you have selected.

You can also click the + button at the right side of the Spotlight criteria area to add another rule to your search. You can add as many rules as you want, and change the rules as you need. Figure 5.10 shows a whole set of different rules added to a Spotlight window.

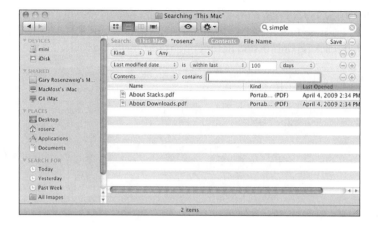

Figure 5.10

A Spotlight window can have as many rules as you want to narrow your search.

So, for instance, you could search for files with "taxes" in the name, that are of the kind made by the application Numbers, and were created in the last 12 months. In Figure 5.10, the search will look for files of any kind with any content modified in the last 100 days.

Using Ctrl-click or the right mouse button on a Mighty Mouse, you will get a contextual menu with choices like Open, Open With, or Open Enclosing Folder.

Spotlight Menu

Another way to search is to use the Spotlight menu found at the upper-right corner of your screen—it looks like a magnifying glass. Click once on that, or use Command+Spacebar to open a search field. Type your search term(s) in that field, and search results will populate a menu flowing down from the upper-right corner as in Figure 5.11.

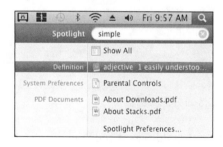

Figure 5.11

The Spotlight menu offers a quick but comprehensive way to search all your hard drive content.

You will see files, folders, applications, and even things like contacts, calendar events, and email. A Spotlight menu search is pretty comprehensive.

You can use the arrow keys to move through the Spotlight menu contents, or use the mouse to select something. Pressing Return or clicking once on an item opens it. Holding down the Command key plus clicking or pressing Return opens the enclosing folder for the item.

USING SPOTLIGHT AS A LAUNCHER

You can use the Spotlight menu as an application launcher. For instance, type **TextEdit** or even a portion of the name, like **Tex**, and you will see the TextEdit application appear in the Spotlight menu, and it will be selected by default. Just press Return and it launches.

So the complete sequence could be: Command+Spacebar, T, e, x, Return. That's all it would take to launch TextEdit from the keyboard.

Spotlight Elsewhere

The Spotlight search field also appears in other places besides the Finder. For instance, it can be found in Open dialog boxes for all applications. Figure 5.12 shows the Open dialog you get when trying to open something in TextEdit.

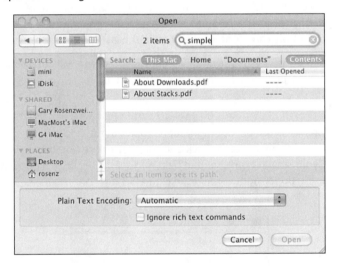

Figure 5.12

The Open dialog in TextEdit includes a Spotlight search field.

So instead of searching for a TextEdit document and then opening it, you can simply run TextEdit and then search using its Open dialog.

Another program that uses Spotlight is Mail. There is a search box in the upper-right corner of Mail that will result in a Spotlight search—but only of Mail messages.

Even the System Preferences has a Spotlight search field in it. This only shows results that apply to finding the right System Preference subpanel. It is very handy when you can't remember where something like "sleep" settings are. You just type "sleep" into the search field at the top of System Preferences and you'll be pointed in the right direction.

Saved Searches and Smart Folders

Suppose you find that you repeat a specific search relatively often. For instance, you always want to see what PhotoShop files you have created in the last seven days.

All you need to do is to perform this search once in a Spotlight window. Then, click on the Save button to the right and you will be asked to name the search and decide whether you want to add it to the Finder window sidebar.

As you can guess, when the search is in the Sidebar you can repeat it very quickly and easily. The Sidebar item is just an alias to a small file that contains the search definition. This file can be put anywhere, though the default location is your user Library folder, in a folder named Saved Searches. But you can decide to put them on your Desktop or anywhere else. Then just double-click on one to open a Spotlight window with that search.

A Smart Folder is the same thing as a Saved Search except that you start by creating the file first and then define the search criteria, whereas with a Saved Search, you define the criteria first and then save it as a file. To create a Smart folder, open the finder and choose File, New Smart from the menu.

Deleting Files

The basic process for deleting files consists of two steps: Move the file into the trash folder and then empty the trash.

The Trash

The Trash folder is a holding place for files that you no longer need. It is represented on the Dock by a trashcan icon all the way to the right side of the Dock. Double-click on that and you'll get a Finder window that looks pretty much like any other Finder window—you can even set it to icon, list, or column view.

The Trash folder is similar to the Windows Recycle Bin, but it isn't an icon on the desktop, but instead in the Dock. It also won't automatically delete files as it grows in size like the Recycle Bin.

There are many ways to put a file in the Trash. You can simply drag its icon from any Finder window or the Desktop into the trashcan icon on the Dock. You can also select the file and press Command+Delete on the keyboard. Another way is to right click or Ctrl-click on the item and choose Move to Trash or choose File, Move To Trash from the menu bar.

When a file is in the Trash, there is no rush to empty the Trash for most casual computer users. The whole idea of the Trash is to give you time to change your mind. It may turn out that you threw away the wrong file, or that you actually did need that file a few weeks later.

It is not uncommon for the Trash to hold days, weeks, or even months worth of old unwanted files.

Emptying the Trash

When you do want to empty the trash, all you need to do is choose File, Empty Trash. Or, you could Ctrl-click on the trashcan icon in the Dock and choose Empty Trash. Or, you could open the Trash Finder window and look for the Empty button on the right side near the top.

One option is to use File, Secure Empty Trash instead of just plain Empty Trash. The difference is that Secure Empty Trash overwrites the blocks on your hard drive that contain the files, making it impossible to recover the file contents. Otherwise, Empty Trash just tells the finder to forget that those files existed and reuse those blocks the next time it needs them for something else.

> **NOTE**
>
> Secure Empty Trash might seem as if it is only useful if you are paranoid. But it is easier to recover files than you may think. You can buy inexpensive programs that help you record files, or parts of files, that have been deleted. They are easy to use and come in handy when you accidentally delete something.
>
> But using Secure Empty Trash ensures that even these programs cannot recover what was deleted.

Now that you know how to work with files, let's look at the larger picture and learn how to control programs and windows open on your Mac.

WHO SHOULD READ THIS CHAPTER:

If you want to learn how to switch between programs and manage a whole bunch of windows on your screen at the same time, this is the chapter for you. If you think that managing lots of things at once on your Mac will be too much, you may also want to read this to find out how easy it is!

6

Controlling Windows and Applications

While working on your Mac you may typically have several applications open. For instance, you might have Mail and Safari open at the same time, so you can check your email and surf the web. You, may even have TextEdit open and be in the middle of writing a document, and iTunes open as well playing some music.

Multitasking is normal for a Mac user, and your computer and OS are built to handle it. Let's look at how you can manage multiple programs and windows in Mac OS X.

Hiding Windows and Applications

The key to managing multiple applications running at the same time is to realize that you don't need to *see* all of the applications. If you are running Mail, Safari, TextEdit and iTunes, you may only need to see Safari if you are just browsing the web at the moment.

For the rest of the applications, you can simply hide them.

Hidden applications are still running; you just can't see their windows. They can continue to "do" things, however. For instance, iTunes can continue to play music through your speakers or headphones, or it can continue to import songs from a CD, download podcasts, or burn a music CD.

So it is just a matter of controlling what you see and what is cluttering up your screen.

To hide an application, the standard menu choice is in the application's menu, and is shown as Hide followed by the application name. So for iTunes it is iTunes, Hide iTunes.

There is also a standard keyboard shortcut of Command+H, although it doesn't work in some third-party applications.

> **NOTE**
>
> When an application is hidden, you can unhide it by simply switching to that application again. You can use the Application Switcher or the Dock to do this. We'll look at both in the next section.

You can also hide individual windows of applications by clicking on the yellow minimize button at the top-left corner of the Finder, as you learned to do with Finder windows in Chapter 4, "Getting Around."

This places the window into the Dock, and you can find it there and click on it to expand the window again.

In addition to the Hide menu choice, you can also select Hide Others and Show All. The first hides everything except the current application. The latter makes all hidden applications visible.

Moving Between Windows and Applications

If you have multiple applications running, it is important to know all of the ways you can switch between them. Typically, you would use either the Dock or the Application Switcher.

However, you can also just use your mouse. If you can see a window from an application, just click in it to bring that application to the front as the one you are currently using. This is the simplest way to do it, as long as the application isn't hidden.

The Dock

Another way to do it is to look at the Dock. All of your running applications appear in the Dock, regardless of whether you put them in there. So, for instance, if you run the Terminal program, which is not normally in the Dock, it is temporarily added to the Dock as long as it is running. This is like looking at the buttons in the Windows taskbar.

> **NOTE**
>
> A small light appears in the Dock under any application that is running. This way you can see what might be running that you forgot about.

You can click on any running application in the Dock to both unhide it and bring it to the front. If any windows are minimized, you can see them on the right side of the Dock as well, and click on those to expand them.

The Application Switcher

The Application Switcher is a device that allows you to quickly move from one running application to the next. To activate it, press Command+Tab. It is like using Alt+Tab in Windows. Figure 6.1 shows the Application Switcher activated over a busy screen.

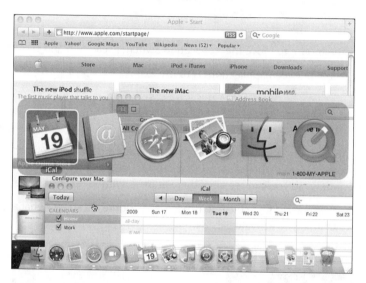

Figure 6.1

The Application Switcher temporarily appears over everything on the screen when you are using it.

After the Application Switcher is active, continue to hold down the Command key. From that point, you can use any number of other keys to navigate through the list of applications (see Table 6.1).

Table 6.1   Application Switcher Shortcut Keys

Key	Action
Tab	Move right
~	Move left
Shift-Tab	Move left
Left arrow	Move left
Right arrow	Move right
Home	Move to the first icon
End	Move to the last icon
Return	Switch to the selected application
H	Hide the selected application

Continues...

Table 6.1   Continued

Key	Action
Q	Quit the selected application
Esc	Quit the Application Switcher
.	Quit the Application Switcher

You can also use the mouse to move the Application Switcher selection and click to switch.

Another way to switch between applications is to use Exposé.

Exposé

Exposé, like the Application Switcher, is a device in the Finder. It deals with windows—all of the windows open from all of your applications. What Exposé does is to temporarily shrink and rearrange your windows so you can see all of them at once, without anything overlapping.

The default keyboard shortcut for activating Exposé is F9. Figure 6.2 shows what a cluttered Mac screen may look like after you activate Exposé.

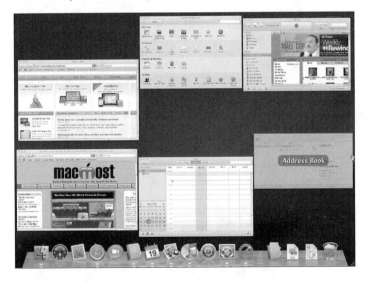

Figure 6.2

Exposé will shrink and move all of your windows so they no longer overlap.

The most basic reason to use Exposé is to find a window that you may have misplaced. Press F9 and then use the mouse to click on the window you want to bring to the front.

Alternatively, you can only look at windows from the current application by pressing F10. You can clear away all windows and only see the desktop by pressing F11. Press the same F10 or F11 key a second time to deactivate Exposé without performing an action and all your windows will return to their previous locations.

> You can also use the scroll ball on an Apple Mighty Mouse or a two-finger drag on a MacBook trackpad to move between windows after Exposé has been activated. You can then press F9 or F10 a second time to jump to that window. Alternatively, you can press and hold F9 or F10 and then release the key when you have selected the window you want.

Besides switching windows, there are many more ways to use Exposé for similar functions.

Moving Files

Select a file in a Finder window and start dragging it. While dragging, press F11 to move all of the windows away and see the Desktop. You can now drop the file on the Desktop.

This also works the opposite way. You can press F11, select and start to drag a Desktop file, and then press F11 again to move the windows back in place and drop the file into one of those windows.

You can even use this to drop files into other applications. For instance, an image file can be dropped onto Photoshop or any file can be added to a Mail message where it becomes an attachment.

Group by Application

When you press F9, you will see all of the visible windows crammed on to your screen. But then press the Tab key. This switches to showing only those windows in a single application. This is the same as pressing the F10 key to start Exposé.

Press Tab again and you'll move to the next application. This comes in handy when the windows are too small to allow you to figure out which one you want. Press F9 again or the esc key to exit.

Exposé Preferences and Active Screen Corners

You can set the keyboard shortcut preferences for Exposé by going to the System Preferences in the Apple menu and choosing the Exposé & Spaces preferences. Choose the Exposé tab and you'll see the preferences as shown in Figure 6.3.

In addition to the three keyboard shortcuts for activating Exposé, you also get to choose a keyboard shortcut for the Dashboard, which we'll look at later in this chapter.

At the top of the Exposé preferences window is a set of four options called *Active Screen Corners*. These are Desktop commands that you can activate by simply moving your mouse into a corner of your screen.

You can choose from the complete set of Exposé functions: all windows, application windows, and the desktop. These are the options that correspond to pressing F9, F10, and F11. You can also choose to launch the Dashboard.

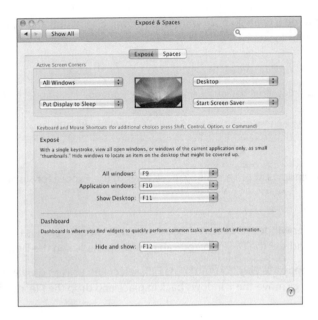

Figure 6.3

Exposé preferences include the preferences for active screen corners. If you have never set these before, each of them may be blank.

A corner can also be used to start or disable the screen saver. Setting a corner to start the screen saver would mean that you just move your mouse into that corner to start it. But setting a corner to disable the screen saver would mean that moving your cursor into that corner would stop the screen saver from starting when the time came. This is handy while giving a presentation.

You can also set a corner to activate the sleep mode of your computer. This is handy when you are trying to conserve every bit of power in your MacBook's battery while traveling.

Spaces

Most Mac users have a single display—the built-in screen of a MacBook or iMac. But sometimes a single screen isn't enough to hold all of your application windows.

Spaces is another way to organize all of those open windows. It is like having more than one screen, or doubling or quadrupling the size of your screen.

To use Spaces, first make sure it is turned on. Go to the System Preferences, choose the Exposé & Spaces preferences, go to the Spaces section, and click Enable Spaces. You can also choose how many spaces you want by adding or subtracting rows and columns.

Switching Spaces

When you press F8, your screen changes to show all of the Spaces available. Figure 6.4 shows what this looks like with four different Spaces.

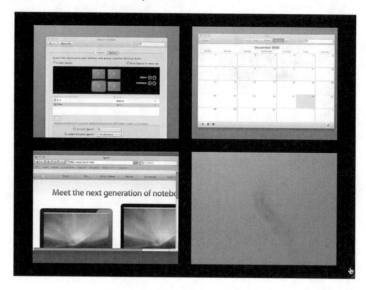

Figure 6.4

When you activate Spaces you get to see all of the Spaces and select the one to go to.

When viewing all of the Spaces available, you can also drag windows from space to space. The idea is to organize things according to what you need to see at the same time.

For instance, you might want to have Safari open in one Space along with Mail, while you have a word processing window in another Space where you are working on a document. Then you can switch between the spaces as you need while working.

Assigning Applications to Spaces

The Spaces preferences also allow you to preassign Spaces to applications. So when you launch that application it is automatically put in that Space. Figure 6.5 shows the Spaces preferences tab of the Exposé & Spaces preferences window.

To add an application to the list, first make sure that application is running. Then click the + button under application assignments. When it is in the list, you can choose the Space in the second column. If a program is not running it can still be assigned to a space by selecting Other and then navigating to the program file and selecting it.

You can also choose Every Space, which would make the application and its windows available in all Spaces. This enables you to have a word processing program open everywhere, while putting different Safari windows in different Spaces as you do research for a document.

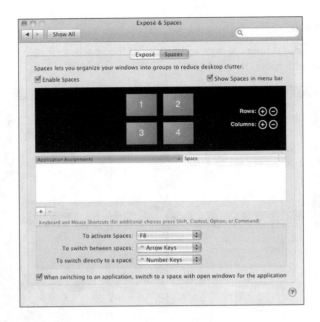

Figure 6.5

In Spaces preferences you can set the number of screens and assign applications to each Space.

Navigating Spaces

After you have Spaces enabled and windows spread out among several Spaces, you can navigate through the screens using a variety of different techniques.

The quickest way to go from one Space to the next is to use Ctrl-Arrow to move around. The screens slide in from side-to-side or up-and-down.

You can also check off the Show Spaces in Menu Bar option as seen in Figure 6.5. Then you get a little menu on the right side of the menu bar that lets you choose a screen by number.

You can also press the default F8 key to display all screens at once, and then you can choose one by clicking on it. This is what Figure 6.4 shows.

Yet another way to go to each screen is to check off the option at the bottom of the preferences as shown in Figure 6.5 and then press Ctrl plus a number to jump to that screen.

Finally, you can simply switch to an application on another screen to jump to that screen. For instance, if Safari is on screen 2, but you are looking at screen 1, switching to Safari using the Dock, Application Switcher, or any other method will take you to that screen.

Dashboard Widgets

In the next chapter we take a look at some of the applications that come with Mac OS X. But bridging the gap between those full-fledged applications and the Mac OS X tools and gadgets are something called Dashboard widgets.

A widget is a small application that does something simple, like a calculator, weather display, or a clock. The Dashboard is the program that contains all of the widgets in Mac OS X. You can usually run Dashboard from the Dock by clicking on the second icon from the left, which looks like a gauge on a car's dashboard. Figure 6.6 shows the Dashboard once it has been activated.

Figure 6.6
The Dashboard shows the default widgets of the calculator, weather display, calendar, and clock.

The Dashboard and all of its widgets appear on top of everything else on your desktop and running applications. Widgets can even be semi-transparent at times, revealing what is behind them. Clicking anywhere besides a widget closes the Dashboard.

Using Dashboard Widgets

For those widgets that require some input, like the calculator, simply click on the widget to focus on it and type in data. Other widgets, like the calendar, have buttons on them. In the calendar you can move backward or forward through the months.

Often, widgets link to web pages. For instance, you can click on the city name area in the weather widget to go to a web page that gives you more details about the weather.

Widget Preferences

Many widgets can be customized. For instance, the weather widget allows you to enter your city name and whether you want the temperature in Fahrenheit or Celsius.

To access these preferences, roll your mouse over the widget and look for a little "i" button. Different widgets are designed in different ways, so you may have to hunt for it. Some widgets don't have any preferences and so won't have a button.

When you click on the preferences button, the widget will flip over and allow you to enter in some data. Some widgets allow you to enter quite a bit, such as the stocks widget, which allows you to enter a whole list of stocks to track. Other widgets only contain information instead of preferences.

Adding Widgets

Although the Dashboard only shows four widgets by default, there are many more on your Mac that you can activate and use. To see them, click the circled + button at the bottom-left corner of your screen while the Dashboard is displayed.

Now you will see a whole list of widgets along the bottom of the screen. You can click on another button at the right side to scroll along and see even more. There are typically three screens of widgets preinstalled on a new Mac.

To add one of the widgets to your Dashboard, just click on it and it will pop into place. You can then drag it around the screen for better positioning.

> **NOTE**
>
> You can add more than one copy of the same widget if you like. This allows you, for instance, to track the weather in several places, or to have multiple calculators in the Dashboard.

You'll also notice a circled X button on each Dashboard widget at this point. You can use this to remove any widget. They will still appear along the bottom of the screen whenever you want to add more widgets, so they are easy to get back.

In addition, you can click on the Manage Widgets button that places a control panel for all of your widgets in the middle of the screen, like in Figure 6.7. This is in itself a widget also.

The Manage Widgets widget allows you to add or remove widgets from your bank of widgets that can then be added to the Dashboard. So you really have two layers of widgets. The first is those that are available to you and are on your Mac. The second layer is those that are currently visible in the Dashboard.

> **NOTE**
>
> To permanently remove a widget from your Mac, you can use the Manage Widgets widget and click on a red circle that appears to the right of a widget name. But this circle only appears for widgets you installed. You cannot remove widgets that are preinstalled with your Mac.

Figure 6.7

You can add or remove widgets with the Manage Widgets.

Finding New Widgets

There are many more widgets that you can get for your Mac by simply clicking the More Widgets button at the bottom of the Manage Widgets widget. This opens Safari and takes you to http://www.apple.com/downloads/dashboard/.

From here you can browse through many categories of widgets. There are thousands available from which you can choose.

Make Your Own Widgets

As you browse through the available widgets, you may start to notice a pattern. Most of them are ways of displaying information from the Web. The weather and stocks widgets are great examples.

You can make your own widgets that show you information from the net very easily, no programming required.

A Web Clipping is a Dashboard widget created from a section on a web page. To do so, launch the web browser Safari. Choose File, Open in Dashboard. You will then be able to roll your cursor over various parts of the web page you are looking at and select them.

For example, look at Figure 6.8. Safari is looking at http://macmost.com. The Web Clippings button has been clicked and the cursor was moved over the center area. Click on that area and then click the Add button. A Dashboard widget will be created that shows the selected area, but in the Dashboard rather than in Safari.

Figure 6.8

You can turn any part of a website into a Dashboard widget.

You will also have the chance to adjust the area before clicking Add. This allows you to grab parts of web pages that are not easy for Safari to make out, or combine several pieces of a web page.

Dashboard widgets are useful little programs, but they are not really full applications. Plenty of those come with your Mac. The next chapter takes a look at them.

WHO SHOULD READ THIS CHAPTER:

This chapter will familiarize you with the applications that come with your Mac. Even if you think you know it all, there may be some applications you have never tried, or some functions that you didn't know these applications could perform.

7

Applications That Come with Your Mac

Your Mac comes pretty fully loaded with applications. You've got everything you need to surf the Internet, send email, collect music and videos, create text documents, keep an address book and calendar, and organize your digital photos. You can even edit your own videos and make your own DVDs—complete with an original musical score!

Many of these applications are complex enough that they can have an entire book written about just that one application. We won't go into that kind of detail here. Some of them will have entire chapters dedicated to them later in the book.

Internet Applications

For many people the main reason they buy a Mac, or any computer, is to access the Internet. You might need to surf the web, send email, and download music and video. With so much being possible using web applications alone, you may not need anything else.

Safari

It is entirely possible to get a lot out of your new Mac without using anything other than the Safari web browser. Safari will allow you to access the whole web, including web-based email and web-based applications.

> **NOTE**
>
> In Windows, the default browser is Internet Explorer. Many Windows users don't even
> know it is called that; they just know it as "the Internet" and click on the "e" icon to launch
> it. Likewise, many Mac users may think of Safari and its compass icon as "the Internet" and
> do not think of it as an application.

Chapter 10, "Using Safari, the Mac Web Browser," goes into detail about Safari and how to use it.
But basically, you view Internet web pages in the main window of Safari, using the address bar at
the top to enter the web address, or URL, of the website you want to visit. Figure 7.1 shows Safari
with Apple's home page at Apple.com.

Figure 7.1

The address bar at the top of Safari shows the web address, also known as the URL, for the web page you are visiting.

SAFARI BASICS

When you launch Safari, you'll be taken to your web home page. You can change this in the
Safari preferences, but it usually starts as a page at Apple's website.

Then you can click on the address bar at the top and type in the web address you want, such as
http://www.google.com or http://www.yahoo.com, to go to that website.

> **NOTE**
>
> You can always leave off the "http://" before a URL when typing it in the address bar.
> Safari will add it for you. And, you can usually leave off the "www" as well—most websites
> are configured to not need it. So "apple.com" is just as good as typing
> http://www.apple.com. Much of the time you can even just type "apple" and it will get
> you there too.

You can click on any link on a website to continue navigating, or "surfing" the web. You can use the left arrow button at the top of the Safari window to go back to the previous page. You can also use the History menu to go back to any specific page you recently visited.

SAFARI USES

A web browser is probably the most versatile of any application. After all, it is just a window to the Internet, and the Internet is vast and has a ton of different uses.

Consider, for instance, that many, if not most, people have email through a web-based email service like Yahoo Mail, Gmail, MSN, and so on. They would use a web browser to access their email, then, not a Mail client.

Also consider that many basic applications now exist as web applications. Google Docs (http://docs.google.com) and other sites offer word processing and spreadsheet programs that run inside a web browser. Even Adobe's Photoshop now has a web browser version (http://www.photoshop.com).

SAFARI TRICKS

You can have more than one Safari window open at the same time. When you first run Safari, you get one window. Then choose File, New Window or press Command+N to open a second or third.

In addition, you can use tabs to view many web pages in the same Safari window, switching between which page is shown at any one time. Switch on tabs by going to the Tabs preference pane in the Safari preferences. Then use Command+T to open a new tab. Click on the tabs themselves at the top of the browser to move between them.

A lot more tips and tricks will be revealed in Chapter 10. For now, let's move on to some more applications.

Mail

The Apple Mail program is an application used to access standard or corporate email. If you prefer to access your email through a web interface like Yahoo Mail or Gmail, and you may never need to use Mail. On the other hand, you can use Mail as an application to access these services as well.

A bit of a set-up process is required before you can use Mail, but once that is done you should be able to access and work with your email quickly and easily with Mail.

In Windows, the equivalent program to Mail is either Windows Mail, Outlook, or Outlook Express. Microsoft also makes a Mac version of Outlook, but it is called Entourage and comes with Office for Mac. All of these programs do basically the same thing: access your server-based email.

Chapter 11, "Getting and Sending Email," deals with setting up Mail so it can access your email provider. Mail can access POP or IMAP email, the primary two ways you will get email from Internet service providers like your DSL or cable company, or your office. It can also handle Microsoft Exchange email and Apple's MobileMe email service.

MAIL BASICS

When you have Mail configured with your email account, the two main things you will do are read incoming email and compose new messages.

> **NOTE**
>
> Mail can access four different types of email accounts: POP, IMAP, Exchange, and MobileMe. The first is the most common type from a standard Internet provider and also for company email. A more advanced server may use IMAP or Exchange, especially if email power users are on the system.

To get email, click the Get Mail button at the top of the Mail window, or choose Mailbox, Get All New Mail from the menu bar. Mail will attempt to connect to your server and retrieve your new email.

The main Mail window shows you a list of email you have received. Figure 7.2 shows what this may look like. Click on a message to view it in the bottom portion of the window, or double-click to open the message in a new window.

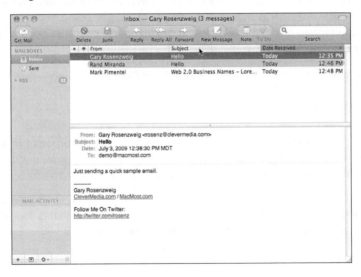

Figure 7.2

The main Mail window shows mail accounts and folders on the left, and the list of incoming messages on the right.

To compose your own message, click the New Message button at the top of the window or choose File, New Message. This opens up a new window where you can compose your message, starting with specifying who the email should go to and what the subject of the email is.

When you are done with the new message, click the Send button that appears at the top of this window.

Rather than create a new email message, you can reply to a message you have received by clicking Reply. The same message composition window will appear, but the "to" address is already filled in and so is the subject line. The old message will even be placed in the body of the new message so you can refer to it and send it along as a reference to the person to whom you reply.

MAIL USES

Email is probably the predominant way that people communicate with each other so far in the 21st century. It is used for both personal and business correspondence all over the globe.

You may use email to communicate with the owners of a website—such as sending a question about a product you see at an online store. You can also subscribe to email newsletters of various topics and groups.

Of course email is used for something else by a not-so-legitimate part of the business world. Spam, or junk email, is a big problem and sooner or later you will get some of this. Apple's Mail program includes a junk mail filter that attempts to toss these into a special mail folder so you don't have to deal with them.

MAIL TRICKS

Email isn't always about words. You can use email to send files as well. Adding attachments to a message can be done in many ways, but the simplest is to just drag and drop a file from a Finder window into a Mail message window.

In the Mail preferences you can set a signature to use for each message you compose. This bit of text automatically appears at the bottom of a new message when you start composing it.

You can create mail folders in the left sidebar to organize your email. After you read a message, for instance, you can file it away in different folders as an archive of all of your messages. There's really no reason to throw away old messages completely, as they don't take up much hard drive space and it can be useful to refer to them later on.

In Chapter 11 we'll look at more advanced techniques for organizing your mail messages.

iTunes

The iTunes application is a media manager, podcast subscription tool, synchronization tool for iPods and iPhones, and storefront for Apple's iTunes Music Store. Chapter 17, "Managing Your Music and Video," goes into detail about iTunes.

> **NOTE**
>
> There is nothing quite like iTunes in Windows. Well, besides iTunes itself. Windows users can download iTunes for free. It is required, in fact, if they want to sync an iPod or iPhone to their PC.
>
> But besides iTunes, the closest application to iTunes that comes preinstalled on all Windows computers is Windows Media Player. It can import music from CDs, organize a media library, and do other similar basic functions.

ITUNES BASICS

Figure 7.3 shows the iTunes application. On the left is a sidebar showing different sections of your media library, a link to the iTunes store, and other items. The majority of the window is taken up by the iTunes store itself, which comes up by default when you first launch iTunes.

Figure 7.3

The iTunes application is a window to the iTunes Music Store run by Apple.

You browse the iTunes Music Store much as you would browse a website in Safari. Click on items that interest you to find out more about them. Click on links on the left and right side of the store to go into categories or to search or perform other functions.

If you click on one of the choices under Library all the way over on the left, such as Music or Movies, you will be shown items in your personal media library on your Mac. You may start off simply with nothing in your library.

The two main ways people add music to their media library is to rip them from their CD collection or buy them at iTunes. Ripping a CD you already own is as simple as inserting the CD into your optical media drive and looking for the Import button that will then appear in the iTunes window. Chapter 17 shows you how to customize your settings to import music in different formats.

ITUNES USES

You can use iTunes to store all of your digital music and videos, whether you pulled them from your CD collection or bought them from the iTunes Music Store. You can then organize, search, and play back that media in iTunes.

You can also subscribe to podcasts—regularly updated audio and video shows produced by other people all over the world on various subjects. You can search for and subscribe to podcasts so that iTunes automatically downloads any new episodes as they're made available.

If you have an iPod or iPhone, iTunes is the application that you will run to synchronize it with your Mac, bringing in music, video, and even data like contacts and calendar events.

iTunes also works as the way you access the iTunes Music Store, Apple's media empire that lets you download music, movies, and TV shows—for a price. You can browse through the store in iTunes and purchase items that will also download through the iTunes application.

ITUNES TRICKS

iTunes attempts to organize your media whether you like it or not. For instance, if you drag and drop a music file or a video file into iTunes, it will copy it to the iTunes folder, inside your Music folder, and rename and organize the files. If you prefer to leave your files where they are and organize them yourself, look at the options in the iTunes preferences under the Advanced tab.

Even if you are not yet ready to purchase music or import your CDs, you may want to check out the podcasts section of the iTunes Music Store. Podcasts are almost always free and there is a ton of great content out there. Just think of your hobby or a topic that you are interested in, and chances are that someone is podcasting weekly about it. There are even podcasts that introduce you to new music.

When you have some music in iTunes, you can use it to listen to music while working on other things on your Mac. Just browse through your library and select an artist, album, or song and double-click to start playing it. You can also play the music from an audio CD in your optical drive without importing it. Then you can hide iTunes and it will keep playing. Or, you can click the green + button at the top of the iTunes window to change iTunes to a mini player window.

iChat

iChat is one of those applications that you may never use—or you may use it more than anything else. iChat is a way to connect to other people's computers (and mobile phones) and send them instant messages.

> **NOTE**
> Windows Messenger is a comparable program that comes with Windows. It focuses on using the MSN messaging system, while iChat focuses on using MobileMe and AIM.

ICHAT BASICS

There are several systems that iChat can communicate with: MobileMe, AIM (AOL Instant Messenger), Jabber, and Google Talk. You can also use Bonjour, which is a system function for allowing Macs to communicate with other Macs on the same local network. So if you want to chat with other people in your office or house, you may be able to use Bonjour instead of signing up with one of the other services.

> **NOTE**
> MobileMe costs money to join, but you can get AIM, Jabber, and Google Talk accounts for free.

When you have an account on one of these services, you can go to the iChat Preferences and add that account. Then you will see a window appear in iChat that lists your friends and you can click on anyone listed as "online" to start to chat. You can also add more friends to the list.

ICHAT USES

But iChat is much more than just text chat. You can chat using audio and video too, providing you and your friend have the right hardware. If, for instance, you both have Macs with iSight cameras, starting a video chat is as easy as starting a text chat. Then there you are, chatting face to face with someone that could be anywhere in the world.

You can even have text, audio, or video conversations with more than one person at a time. For video chats, each person is put in his own box in a 3D space. You can have a business meeting or a family reunion with iChat.

ICHAT TRICKS

You can be yourself when video chatting—or not. Choose Video, Show Video Effects to apply odd and interesting filters to your video feed. Squeeze, bulge, or twirl yourself around. Make your skin look a little green, or place yourself on a roller coaster ride.

If you find yourself in a chat working to help someone on another Mac troubleshoot something, you can see exactly what he is seeing by sharing his screen. Look under the Buddies menu for the Share Screen and Ask to Share Screen menu choices. After confirming the choice, you get to see your friend's Mac's screen and help him through a problem. Alternatively, you could watch him make a presentation or show you a website.

We'll be taking a closer look at iChat in Chapter 12, "Instant Messaging and VOIP."

Basic Applications

There are many programs that come preinstalled with Mac OS X. These are not fancy or heavily promoted applications, but things that simply help you use your computer for basic tasks.

You will find, however, that there is a lot of power in these applications. Let's look at each one and learn how to use them.

TextEdit

For decades both Mac and Windows systems have come with simple text editors: SimpleText for Mac and Notepad for Windows. These were not really competitors to full-fledged word processing programs, but just something simple and basic.

However, with Mac OS X, Apple provides something that goes beyond a simple text editor. TextEdit can be used to create pretty decent documents with fonts, styles, lists, tables, and even inserted images. You can spell check and even open or save in Microsoft Word format.

The current equivalent to TextEdit in Windows is a program called WordPad. It, too, can work with rich text (RTF) and Word documents.

We'll go into more detail about TextEdit in Chapter 14, "Word Processing and Printing." We'll also look at some alternatives such as professional word processors like iWork's Pages and Microsoft Word.

TEXTEDIT BASICS

TextEdit has two modes: plain text and rich text. When you have a document open you can switch between the modes in the Format menu. Figure 7.4 shows a rich text TextEdit document.

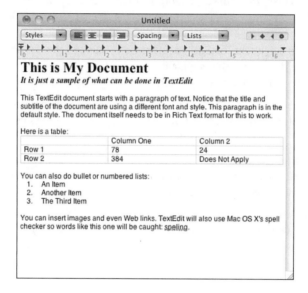

Figure 7.4

This TextEdit document shows examples of different types of formatting, tables, and lists.

To create a new document, open an existing document, or to save the document you are work-ing on, use the File menu. When you have a document open, you can just use the keyboard and mouse to type and move around in your document.

On the Format menu, you'll find choices for changing the font and style of selected text. The Format, Text submenu is where a lot of the special features hide, such as creating lists and tables.

There is a spell checker built into Mac OS X that works particularly well in TextEdit. If you type a word that it doesn't recognize, it appears underlined in red. You can Ctrl-click on that word for spelling suggestions. You can also choose the Edit, Spelling, and Grammar submenu for more choices.

TEXTEDIT USES

TextEdit can handle small and medium-sized word processing. If you plan to write a book or use documents as part of your everyday business dealings, you will probably want to get something more full-featured like iWork's Pages, Microsoft Word, or OpenOffice.

TextEdit can also be useful to open Microsoft Word documents. You'll find that Windows users easily forget that Word is not a program usually found on Macs (and even many Windows machines!) and will send you email attachments in the .doc format. But TextEdit can open them, even if it can't render some of the more tricky layout bits.

TextEdit is also a great way to create personal notes and documents. You can make to-do lists, packing lists, write little memos to yourself and others, and so on. It can be your go-to application for whenever you want to write something down and store it in a file.

TEXTEDIT TRICKS

To place an image into a rich text TextEdit document, all you need to do is drag the image file from the Finder to the document. This is typical of many Mac applications—when there isn't an explicit menu choice or command to do something, usually drag and drop works.

You can also copy and paste an image into a TextEdit document. For instance, if you select a part of an image in Photoshop and then copy it, you can then paste it into the cursor position in TextEdit. It's that easy.

If you are looking at a large document in TextEdit, you can search for a word or phrase by choosing Edit, Find. Then you can continue to use other Edit menu commands and their keyboard shortcuts to look for all of the occurrences in that document.

You can even create rich text documents and save them as .html files to post on a website. The formatting will be converted to HTML format so the page appears with your formatting when viewed in web browsers.

Preview

Besides text documents, there are two other types of documents that you may need to view on your computer. The first is images, from tiny little thumbnails to huge high-resolution photographs.

Another type of document, often called a PDF file or an Adobe Acrobat file, is a document that mixes text, images, and complex layout. It could be something like an eBook or magazine, or just a government form downloaded from a website.

Preview is the application that comes with Mac OS X that allows you to view these types of documents. It also allows you to perform some editing and even add annotations to these documents.

In Windows, without any other programs installed, users would probably use Windows Picture and Fax Viewer to look at images. PDFs would require a download, such as Adobe's free Acrobat Reader. Often on websites you'll see messages saying that you need Acrobat Reader to view a file. On a Mac, you won't need to download that program as Preview opens almost all PDF files.

PREVIEW BASICS

Most of the time that you use Preview you won't need to launch it yourself at all. Just double-clicking on a PDF or image file will launch Preview and open the document with it. Figure 7.5 shows a PDF document from the Apple website opened in Preview.

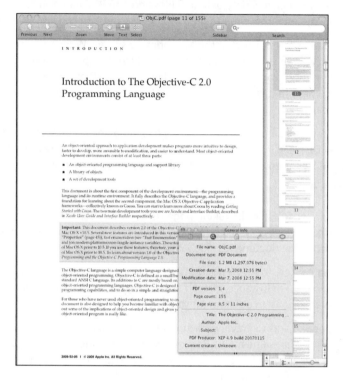

Figure 7.5

You can navigate through a document in Preview using the buttons at the top or the thumbnails in the sidebar.

You can open and close a right sidebar with View, Sidebar. This shows thumbnails of each page so you can jump from page to page. Otherwise, you can use the buttons at the top, or Go, Go to Page to jump to a page number. You can also use Edit, Find to search the document.

Often you will need to zoom in or out to be able to read the text in a document. You can use the zoom buttons at the top of the page or the View menu to change the zoom.

There are actually three modes you can be in while using Preview, shown at the top of the Preview window. The first, Move, simply lets you navigate around in the document. If you have zoomed in too much to be able to fit a page in the window, you can use the mouse to move the page around inside the window.

The second mode, Text, allows you to use the mouse to select text in the document. Then you can copy and paste it into your own documents or email messages. You cannot, however, edit the text in a document. If a PDF has blank fields to fill in, like a form, you can use Text mode to fill in those fields.

The third mode is Select, which allows you to select an area on the document. You can then use the Tools menu to crop that page to fit the selected area, or the Edit menu to copy that area.

PREVIEW USES

Preview can be used to open a variety of image files and also PDF files. You can fill out PDF forms that you may run into from time to time on the Internet. You can also do a bit of editing.

The Preview application is also a part of the Mac printing system. When you are working in another application, and you choose to Print, you are given the option of seeing a preview of that printout. This preview is actually Preview—it launched the Preview Application and "prints" the pages to a document that is then opened by Preview. So you have the chance to look at it before you waste paper.

You can also use Preview as a more advanced way to send a document to a friend or colleague. You can open the PDF file in Preview and then use the annotation features to mark areas of interest and leave notes. Then you can save the document and send along your version.

PREVIEW TRICKS

You can create your own PDF files by taking pages from other PDF files. Just open the large file and select a page in the sidebar. Then choose File, New From Clipboard. Now you can drag and drop other pages from one document's sidebar to the other.

When you are using Preview to preview a printout, you can save the document in addition to, or instead of, printing it out. For instance, instead of printing out a document, you can use Preview to save it and then email it as an attachment to someone.

You can even add bookmarks to Preview documents. Choose Bookmarks, Add Bookmark and it will appear in the list in that same menu. Because many user manuals and instruction booklets now come as large PDF files, and you can buy books as eBooks in PDF format, this could be a great way to remember where important pages are located.

Address Book

Managing your personal information is something that your Mac can do well. It starts with the simple Address Book application. This just stores a list of your contacts—although it can be a detailed list. Figure 7.6 shows the main Address Book window.

The Address Book starts with just you and Apple Inc. From there, you can add other people you know. You can even use the File, Import feature to import contacts from other programs or computers.

The equivalent to Address Book in Windows is... Address Book in Windows XP and Windows Contacts in Vista. A program of the same name exists on both platforms. If you have been using Windows Address Book, you can use File, Export in that program to create a file that you can then import into your new Mac Address Book.

Figure 7.6

The Address Book can store information about people and companies in a small database.

ADDRESS BOOK BASICS

The three columns in Figure 7.6 represent groups, contacts, and contact information. Click the + button at the bottom of the second column to add a new contact. Then click the Edit button at the bottom of the second column to edit that contact's information.

When you are editing information, you can add or remove fields. For instance, one contact may just be a name and an email address. Another may be a name, physical address, and phone number. You can even add notes and custom fields to each contact.

Much of the time, however, you will not even need to use Address Book to add new contacts to this database. For instance, when reading your mail in Apple Mail, you can choose Message, Add Sender to Address Book. This creates a new contact and puts the email sender's name and email address in it.

Sometimes you will even get an email with a .vcf or .vcard file attachment. This is a virtual business card and contains a whole set of contact information that you can add to your Address Book by simply opening the attachment. You can also export any contact in your Address Book as a vcard using File, Export or by simply dragging it to the Finder.

ADDRESS BOOK USES

The address book is used whenever another Mac OS X program needs some contact information. For instance, in Mail, you can start composing a new message and click the Address button at the top of that window to select a recipient from your Address Book database. Even if you start typing an email address instead, you will get some help from your contacts list as it tries to complete the address as you type.

The Address Book is also where you store information about yourself. Your own card has special significance in the Address Book and can be used to automatically insert information about you in other programs.

If you own an iPhone, or even an iPod, the Address Book will synchronize information through iTunes with the device. So you can add new contacts while on the go, or access your Address Book from your iPhone. It also syncs with the MobileMe service so you can access your contacts from anywhere with a web browser.

ADDRESS BOOK TRICKS

You can create a group in Address Book and use that group to quickly send email to several people. For instance, create a "Family" group and drag and drop several contacts into it. Then the next time you want to send them all an email, just type **Family** in the "To" field of an email and you'll see all those contacts appear.

You can also create Smart Groups. These are like Smart Folders in that they use searches to find items that have something in common. For instance, you could create a Smart Group of only people with addresses in your state and use that to invite people to a party.

The iPhone has a Contacts App that comes preinstalled. This syncs with your Address Book on your Mac. If you go to a contact on your iPhone, click Edit and then look for the box that says Add Photo. Now you can take a photo of that person if they are standing right there, or use one in your iPhone's camera roll that you took before. Not only will that photo show up when that person calls you on your iPhone, but it will show up in your Mac's Address Book after you sync. Otherwise, you can also drag and drop photos from iPhoto into Address Book to use them.

iCal

iCal is a calendar program that comes with Mac OS X that helps you organize your schedule. It is basically a list of events, but presented in many different formats so you can see what you've got coming up. Figure 7.7 shows the calendar in month view.

Figure 7.7

iCal is shown here in Month view with the Calendar List sidebar.

> Although no calendar program comes with Windows XP, Outlook has a calendar, and Windows Vista and Windows 7 users can use a program called Windows Calendar.

ICAL BASICS

To add an event in iCal, just double-click in the date or time slot (depending on your view). This opens a little window where you can enter some basic details about the event. You can also choose File, New Event or press Command+N.

After you've put events on the calendar, you can click and drag them around to change times. You can also have multiple "calendars" overlapping each other. By default, there are Home and Work calendars as shown in Figure 7.7. You can select to only show one of these, or any combination.

There are a variety of views for iCal including by day, week, and month. You can also choose to show or hide the left sidebar seen in Figure 7.7 that shows the list of calendars and the mini monthly calendar.

Events can be set for a specific time, or just attached to a day, like someone's birthday. You can also have them span a number of days.

The events themselves can have a variety of alerts attached to them. For instance, you can have an email sent to you, or have your Mac show a dialog box and play a sound. You can set these alarms to go off a certain amount of time before the event as well.

ICAL USES

You can use iCal to keep track of your appointments, of course, but you can also use it for other purposes. For instance, many people use it as a simple alarm clock, setting events to occur at certain times to remind them to do something.

You can subscribe to calendars with iCal, and many calendars exist. Choose Calendar, Subscribe and enter the URL for the calendar. Or, choose Find Shared Calendars to see what is available. There are holiday calendars, national calendars, sports teams, movie release dates, and so on. You can publish one of your calendars if you have a server to do so.

iCal also has a built-in to-do list function. You can add to-do items and check them off as you accomplish things.

ICAL TRICKS

You can add birthdays to your contacts in Address Book and then select iCal Preferences and check off Show Birthdays calendar to see all of those birthdays in iCal.

You can add multiple alarms to any event. For a big meeting, you could schedule an alarm for the evening before, another for before lunch (so you remember not to eat garlic) and then one 15 minutes before the meeting.

There are also some advanced scheduling and invitation functions in iCal, which grow even more powerful if an entire office is using it to schedule meetings.

iLife Applications

The next set of applications is all part of a single package that Apple calls iLife. You can buy it in stores and online in a box. But Apple also includes the current version of iLife with all new Macs.

All of these apps are creative in nature. You use them to create videos, DVDs, music, and websites. Only iPhoto can be considered a utility—allowing you to store and organize your digital photos. But even then you can use iPhoto to create a lot of things with those photos, like slideshows and printed books.

iPhoto

If you take a lot of digital photos, then iPhoto is an application you will want to get to know well. It is how you will import photos into your Mac and organize them. You can even touch them up and adjust them, and create slideshows and order prints.

> **NOTE**
>
> In Windows XP, when you plug in a digital camera you are asked if you would like to import those photos and put them into your My Pictures folder. You can then use various other programs to work with those photos. There's nothing quite like iPhoto for taking care of your photo library. Windows Vista, however, has Windows Photo Gallery which is similar to iPhoto.

There is enough functionality in iPhoto for it to warrant its own chapter. You can read about iPhoto and what it can do for you in detail in Chapter 16, "Importing and Managing Photos." In the meantime, here are the basics.

IPHOTO BASICS

You can get your photos into iPhoto in many ways. The usual way is to connect your digital camera to your Mac using the USB cable that usually comes with such cameras. You should get prompted as to whether you want to import the photos from the camera.

Alternatively, you could drag and drop photos you already have on your hard drive into iPhoto. When you have some pictures in there, you should see something like in Figure 7.8.

To see a specific photo, double-click on its thumbnail to go into close-up mode. Or, simply click on it once to select it, and then click on the Edit button at the bottom of the iPhoto window to go into edit mode.

In editing mode, you can perform a variety of functions. For instance, you can rotate or crop the photo, straighten a crooked photo, adjust the color, remove red-eye, and even retouch areas of a photo. You'll find out more about each one of these in Chapter 16.

IPHOTO USES

iPhoto can be used as a media library for all of your digital pictures. You can also use it to store video, particularly video that you take with your digital camera that will be imported alongside the pictures.

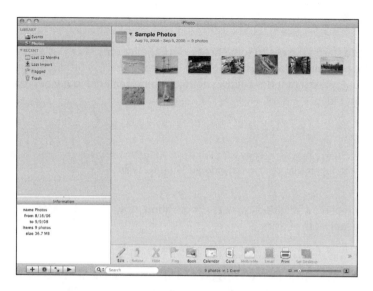

Figure 7.8

iPhoto in Photos mode, showing each event as a group of picture thumbnails.

When you have photos in iPhoto, you can organize them by naming them, and even adding key-words to them. For instance, you could add the names of people in the photos. Then you can search your photos by those names.

You can also print out photos if you have a decent printer, or use the Book, Calendar, or Card functions to order printed products using your photos from Apple.

You could also email photos or send them to the web using the MobileMe service. In Chapter 16 you'll learn how to use other services as well, such as Flickr or Picasa.

IPHOTO TRICKS

Using the + button at the bottom-left corner of the iPhoto window, you can create a variety of different types of "albums." You can create a normal album and decide which photos go into it. You can also create a Smart Album and put search results into the album, and it will automatically update as you add new photos that meet the same criteria.

You can also create a slideshow of photos. You can choose the transitions to use in the slideshow and other visual effects. You can even choose the music from your iTunes collection. You can then turn the slideshow into a video file with the File, Export function, or send it right to iDVD with the Share, Send to iDVD function and create a DVD slideshow.

You can also rate your photos. Why would you want to do this with your own pictures? Well, you can rate your very best photos five stars, some other great ones with four stars, and so on. And then when you want to show someone your pictures, you can show them only your best.

iMovie

With iMovie we're starting to get to some heavy-duty applications. iMovie is a complete video-editing tool. It is not quite as fancy as Apple's pro-level tool Final Cut Studio, or even its little brother Final Cut Express. But it does allow you to combine and edit your video clips and produce high-quality video.

> **NOTE**
>
> No video-editing program comes with Windows XP or Vista. However, some PC manufacturers bundle full or trial versions of video-editing software.

In Chapter 21, "Creating with Video," we'll talk more about how to create videos with iMovie. For now, let's have a look at the basics.

IMOVIE BASICS

The iMovie window, shown in Figure 7.9, is divided into many sections. The bottom half holds video segments that you have imported into iMovie. You can do this either by choosing File, Import Movies, or by importing directly from a camera plugged into your Mac.

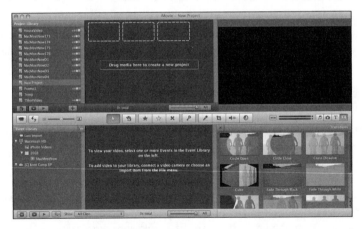

Figure 7.9
The iMovie window allows you to edit your videos and produce finished video projects.

When you have segments in the bottom part of iMovie, you can drag them up to the middle top area. This is the project area and you can arrange video clips here in the order you want them to appear in your final video. To the right of that is the video preview area.

Most of the editing in iMovie involves drag and drop. For instance, to add a transition between clips, click on the transitions button (the last one on the right of the middle toolbar). Then you will see a bunch of transitions graphically represented in the bottom right, like in Figure 7.9. You simply drag one of these to the space between clips in the top middle project area to add a transition.

Learning about using all the iMovie editing techniques takes time and practice. But creating your first edited video can be done quickly by just dragging clips from the library area to the project area and adding transitions. Then you can use the Share menu to export the video to a file or even to MobileMe or YouTube.

IMOVIE USES

Although you can skip iMovie and bring your video clips directly into iDVD to make a DVD, using iMovie allows you to get creative with your videos. It also allows you to export the video in a more suitable format for the Internet.

If you take a lot of video, iMovie is a way to find the best segments and combine them into a narrative. You can even add music and audio narration to your movie.

You can also use iMovie as a video library in much the same was as you would use iPhoto as a photo library. The only problem is that video takes up much more space, and although iMovie can hold years of photos, a single vacation's worth of videos may be too much for a smaller lap-top hard drive.

iMovie is also a great application for creating web video, like the kind you would upload to YouTube. You can shoot a single sequence of video right on YouTube's site, or upload a single file right from your camera. But iMovie lets you get creative and edit shots together and add titles, transitions, and effects.

IMOVIE TRICKS

We'll be looking at a lot of cool things in Chapter 21. But here's a sampling.

You can drag and drop photos into iMovie as well as video. You can even add the "Ken Burns effect" to these photos, which makes them slide diagonally and zoom instead of just staying still. This creates the illusion of movement even for still images.

You can also add titles and text overlays in iMovie. There are a variety of styles to choose from.

Another thing you can do in iMovie is to record yourself directly from the built-in iSight camera included with MacBooks and iMacs. Or, you could hook up a USB or FireWire camera. You can create and edit a video diary right in iMovie.

iDVD

The sister application to iMovie is iDVD. If you are making a physical DVD of your videos, iDVD picks up where iMovie leaves off.

Like iMovie, iDVD doesn't have a similar program on Windows XP that all users have. Instead, some PC makers may include some DVD software, especially if they are including an optical drive capable of burning DVDs. With Windows Vista, you get DVD Maker.

We'll also talk more about iDVD in Chapter 21. Here are the basics to get you started.

IDVD BASICS

iDVD is a simple program that makes very professional-looking DVDs. Notice how store-bought movie DVDs have fancy intros and menu sequences? Well, your DVDs can have those too. When you create a new project in iDVD you get to choose from several iDVD themes.

Figure 7.10 shows the Revolution theme. Notice that there is a tiny "Drop Zone 1" in the middle of the image. Whenever you see something like this, you can drag and drop a piece of video or a photo on to it. This video will play in this area while the menu is displayed.

Figure 7.10

The Revolution theme is one of many you can choose in iDVD.

Most of what you need to do in iDVD is drag and drop like that. You can drag and drop buttons, text, videos, and media onto predefined themes.

Click on the DVD Map button at the bottom of the window (looks like a chart) and you can add more pieces to your DVD. For instance, you could start with a video sequence that leads to a menu. Then the menu can branch out to three different video sequences, depending on which button is selected using the DVD remote control.

A lot of creative control is left up to you, so the best way to learn iDVD is to experiment. You can preview the entire DVD with the Play button at the bottom of the window. So there is no reason for not experimenting with your first production.

IDVD USES

The obvious use for iDVD is to make a DVD of your family or vacation videos. But don't forget to include a lot of photos as well. iDVD can include photo slideshows also. The + button at the bottom lets you add submenus, movies, or slideshows. After you create a slideshow section, you can drag and drop photos from iPhoto onto it. You can even opt to include the full resolution versions of the photos on the DVD as a DVD-ROM section that can be accessed when the DVD is inserted in a computer.

You can also use iDVD in business. Imagine your client's surprise when you hand her a professional-looking DVD that can be shown before your sales pitch during your meeting.

IDVD TRICKS

Even though iDVD is pretty simple, there is an even easier way to use it to create a DVD. The Magic iDVD function allows you to do nothing more than select a theme, movies, and photos and then iDVD does the rest. If you want to impress someone, show them how you can create a 30-minute DVD in about 10 minutes.

You can also use iDVD in the OneStep DVD mode. This just reads the video off a connected FireWire video camera and makes a quick DVD with the contents. This is useful for quickly transferring video to DVD.

GarageBand

One of the coolest programs ever created comes free with every Mac. GarageBand is a music creation program that anyone can use. It can be anything from a fun distraction for 10 minutes as you play with music loops, to a professional recording studio.

> GarageBand is one of those programs that makes PC users switch. Sure, there are professional music and recording studio programs on Windows, but they don't usually come with the machine and they are rarely as fun and functional as GarageBand.

In Chapter 20, "Creating with Audio," you'll learn how to use GarageBand to record audio and make music. But for now, here are the basics.

GARAGEBAND BASICS

The GarageBand window shows tracks in the main area, a toolbar across the center, music loops at the bottom, and usually a little keyboard window floating above it all as shown in Figure 7.11.

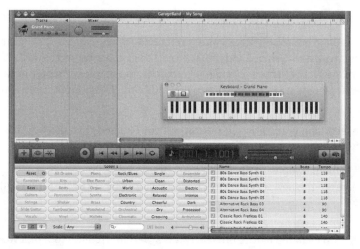

Figure 7.11

GarageBand allows you to create your own songs.

To create a simple little song, use the buttons at the bottom left to narrow down your choices for music loops, which will appear to the bottom right. Then drag and drop those loops to the main area.

When you click the play button in the center toolbar, the music loops will play all at once. You can drag the ends of any sequence to make it loop over and over again. You can drag them to the right if you don't want them to all start at the same time.

Click on the loop button in the center toolbar. This creates a looping area, highlighted in gold at the top of the tracks. Then you can keep the music playing and drag and drop new loops and remove old ones to test the sound.

This is obviously just scratching the surface of what GarageBand can do.

GARAGEBAND USES

You can use GarageBand to simply play with music. In addition to using the built-in loops, you can record your own using a MIDI instrument or analog instrument plugged into the line in or a USB adapter. You can do the same with a microphone for recording vocals.

After you have created a piece of music, you can send it to iTunes and even publish it to the Internet. Or, you can use it with iPhoto, iMovie, or iDVD to provide a soundtrack to a slideshow or movie.

You can also use GarageBand to create your own audio podcasts. When you create a new GarageBand project, you even have the option to start with a podcast setup that will make it easier.

Another use for GarageBand is as an audio editor for iMovie. You have the option in iMovie to send the movie to GarageBand. Then in GarageBand you can see the video portion of the movie, but edit only the audio portion. This allows you to control the sound levels and add more tracks.

GARAGEBAND TRICKS

Although GarageBand is a sophisticated music creation tool, you can use it simply to record and edit audio. Just start a new GarageBand music project, click the + button to add a "Real Instrument," and then click Record to begin recording from the microphone. Check first in the GarageBand Preferences under Audio/MIDI to make sure the Audio Input is set to the microphone.

You can pause recording or record multiple tracks if you like, and then use the Share, Export Song to Disk function to save the audio out in a format that others can listen to.

If you are having fun playing with the GarageBand music loops, you can purchase many more from Apple. There are themed sets like World Music, Symphony Orchestra, and Rhythm Section.

iWeb

The final application included in iLife is iWeb. This is a website creation tool that works well with the MobileMe service from Apple.

> **NOTE**
>
> Although no iWeb-like website-building application comes with most PCs, most web pages are not built with such tools. Sites like MySpace and Blogger are completely contained on the web and don't even care if you are on a Mac or a PC. iWeb provides a somewhat unique approach to combining an application and a service (MobileMe) to build a personal website.

If you do not use the MobileMe service, iWeb probably isn't for you. You can publish the website you create to a folder on your Mac, and then upload that to an actual website, but this makes it very hard to update.

IWEB BASICS

iWeb is what you would call a WYSIWYG website creation tool. This stands for What You See Is What You Get. In other words, instead of editing HTML code, you are editing in a graphical environment, adding elements and arranging things to create your site, which will look just like your editing space when you are done.

Figure 7.12 shows the iWeb window. First you choose your theme, much as you would with iDVD. Then you get to click on text areas and change the text. You can also drag and drop other items, like pictures, into the space. You can use the tools at the bottom to add more text areas and shapes. You can choose View, Show Inspector to bring up the Inspector to do things like turn a piece of selected text into a link to another page.

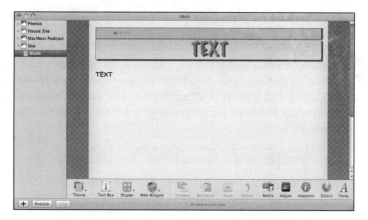

Figure 7.12
You can create your own MobileMe home page with iWeb.

When you have your first page ready, you can choose File, New Page to create another. That's the basic process. Then, when you are ready to publish your site to MobileMe, choose File, Publish to MobileMe. Your site will go live.

IWEB USES

Although iWeb can only create simple websites, there are many such uses for such sites. One great example is a web-based resume or portfolio. iWeb excels at this. By combining the nice themes and your own media, you can quickly get a site up the night before applying for a new job.

Likewise, iWeb is great when you want to help a friend by putting up a quick website or do one for yourself.

IWEB TRICKS

The Web Widgets in MobileMe allow you to add a MobileMe picture gallery at the push of a button. So you could quickly create a web page that includes an entire slideshow without much effort.

Likewise, you can put a Google Map on a web page with another MobileMe Web Widget. This makes iWeb useful as a tool to create an invitation to a party or event.

You can also use the Web Widget button to paste your own HTML right into a section of a page. So if you want to embed a YouTube video or some widget from another website, you can do so easily.

Other Applications

So far we have covered the major applications that come with your new Mac. But there are plenty of other ones that are not used quite as often. Let's take a quicker look at those.

Calculator

The calculator program seems simple at first, with nothing more than the most basic functions. But if you look in the View menu, you'll see that there are Scientific and Programmer versions of the calculator as well. Figure 7.13 shows the scientific calculator. You can even switch into reverse Polish notation which allows you to enter complex formulas without using parentheses by pressing Command+R.

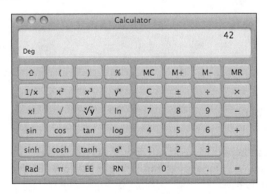

Figure 7.13

The scientific calculator is one of three modes of the Calculator application.

The calculator also includes a menu of conversions. So, for instance, you can take the current number and convert it from kilometers per hour to meters per second.

Dictionary

Another application that adds considerable value to your Mac is the Dictionary. It is the New Oxford American Dictionary, but even better as it weighs less and you can search instead of flipping pages. You also get a thesaurus as well, cross-referenced with the dictionary part.

To make it complete, you've even got the front and back text usually only found in paper versions of the dictionary. And you can add more dictionaries to the application in the preferences. It comes with a special Apple dictionary containing terms that apply to Macs and other parts of Apple culture. There is also a Japanese dictionary if you want that too.

DVD Player

Your Mac is also the most full-featured DVD player you've ever seen. The DVD Player application is a little powerhouse of features. If you just insert a DVD it will launch. Then you can view the DVD in a window, or choose View, Enter Full Screen to have it take over your entire monitor.

Then you can use the Go menu to jump to chapters, move forward and back, and even bookmark your own sections in the DVD. You can't do that with a normal DVD player.

Plus, just about every command has a keyboard shortcut, so if you use DVD Player often enough to learn them all, you've got ultimate control at your finger tips.

Front Row

If an awesome DVD Player application is not enough, you've also got Front Row. This app transforms your Mac into a media center. And I do mean transforms—away goes everything else, to be replaced with a completely different interface, the same one used by Apple TV. Figure 7.14 shows this transformation.

Front Row is another way to get at your music, videos, and podcasts. It is meant to be used with your Mac hooked into a television set. Some people buy Mac minis as an alternative to Apple TV. You get most of the functionality of Apple TV with Front Row, plus all the functionality of a Mac.

> After you launch Apple TV, you may find yourself stuck in it. The secret is to press Command+Esc to quit. You can also use Command+Esc to enter Front Row, which is handy if you find yourself using it a lot.

Front Row is meant to be controlled with the Apple Remote. This little device can be bought from Apple for about $19, but it has also come with some Macs in the past. But you can also use arrow keys and the spacebar to control Front Row.

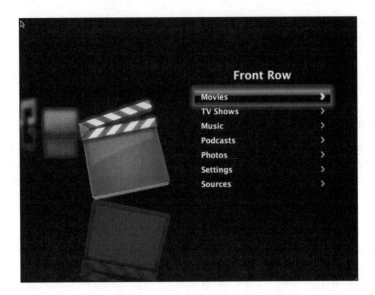

Figure 7.14
Your Mac is now an Apple TV, with the help of the Front Row application.

Image Capture

The Image Capture utility predates iPhoto and acts as a simple way to bring images in from digital cameras, scanners, and other devices. When you launch it, it checks to see what is connected. You can then use some simple windows to bring in all or some of the images, and place them where you want on your hard drive.

Even if you use iPhoto to store and organize your own pictures, Image Capture can come in handy when you want to connect to someone else's camera and pull off an image without adding it to your iPhoto library.

PhotoBooth

PhotoBooth is probably the most unnecessary, but the most fun, of any of the Mac applications. It is basically a toy that allows you to use a built-in iSight camera to take pictures and video. It amplifies the fun by allowing you to apply all sorts of crazy filters, such as in Figure 7.15.

For instance, you can distort your face, or adjust or reverse the color. You can also put yourself on a still or moving background, like the moon or a roller coaster. You can capture still images or video and save them to your hard drive.

If you think this is useless, try running Photo Booth with a bunch of little kids around—hours of entertainment.

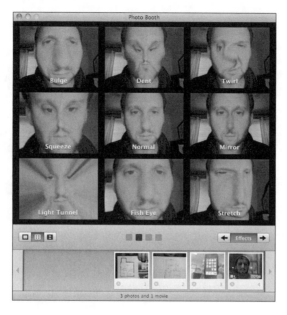

Figure 7.15

Photo Booth allows you to apply all sorts of crazy filters.

QuickTime Player

QuickTime is the technology behind pretty much all video playback on your Mac. The QuickTime Player is a somewhat simple application that just plays back most video formats in a simple window. There are some advanced controls, and the ability to play back in full screen and play back audio files, and so on.

You can also record audio, video, and even your screen with the QuickTime Player. These functions used to be part of QuickTime Pro, a $30 upgrade to the QuickTime Player, but are now included by default.

Stickies

Stickies barely qualifies as an application; it is more of a gadget, or a Dashboard widget that has escaped the Dashboard. It is basically the ability to create little notes and place them anywhere on your screen. Some people never use it, but others find it indispensable.

With Stickies running, use File, New Note to create a new note. You can type or paste anything in there. Then look in the Note menu to make it translucent or give it the ability to float above all other windows. Other menus gives you power to arrange or change the color of notes.

Now that we've looked at all of the major applications that come with your new Mac, we've got a good handle on what comes with your new machine. Next, let's look at what you can bring to your Mac—your files and information from your old Mac or PC.

WHO SHOULD READ THIS CHAPTER:

If you are switching from Windows to Mac and you need to get your files or other bits of information off your old machine onto your new Mac, this chapter shows you how. You'll also learn how to transfer files from a friend's Windows computer to yours without needing to set up a network.

8

Moving from Windows to Mac

If this is your first Mac, but not your first computer, chances are that your old machine runs Windows. You may have old files on your Windows machine—your contact list, calendar events, even your browser bookmarks.

You don't have to leave those behind. You can take them with you to your new Mac. There are many methods for bringing files and information over from your old Windows machine.

Transferring Your Documents

There are two ways to move files from a Windows computer to a Mac: the hard way and the easy way. The hard way is to set both machines up on the same network, get both machines to recognize each other, and transfer files.

You'd think with both Mac and Windows being so mature and advanced that this would be easy. But networks vary so much and are so complex that it can be rather frustrating.

Chapter 13 describes how to network Macs and PCs. If you plan on keeping your Windows computer around and transferring files between them often, you probably want to put the time in now to figure it out. Otherwise, there is an easier way.

The easy method is to use a small and cheap USB flash drive to copy files from your PC to your Mac. They can be bought for $10 to $40, depending on the size. And they will continue to be handy for bringing files to and from work, sharing between friends, and for bringing files along with you away from your Mac.

Copying Files with a USB Flash Drive

When you have a flash drive, the first thing you may need to do is format it in such a way so it can be read by both Mac and Windows machines. Windows cannot read a Mac-formatted disk, but Macs can read a Windows-formatted one. So, if it needs to be formatted at all, you need to format it as FAT32.

You can do this in Disk Utility on your Mac, where it is called MS-DOS (FAT) format, but it is probably easier to just reformat the drive on your Windows machine. It may even already be formatted FAT32 if you just brought it home from the store.

Connect the drive to a USB port on your Windows machine. If it is not in a Windows-readable format, you will be asked to reformat it now. Go ahead and do that, but realize that any data you may have had stored on the drive before will now be gone.

Now you should see the drive show up under My Computer on your Windows machine. In Windows XP, it will look something like Figure 8.1, where you can see the drive as F:.

Figure 8.1

In Windows XP you can see a flash drive show up under My Computer.

Also in My Computer you should see a folder with your name followed by the word "Documents." If you have stored all of your files in Windows in your document folders, they should all be there.

Simply drag and drop the whole folder with your name on it on to the removable flash drive. They should copy right over.

Then, think about where else on your Windows machine you would have documents. Have you been storing files in some other part of the drive, outside of you're Documents folder? Think about it and also look around to see what you can find. You can always come back later if you are not getting rid of your PC right away.

> If you have too many files to fit on your flash drive at one time, you may have to only copy portions at a time—like photos for one trip, documents for another, music for a third, and so on.

Then remove the drive by right-clicking on it in the My Computer window and selecting Eject. Wait a few seconds and then disconnect it from the USB slot.

Next, plug it into your Mac's USB slot. It should appear as a device on the left side of all of your Finder windows. You can then drag and drop documents from there into any folder on your Mac. I recommend putting them all in a "From Windows" folder in your Documents folder in your user folder.

If you also want to bring over photos, videos, and music, you can place them in those folders as well, though you should read later in this chapter about how to get photos and music into iPhoto and iTunes.

Alternate File Transfer Methods

A flash drive isn't the only way to transfer files from a Windows machine to a Mac. Here are some more options.

- **Full-sized hard disk**—You are buying an external drive to use for Time Machine backups anyway, right? Before you start, just format it for Windows as FAT32 the same way you would format a flash drive. Then use the full-sized drive to get your files over to your Mac before letting Time Machine reformat it for backup use.

- **Local network**—If you can connect both computers to the same network, turn file sharing on for both, and you can connect successfully, this is the best method. See Chapter 13, "Networking and File Sharing," for details.

- **Bluetooth file sharing**—If your Windows computer has Bluetooth, a wireless communications method, you can attempt to send single files back and forth.

- **iDisk**—If you are a MobileMe user, you can access your MobileMe storage space on both Mac and Windows computers. Then just transfer files from your Windows machine to your iDisk, and then from your iDisk to your Mac.

- **Email**—If you have email working on your Windows machine and your Mac, consider just attaching files to an email and sending them to yourself.

- **File-sharing website**—Some websites allow you to upload files, for a fee, to make them publicly or privately available to others. You could simply send or share a file to yourself this way, from one machine to the next. Check out http://yousendit.com, http://www.box.net, http://www.jungledisk.com, and many others.

- **Special hardware**—For a price you can get a special cable that will allow you to connect a Windows computer and a Mac. One is the Belkin Switch-to-Mac Cable. Another is the iTornado.

- **Burn a CD**—If your PC has a CD or DVD burner in it and you know how to use it, you can burn a CD-ROM or DVD-ROM with all of your files on it. This is also a good way to archive your PC's files before retiring the PC in favor of your new Mac.

- **Apple Genius**—The Apple Store offers to do the file transfers for you for free. Just make an appointment at the Genius Bar and bring both your new Mac and old PC. See Chapter 25, "Getting Help," for more about the Genius Bar.

Moving Contacts and Calendars

Moving files isn't too painful. But moving contacts, calendars, and email can be harder.

For one thing, it depends on which program you are using to store this data. For email, some Windows XP users use Outlook, and others use Outlook Express, a completely different program. Others use a third-party email program. In Windows Vista, Outlook Express was replaced by Windows Mail. But it is pretty much the same thing.

A similar thing happened with Windows Address Book. That's what it was called in Windows XP, but Windows Vista has Windows Contacts instead.

Moving Contacts

Fortunately, thanks to standards, it is easy to move your Windows address book contacts over to your Mac. The first thing you want to do is to find Address Book or Windows Contacts and run it.

You should then see a list of all of your contacts. The goal is to get these over to your Mac. How to do this varies depending on whether you are using Address Book in Windows XP or Windows Contacts in Vista.

You can move your contacts from Windows XP to Mac by using these steps:

1. Connect your flash drive to your Windows machine.

2. Create a new folder on your flash drive. Name it "My Contacts" or something similar.

3. Have that folder open in a window, and the Address Book window next to it, as shown in Figure 8.2.

4. Then select all of your contacts and drag and drop them into the folder. This creates a whole bunch of files with a .vcf file extension. This stands for vCard file. This is a standard way of transporting contact information from one device to another.

5. Now remove the flash drive from the PC and bring it over to your Mac and plug it in.

6. Launch the Address Book. Select the group All Contacts.

7. In the Finder, find the "My Contacts" folder and select all the .vcf files in it.

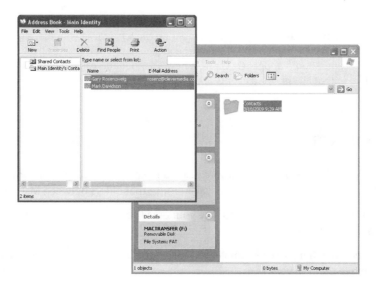

Figure 8.2

This Windows XP address book shows two contacts that are about to be dragged to the Contacts folder created on a flash drive.

   8. Drag and drop all of the .vcf files from the Finder window into the Name column of the Mac Address Book.

It's as easy as that. You now have new Address Book entries for every .vcf file you brought over from Windows.

Now if you are using Windows Vista, steps 1 and 2 are the same, as are steps 5 through 8.

But in order to get vCard files out of Windows Contacts, you need to use the Export button located at the top of the window. It will ask you to select a folder to save all the vCard files to—it then dumps each contact into its own file. So select the folder you created in step 2.

Moving Your Calendar

Windows XP didn't come with a standard calendar program, though users of Outlook have a calendar. Windows Vista has Windows Calendar.

With events in Windows Calendar, you can employ a similar strategy as with Windows Contacts or Windows Address Book. Simply select File, Export and you will get a .ics file, which is a standard calendar format. Make sure you haven't selected any events in the calendar, as you may then only get those events in the export. Otherwise, you should get everything.

Then take that .ics file and move it to your Mac.

Strangely enough, you cannot use File, Import to bring in the .ics file. But you can simply drag and drop that .ics file onto your iCal window and all of the events will appear in your new calendar.

NOTE

Make sure you have selected the right calendar on the left side of your iCal window. For instance, if you have Personal and Work calendars, select the one where all of your imported events should appear. Or, create a new calendar and call it "From Windows" and select that, so that all imported events appear in that calendar.

Moving Your Email

Mail programs on both Mac and Windows are just interfaces for handling mail from servers—so email is really universal itself; it is just the visual interface that differs between Mac and Windows.

To move to a Mac, all you need to do is to take your email settings from your Windows computer and use them to set up Mail on your Mac.

You can, to a limited extent, take old email messages from Outlook Express, Windows Mail, or Outlook and move them to your Mac.

Setting Up Email

In the section "Setting Up Mail" in Chapter 11, we'll look at how to configure Apple's Mail program to connect your mail to a standard POP server. If that is how you get your mail on Windows, from a program like Outlook Express or Windows Mail, you just need to take the information from the Windows side so that you have it ready to enter on the Mac side.

Figure 8.3 shows part of the Outlook Express mail settings. You can get to them by choosing Tools, Accounts and then the Mail tab. You then double-click on the account to get to the settings.

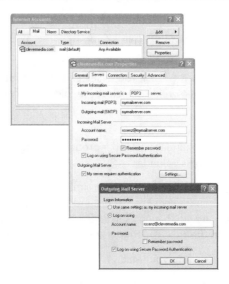

Figure 8.3

The settings in Outlook Express have basically the same information that you will need for Apple Mail.

You should be able to find server information for incoming mail (POP3) and outgoing mail (SMTP), and an ID and password for both the Incoming Mail Server and Outgoing Mail Server. You will have to click on the Settings button under Outgoing Mail Server to get to those settings. You will not be able to see your password, however, so hopefully you remember it.

These map logically to the Incoming Mail Server, User Name, Password, and Outgoing Mail Server information as well in Apple Mail's accounts. The settings and how to get to them are virtually identical between Outlook Express in Windows XP and Windows Mail in Vista.

Moving Old Messages

You can use the same drag-and-drop strategy as the address book to get old mail messages from Outlook Express or Windows Mail to your Mac—sort of.

If you open one of these mail programs that come with Windows, you can select messages and drag and drop them into a folder on your flash drive. Then you can bring them over to your Mac. They will be .eml files. Each file is a single email message.

At first you can't seem to do anything with them in Mail. Dragging and dropping doesn't produce results. But you can double-click on a .eml file and it will open up in Mail—even the header information is all set just as if you got the email on your Mac.

From there, you can choose Message, Move To and put the message into one of your existing Mail folders. You may want to create a specific folder just for this purpose.

So getting one Windows email to your Mac is a piece of cake. But you can only do one at a time. So one, yes. Twenty, maybe. Four thousand—not really.

A better way to do it is to use an intermediary. You can get a program like Microsoft Entourage on Mac, or Mozilla Thunderbird (http://www.mozilla.org/projects/thunderbird/) to import the .eml messages in bulk. Then you can use the File, Import Mailboxes menu choice in Mail to import the whole lot at once.

If you are using Outlook, which is a completely different mail program than Outlook Express, you can get your Outlook mail to Apple Mail with the help of a third-party program like O2M (http://www.littlemachines.com/).

Moving Your Music and Photos

To get your music, photos, and other media files from your Windows computer to your Mac, just follow the suggestion in the first section of this chapter and get those files from your Windows computer onto a flash drive.

Music files on the Mac are handled by iTunes and photos are handled by iPhoto. Both of these program support drag-and-drop import. This means you can simply drag a photo file from the Finder onto the iPhoto library and it will import into iPhoto. Same for music and iTunes.

Organizing Your Windows Photos

What you get when you drop photo files into iPhoto depends a lot on what data is stored in those files. For instance, if they are the original files from your camera, they may have date, time, and even location information. iPhoto will pick that up and use that information.

Separating them into events might be trickier. You may end up with a huge untitled event containing all of your Windows photos. You can leave them like that, or spend the time organizing using the tools in iPhoto.

Music Playback Issues

Music files also include lots of data. An MP3 file usually includes the artist, song name, album name, and other information. iTunes uses this to organize the imported music into artist and album.

However, you may be disappointed to find out that some or even all of your music doesn't play on your Mac. The reason for this is DRM: digital rights management.

If you imported music from CD to your Windows computer in MP3 format, those files will play fine on your Mac. But if you purchased music from an online music service, those files may be protected and can only be played on a computer you registered with that music service. In almost all cases, that will be Windows-specific copy protection. There is simply no way to play those files on a Mac because the program needed to grant you rights to listen to that music is built into Windows.

Transferring Bookmarks

Fortunately, transferring your browser bookmarks is relatively simple. In Windows, you most likely used Internet Explorer for web browsing. On Mac, you'll be using Safari.

To get your bookmarks out of Internet Explorer, it depends on which version of Internet Explorer you are using. In IE7, you would select the Add Bookmark button near the top left of the window. It looks like a star with a plus sign next to it. One of the options is to Import and Export Bookmarks.

Follow the dialog to export all or some of your bookmarks to a file. Figure 8.4 shows just one step in the export wizard. You should end up with something like Bookmark.htm.

Then, after bringing the files over to your Mac via flash drive or some other method, you can import them with Safari's File, Import Bookmarks command.

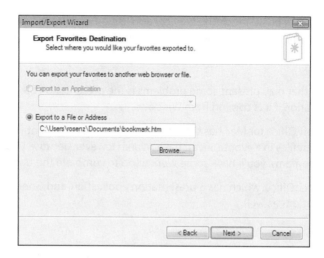

Figure 8.4

Exporting your bookmarks from Internet Explorer is as easy as following a quick series of steps.

Opening Windows Files on Your Mac

So you've got your files from your PC to your Mac. Now what? Despite the windows, icons, and mice, these are different operating systems that run different applications.

You've been used to opening .doc files in Microsoft Word and .ppt files in PowerPoint. The .exe files are executables and the .wmv files are videos. But getting any or all of these to open on a Mac can be tricky.

Document Files

If you have .doc files, they are in Microsoft Word format. You can open them using Microsoft Word on Mac, if you have purchased Microsoft Office for Mac. You can also open them in Pages if you have iWork.

If you have neither Word or Pages, your easiest option is to open them in the free TextEdit program that comes with your Mac. The formatting in complex documents may be lost, but the basics will be there.

You can also open .doc files using open source office software like OpenOffice. You can get that at http://www.openoffice.org. Another option is to use the free Google Docs website at http://docs.google.com to import and view the files.

Another popular type of document file is the .pdf, or Portable Document Format. These are sometimes known as Adobe Acrobat files, though they can be generated by just about any document creation application.

Opening .pdf files is easy on a Mac, as the Preview application handles them. If you like, you can also download the more complex Adobe Reader at http://get.adobe.com/reader/.

Presentation Files

Another type of file that may present some problems is the presentation file—almost certainly a PowerPoint presentation if it is coming from Windows.

Once again, Microsoft Office for Mac has the best solution with PowerPoint for Mac. But you can also open PowerPoint files in Keynote, if you have iWork. However, because visual effects differ between the two programs, you'll have some work to do to complete the transformation.

You can also use OpenOffice, which has a presentation application, and Google Docs to view the simplest of presentations as well.

Spreadsheet Files

If you use spreadsheets at work, chances are that they are Excel spreadsheets. You can get Microsoft Excel for Mac as part of Microsoft Office. And, honestly, it is probably your best option if you need to work with Excel spreadsheets.

Numbers is the spreadsheet program that comes with iWork, and it is very powerful, but quite different than Excel. It will not be easy to take a file back and forth, though it can be done. OpenOffice is closer to Excel if you really need the option.

Video Files

The standard video file format in Windows is a Windows Media file, a .wmv file. You can't play those files on a Mac without adding some extra software. Fortunately, it is free.

Go to http://www.telestream.net/ and download the free Flip4Mac WMV player. It is also shown on the site as the trial version of the Flip4Mac WMV Player Pro. If you don't plan to use it to make .wmv files, but only to watch them, the free trial is all you need.

After installing Flip4Mac WMV you can watch .wmv files in the QuickTime player and in Safari.

For other formats that QuickTime Player cannot handle by itself, try the VLC Media Player, another free download at http://www.videolan.org/vlc/. This can play back DivX and other odd formats.

Executables

If you have .exe files, these are Windows executable files. The equivalent are .app files on the Mac—but Mac users rarely see or notice the .app file extension, so these are just thought of as applications.

There is no good way to do anything with a .exe file in Mac OS X. It is a Windows program and can only be run under Windows.

But there are ways to run Windows on a Mac. We'll explore these in Chapter 18, "Running Windows on Your Mac." Using one of these methods, you can run .exe files.

WHO SHOULD READ THIS CHAPTER:

If you have already connected to the Internet at home or at work, you may decide to skip this chapter. However, if you have a MacBook, you may need to familiarize yourself with your network settings so that you can connect to the Internet at hotspots and hotels.

9

Setting Up Your Internet Connection

Connecting to the Internet is probably one of the first things you want to do with a new Mac. Setting up your Internet connection can be as easy as letting Mac OS X do it for you when you start up for the first time. Or it can be as difficult as calling the customer support line for your cable or telephone company. It depends on your exact situation.

Types of Networks

How you set your network preferences depends entirely on what sort of connection you have to the Internet. A typical American home in 2009 would have a cable modem or a telephone DSL line. Some homes may still use a dial-up connection through a regular phone line. At work you may have a more sophisticated network connection. And when you're on the go, a MacBook may need to connect to a public or private wireless hotspot.

Cable Modem or DSL

When you get a cable or DSL connection from your cable or telephone company, you usually get a "box" hooked up to the cable or phone line. Sometimes this is called a modem, router, or hub.

Follow the instructions that come with this box to hook it up to your service and test it. Usually testing involves looking for a steady green light indicating a good network connection. But this can vary depending on the service and the box.

Some of these boxes have the ability to connect to your Mac wirelessly. You can usually tell by the presence of an antenna. All of these boxes should have one or more Ethernet connectors that you can use to connect an Ethernet cable from your computer to the box.

You should get a set of instructions containing information about the settings required to connect to the network. You can connect your Mac with an Ethernet cable to the box if you don't have the choice of using a wireless connection. Otherwise, you'll be able to establish a wireless AirPort connection.

Alternatively, you can purchase your own wireless base station, such as Apple's AirPort Extreme base station, and plug that into the cable or DSL box. Then your Mac can connect wirelessly to the base station, and your base station connects to the cable or DSL box. This kind of setup is more ideal if you also need other devices hooked up to your connection, such as a second computer, game console, or a set-up video box like the Apple TV.

If you purchase an Apple Airport Extreme, Time Capsule or Airport Express, you'll be able to use Apple' instructions and handy Airport Utility software to set up and configure your wireless network.

> **NOTE**
> Often the settings provided by Internet service providers include descriptions and screenshots that are specific to Windows. But the same settings are used by both Mac and Windows machines. In this chapter you'll learn how to put the right setting in the right place, even if your ISP doesn't have any Mac-specific instructions.

Wireless Hotspot

Wireless hotspots can be found in places like coffee houses, restaurants, libraries, and other places where you might take a MacBook. But some living spaces might also have wireless Internet connections set up; college dorms, for instance, or even some apartment complexes or small communities. Some larger towns and cities are blanketing their streets with wireless networks that you can connect to.

In these cases, no other hardware is needed to connect your Mac to the network. You can do so by establishing a wireless connection to the wireless network. In the case of a Mac Pro, however, you may need to purchase an AirPort card, or you would be without the ability to connect to wireless networks.

> **NOTE**
> Make sure you have permission to connect to a wireless network. If you see a network show up on your Mac and you don't know who it belongs to, don't connect to it. On the one hand, you shouldn't take advantage of someone who has not locked down their wireless connection by stealing their bandwidth. On the other hand, it could be someone hoping that you connect to their network so they can sniff your data and get passwords and credit card numbers.

Most wireless connections are easy to hook up to, requiring only a password. Your Mac is able to figure out the rest of the settings just by talking to the wireless base station.

Dial-Up Modem

In some areas DSL and cable modems have not yet arrived. In addition, hotspots may also not be available. In this case you may have to fall back to the 90s and connect via a regular telephone line with an old-fashioned dial-up modem.

Macs no longer come with telephone modems. Instead, you can buy one from Apple that connects via your USB port. It costs about $50.

Connecting with a dial-up modem requires a service on the other end to which you can connect. That service should provide you with a phone number to use, plus other settings that need to be set to complete the connection.

Business Network

If you connect your Mac to the Internet at work, chances are you may never see the equipment to which you are connecting. Instead, you just have an Ethernet port in your office or cubicle, or you have a wireless connection that appears in your list in your AirPort settings.

Your company may provide you with a page of settings that you will need to connect your Mac to the network. Or a helpful IT (Information Technology) person may come around to lend a hand.

Other Connections

There are many other ways to connect to the Internet. You can use a satellite television service, for instance. Some communities have broadband over power lines. You can also buy wireless cards or USB sticks that establish a connection through a mobile phone network.

Whatever the connection type, you should always obtain a list of settings from your ISP so that you can configure your network preferences properly.

More sophisticated ISPs may include Mac applications that set up your Internet connection automatically. For instance, mobile phone wireless cards require you to run a special program that configures everything for you and even gives you extra features like access to a GPS indicator built into the card.

Network Preferences

Connecting to the Internet is a matter of matching settings and numbers that your Internet service provider gives you with preferences on your Mac. You do all of that through the Network preferences.

Services List

The Network pane of the System Preferences window is shown in Figure 9.1. It is divided into two main parts. On the left is the list of services available to your Mac. On the right is information about the selected service.

Figure 9.1
The Network preferences shows you services on the left and details on the right.

Typical choices you will see here are AirPort and Ethernet. The first is your wireless connection. The second is a connection wired to your Ethernet port.

> **NOTE**
>
> The order in which these services appear is very important. If you have more than one connection available at a time, like a wireless connection and a wired Ethernet connection, the highest one in the list will be used.

These are the two most common ways to connect to the Internet. Let's take a look at a wired Ethernet connection first.

Ethernet Connection

If you click on the Ethernet service, what you see on the right depends on what type of connection you have. The Configure IPv4 setting is what you use to indicate the type of connection. Usually you can choose from DHCP, DHCP with manual address, BootP, and Manually.

DHCP

DHCP is the most common way to connect. This means that the router (cable or DSL box) takes care of most of the settings. If you are instructed to set your connection to plain DHCP, that may be all you need to do.

Figure 9.2 shows how your Network settings may look with a simple DHCP setup. All you have to do is set Configure to Using DHCP and the rest is filled in by your Mac from information it gets from the router. The DNS Server and Search Domains most likely can be left blank as the router is handling them as well.

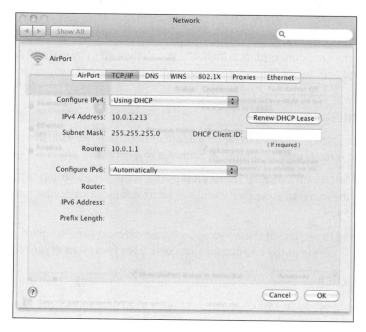

Figure 9.2

With DHCP you can rely on your router to fill in all the hard stuff.

MANUALLY

In an office situation, you may be given instructions to use the manual setting for connecting to the Internet. In this case you need to set the details from Figure 9.2 by yourself.

> **NOTE**
>
> It is becoming less and less common as Mac market share grows, but some ISPs and company IT personnel will claim that they can't help you because you are on a Mac. Or, they will blame any problems you are having on the fact that you have a Mac.
>
> But Macs connect to the Internet in the same way that Windows machines do. The settings you use to connect via Windows are the same as the settings you use on a Mac.
>
> So don't let customer support blame the Mac. If you have to, ask to speak to someone else who may be familiar with the Mac preferences. Or, just ask them to talk more generally about your network settings, and not worry about the specific Windows names and prompts.

After changing the Configure setting to Manually, you then need to fill in the IP Address, Subnet Mask, Router, and DNS Server. These numbers should all be provided to you on some sort of instruction sheet.

BOOTP AND DHCP WITH MANUAL ADDRESS

It is unlikely that you will be asked to set up a BootP, or bootstrap network. This protocol predates DHCP and is rarely used to connect a computer to a network.

Likewise, using DHCP with a manual address is rare. This is the same as using DHCP, except that you are forcing the router to accept a particular IP address for your computer, rather than it assigning one to you.

But if you do need to use one of these two options, you will most likely be given all of the information by your IT person or the instructions that come from your Internet service provider.

AirPort Connection

Establishing a connection to a wireless network is very much like connecting to a wired network, except for two differences.

The first is the lack of wires. No surprise there.

But the second is a byproduct of that—security. Without wires means that anyone nearby can see and/or use the wireless network you set up. So you need to secure it to make sure that only someone with a password can get in.

CHOOSING A WIRELESS NETWORK

If you select the AirPort service on the left side of the Network preferences window, you get very little information on the right side, as you saw in Figure 9.1. You can choose which network you want to use from the Network Name pop-up menu.

When you do this, you will be prompted for a password, if security has been set up on the wireless router.

> **NOTE**
>
> Your Mac will remember passwords for wireless connections. So, chances are that you only need to enter this password one time. If you do so during your initial Mac setup, it also knows your wireless network's password.

When you choose a wireless network, you should see the indicator to the left of AirPort in the services list change to green, meaning that you are connected.

> **NOTE**
>
> Just because you get a green light next to a service in the Network preferences doesn't mean you are connected to the Internet. It just means that you are connected to the router. Figuring out whether the router is connected to the Internet is something that depends on the service and router. Check the documentation that came with your service. However, it is easy to figure out if it is working—just try to use Safari to browse to a web page.

ADVANCED SETTINGS

Wireless networks can be set up in the same way as wired networks, using DHCP, manually entered IP addresses, or things like BootP. To get to these settings, click on the Advanced button shown in Figure 9.1. This gives you a whole set of new controls, which are similar to the one shown in Figure 9.2.

Under the TCP/IP tab, you can change the Configure IPv4 settings to be DHCP, DHCP with manual address, BootP or Manually. You also have a variety of other tabs to change different settings if you are instructed to do so by your ISP, IT person, or router instructions. Chances are you won't need to touch any of this.

Dial-Up Modem Connection

If you need to connect to the Internet using a regular phone line, you first need a modem. Macs no longer come with built-in telephone modems, but you can purchase a USB modem for your Mac for about $50 from Apple.

Setting up a wired or wireless connection sometimes requires information like an IP address or wireless password. But setting up a connection over a dial-up modem requires something even simpler: a phone number.

When you create a modem connection, you need to supply a phone number to call, an account name, and a password. Figure 9.3 shows this service's preferences.

You would get this information from the Internet service provider with which you signed up.

Also in Figure 9.3 you'll notice the Show Modem Status in Menu Bar option. You'll want to turn this on. Then up in your menu bar you'll see a little modem icon and you'll be able to use that menu to start the process of dialing in to your ISP.

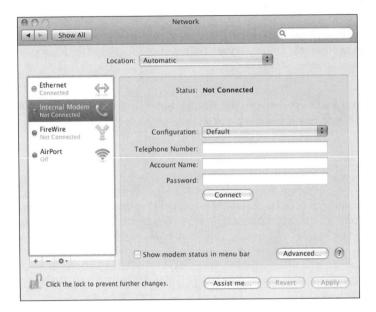

Figure 9.3

The Modem connection preferences start with a phone number.

Using Locations

So what happens when you have a MacBook and you need to move from one location to another? At work you may have a static IP address and use a wired Ethernet connection. Then at home, you may have a wireless AirPort Extreme router. You may even have a USB modem for use when traveling as well.

In Network preferences you can set up different locations with different lists of services available for each. The Location selection pop-up menu can be seen at the top of Figure 9.2 and is usually set to Automatic.

You can click on the pop-up menu and choose Edit Locations to create a new one. For instance, you can create one called Home, another called Work, and another called Travel.

So, for instance, you may have wired Ethernet connections both at home and at work, but the work connection needs a manually set IP address and the home connection needs a DHCP connection.

Without the Locations functionality, you would need to go into your Network settings each time you moved your MacBook. You'd then need to change from one set of settings to another. In the case of the manual IP address, you'd need to remember and retype several sets of numbers every time you change.

But with Locations, you can simply set your home location's Ethernet connection to DHCP and your work location's Ethernet settings with the manual numbers. Then you just switch the location using the Network preferences or the Apple menu Location submenu.

Network Setup Assistant

If you are still having trouble setting up your Mac to connect to the Internet, there is another way to do all of this.

In the Network preferences, there is a button you may have noticed labeled Assist Me. Click on that and you'll start a step-by-step process of establishing a connection to the Internet based on your answers to some questions. Figure 9.4 shows the Network Setup Assistant in action.

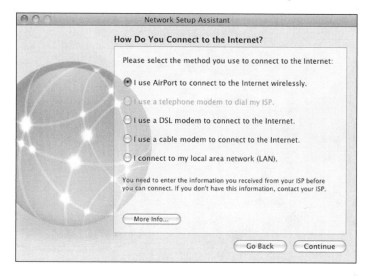

Figure 9.4

If you need more help setting up your Internet connection, try the Network Setup Assistant.

That's all you should need to know to get connected to the Internet. But when you are, there are some things you may want to do with that connection, such as surfing the Web, which we'll look at in the next chapter; sending email, which we'll look at in Chapter 11, "Getting and Sending Email"; and other functions like chat and file sharing, which are the subjects of Chapter 12, "Instant Messaging and VOIP," and Chapter 13, "Networking and File Sharing."

WHO SHOULD READ THIS CHAPTER:

In this chapter we'll learn the basics of web surfing using Safari.
If you are already familiar with web browsing, you can probably
skip the first section and go straight to "Bookmarks."

10

Using Safari, the Mac Web Browser

Perhaps the most essential application on any computer is the web
browser. Macs come with Safari, the default web browser created by
Apple and distributed free with every Mac and every copy of Mac OS X.

Browsing

The World Wide Web is just a huge collection of pages of text and
images. Pages may also contain links to other pages. You can use
search engines to search through the billions of pages of information
to find answers to questions, products to buy, or entertainment to
pass the time.

Understanding Web Terminology

To explain what the Web is, and how it works, it is important to
understand the terminology. A whole set of new words, and new def-
initions for some existing words, has sprung up to define the Web.

The *World Wide Web (WWW)* is a part of the Internet that contains
interlinked documents you can view and interact with. Other parts of
the Internet include email, instant messages, file downloads, streaming audio and video, and a variety of other things. You view these
interlinked documents by using a specialized application called a
browser, such as Safari, Firefox, or Internet Explorer. A *web page* is a
single document that you can view in your web browser. You can

usually scroll down, sometimes quite a bit, so that a single web page could actually take up several pages, or even hundreds of printed pages.

Web pages contain *links*, also called hyperlinks, which are pieces of text or images that, if you click on them, take you to another page. Usually text links are underlined and often blue in color. Sometimes links perform actions on the same page rather than taking you to a new page.

> **NOTE**
>
> When the Web started, it was simply pages of information with links to other pages. But now the pages themselves are interactive with functionality previously only seen in desktop applications. For instance, a page might contain a game, a word processing area or perform a series of calculations based on your input.

Each website has an *address*, also known as *URL (Universal Resource Locator)* or *URI (Universal Resource Identifier)*, which is its location, such as http://www.google.com or http://macmost.com/macmost-now-178-hidden-finder-menu-choices.html. You can type an address into the address bar at the top of your web browser to go directly to a page. The first part of a web address is the *domain*, such as Apple.com or MacMost.com. A *website* is a collection of web pages usually located on the same web server using the same domain name. Examples would be Apple.com, Google.com, or MacMost.com.

A *server* is a physical computer connected to the Internet that serves up the contents of a website or multiple websites. Larger sites may require more than one server to accommodate a large flow of traffic. A web *host* is a company that provides servers to other companies to allow them to serve up web pages. Large companies will host their own servers, and smaller companies will pay a web host to rent space on a server from them.

You can save the address to a web page to a list of *bookmarks* in your browser so that you can quickly find it again. The web page that your browser goes to automatically when you start is called your *home page*. A *search engine* is a website that specializes in allowing you to type a phrase and then it will return websites and pages that it thinks will match what you are looking for.

> **NOTE**
>
> Your browser stores web pages you have recently visited in the browser's *cache*. This allows your browser to load these pages again quickly instead of loading them from over the Internet.

Web pages and websites often store information on your local Mac in a *cookie* so that it can be recalled the next time you visit a site. For instance, your login name at a site may be stored so that the next time you visit, you are automatically logged on. On some web pages you will find a *form*, which is a series of fields, check boxes, or popup menus that allows you to enter information and submit it to a website. Other websites may require you to use a *plug-in*, which is a separate piece of software that integrates with your web browser to add more functionality. Examples are Flash and Shockwave.

An Internet *forum*, also called a message board, allows a website's users to post questions or reply to questions posted by others. All of the posts are shown on the website so that others can read them later on. A *blog* is a website or part of a website where regular articles are posted by one author or a group of authors. Blogs and other websites sometimes allow users to leave *comments,* which are small text messages, commenting on the content. These messages can be viewed by others visiting the pages as well.

Hypertext Markup Language, or *HTML*, is the code used by website developers to define what is on a web page and how it looks. *Hypertext Transfer Protocol (HTTP)* is the language that servers and browsers use to communicate and send web pages and information back and forth. And *JavaScript* is the programming language that developers use to embed simple functionality into web pages.

Now that you know the basic terminology, let's start surfing the Web.

Navigating the Web

When you start up Safari 4 it shows you the Top Sites page. This is a 3D view of your most frequently visited sites. But when you first run Safari it simply shows you some popular sites until you have used it enough. You can see it in Figure 10.1.

Figure 10.1

Safari 4 will show you the Top Sites page by default, giving you a place to start your web surfing.

To visit one of the websites shown, just click on the site's preview image. To go to a specific website, simply type the address of that website in the address bar at the top of Safari. In Figure 10.1 this reads "Go to this address" but you can click on that and replace it with something else, like http://macmost.com.

NOTE

When typing web addresses, you can leave off the "http://" if you like. Safari assumes that it is there. Most websites also allow you to leave off the "www." as well. So you can type http://www.macmost.com, http://macmost.com, or simply macmost.com in the Safari address bar and end up in the same place.

After typing in a web address, press Return to go to that page. It may take a second or three for the page to complete loading, depending on the speed of your Internet connection and the speed of the server where the web page is located.

When you are at a new page, you can scroll up and down, and sometimes left and right, using the scroll bars at the right and perhaps the bottom of the window. You can also click on links in the web page to go to new pages.

Links are traditionally blue and underlined. But that is becoming rare as websites develop their own color schemes and styles. However, links are usually indicated in some way. For instance, at the MacMost.com home page, seen in Figure 10.2, the text headlines are all links and appear in red on your screen. If you roll over this text with your mouse, the cursor changes to a hand to indicate that the words are clickable. In addition, an underline appears and the words change color slightly to further indicate that it is a link.

Figure 10.2

Some links on web pages are indicated by a change in the appearance of the cursor and the text when you roll over them.

Click on a link and it usually takes you to a new web page. But web pages are now so sophisticated that a link can do any number of things. For instance, a link may simply produce a small box on the page with more information, or change the contents of another section of the page.

Searching

The usual way to surf the web is not by knowing a web address and typing it in. It is by search-ing. And you can search the web using only the search field to the right of the address field at the top right. You can see it with the magnifying glass icon in both Figure 10.1 and Figure 10.2.

Just type in a search term there and press Return. The result is then returned in a web page from Google. You can see it in Figure 10.3.

Figure 10.3

The results of a search for Apple, using the default search engine, Google.

The search results are just a web page like any other—with text and links. Click on a link to go to that page.

The search engine that Safari uses is Google. But you can still search with any other search engine by just going to that engine's website, such as http://search.yahoo.com, http://www.ask.com, or http://www.altavista.com.

Knowing how to phrase a search query is the key to finding the information you are looking for.

For instance, if you are searching for ways you can control the Finder using only the keyboard, you can search for "finder keyboard" or "finder shortcuts." Or, you can just type in "controlling the finder with the keyboard." Each one returns different results, so you may need to try more than one search query before you find the information you are looking for.

Filling in Forms

Forms are lists of questions on a web page for you to answer. It can be as simple as a text field, like the one you see when you go to Google.com and type your search query. Or it can be as complex as a mortgage application.

Figure 10.4 shows a more typical long web form. You can see there are many fields, some are only one line and others are set up so that you can enter whole paragraphs. You also have boxes to check and sometimes pop-up menus with multiple choices.

Figure 10.4

Forms, especially longer ones, can have many different types of input fields.

When you are typing into fields, you can use all of the standard text editing tools—like cut, copy, and paste. You can even use the built-in spell check that is part of Mac OS X. Misspelled words should be underlined in red, and you can Ctrl-click on them to bring up a list of suggestions.

> **NOTE**
>
> Some forms are used to upload files. For example, you may be able to choose an image file to use in your profile on a social media website like Facebook. When you see a file upload button, you can click it to select a file. You can also drag and drop the file from the Finder onto the button. But if you miss the button, Safari will assume you want to load the file into the current Safari window, so be careful.

You can fill in forms relatively quickly using only the keyboard. The Tab key and Shift+Tab move you forward and back in the list of form input fields. In the case of check boxes, usually you can press the spacebar to make a selection. For pop-up menus, you can use the arrow keys and the spacebar to browse the selections and choose one.

If there is a Submit button at the end of the form, you can tab forward to it and press the space-bar to click it rather than the cursor and mouse button.

Safari also remembers how you fill out some form fields. For instance, it may automatically fill in your name or address when you return to the same form a second time, or it may assume the answers to these fields when you visit a new form for the first time.

> Sometimes Safari's AutoFill feature fills in form fields for you, and sometimes it won't. The reason lies more with the website than with you or your Mac. One site may define an address field as "address" while another defines it as "streetaddress." Safari can't be sure that these fields are the same thing, so it may not use AutoFill.

You can control the AutoFill feature of Safari in the Safari preferences.

Viewing Your History

Safari remembers which pages you visited and makes it easy for you to return to a previous page. At the top of the Safari window is a pair of arrow buttons: Previous and Next.

After navigating to a series of pages, you can always use the Previous button to go back one page. It doesn't matter if that page is on the same website.

If you press down and hold the Previous button, you will get a list of the last 10 pages you visited, so you can jump back several pages at a time.

The Next button works in the same way, but is only active if you have recently used the Previous button. Otherwise, there is no "next" page to go to.

In addition, you can use the History menu to get a more complete list of the web pages you have visited. It shows the last 20 pages, plus "Earlier Today" and then pages by date after that. You can use Show History in that same menu to get a complete list of all pages that Safari has been to recently. You can even search this list.

> You can control how far back Safari's memory goes by looking in the General tab of the Safari preferences. You can also turn on Private Browsing in the Safari menu, which prevents Safari from adding any pages to your history at all.

We'll learn about more browsing techniques later in this chapter. But before we go any further, let's look at the larger subject of browser bookmarks.

Bookmarks

When you visit a web page you want to return to later, you may want to create a bookmark for it. A bookmark is simply a link to the page that you save in one of many bookmark locations in Safari.

Bookmarking a Web Page

To bookmark a page, choose the Bookmark menu in Safari and click on Add Bookmark.

The title of the web page and a pop-up list of bookmark locations appears. You can change the title, if the title of the page doesn't suit you, and you can choose between three main locations: Bookmarks Bar, Bookmarks Menu, or one of any bookmark folders that you can create.

Or, you can click on the + button to the left of the address at the top of the Safari window and choose Bookmarks Bar or Bookmarks Menu to add it to either place.

The Bookmarks Bar is the bar right underneath the address and search bar in Figures 10.1 and 10.2. It comes preset with bookmarks to Apple, Yahoo!, Google Maps, and a few other places.

When adding a web page to the Bookmarks Bar, it might be best to pick a short name. For instance, use "MacMost" instead of "MacMost: Apple Macintosh, iPod and iPhone News, Reviews and Commentary." This way you can fit more bookmarks on the bar.

The Bookmarks Bar is probably where you want to keep pages that you visit frequently. For instance, you might have bookmarks to a local news station's weather page, or the main page to a site you check every day.

Less important bookmarks can be stored in the Bookmarks Menu. These links will appear when you choose Bookmarks from the menu bar.

In addition, you can create any number of your own bookmark folders. Just choose Bookmarks, Add Bookmark Folder. Creating new folders will help you manage your bookmarks.

Managing Your Bookmarks

After you've bookmarked more than a few pages, you will want to organize those bookmarks. You can do so by creating folders, and also by viewing them using the Bookmarks, Show All Bookmarks menu command.

Figure 10.5 shows the Safari window after Show All Bookmarks has been selected. The left lists collections of web addresses that you can access. In this case, you see the History, Bookmarks Bar, Bookmarks Menu, and even a collection that represents web addresses in your Address Book. On the right, you see both a cover flow view and a list view of the selected collection.

You can manage your bookmarks by selecting them and clicking only once on one of the fields—like the name or address of the bookmark. This allows you to edit the information. Double-clicking activates the bookmark and takes you to that web page.

You can also drag and drop the bookmarks to move them around in their own lists, or to move them from one list to another.

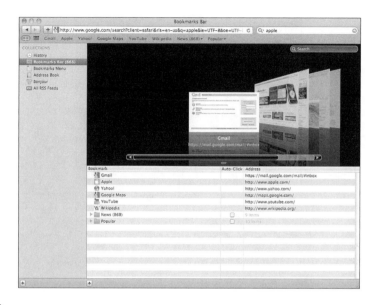

Figure 10.5

The bookmarks list in Safari takes over the whole window and shows you various collections of web addresses, such as your history and the bookmarks menu.

Importing and Exporting Bookmarks

If you are switching from another computer, you may want to take your bookmarks with you. You can export bookmarks from almost any other browser. You'll get a single file, usually in .html format.

After you bring that file over to your Mac, you can use the File, Import Bookmarks to bring that into Safari. These new bookmarks will probably be placed into a special folder. You can then use Bookmarks, Show All Bookmarks to reorganize them if you want.

You can also use the option Export Bookmarks under the File menu. This could be used to bring your Safari bookmarks to another browser, or another computer. You could also use them as a backup.

When you export bookmarks from Safari, you get an .html file as a result. If you have your own web space, you could upload this file as-is and then access it while on the road, using other computers. This is a good way to make sure your bookmarks are available to you while traveling. Just be sure you are OK with your bookmarks falling into someone else's hands if your website is a public one.

Changing Your Home Page

There is one other bookmark-like function in Safari called your home page. If you go to the Safari preferences, under the General tab, you'll see it listed with a Set to Current Page button under it as in Figure 10.6.

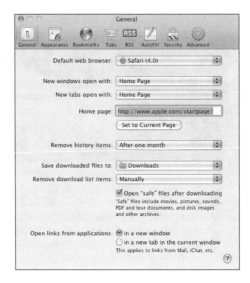

Figure 10.6

The General preferences for Safari allows you to set your Home page.

The page specified here can be used when you start Safari or when you open a new tab or window. You can use the settings shown in Figure 10.6 to determine what you want to happen when you open a new window or tab. You can choose to have it start with the home page, but you can also choose an empty page, the same page as the previous window or tab, or the list of bookmarks.

One thing you might consider doing with your home page is using one of the services that let you create a custom home page with news and information tailored to what you want to see every day, for instance, iGoogle.com or my.yahoo.com.

After you have mastered web navigation and bookmarks, there are some more advanced Safari features you may want to learn about.

Editing Your Top Sites Page

Your Top Sites page can be returned to at any time by clicking on the icon of 12 dots toward the left side of the Safari toolbar. You can also edit your Top Sites page to display sites you want to see, rather than having Safari decide which sites to show you.

To do this, click on the Edit button that appears at the bottom left corner, as you can see back in Figure 10.1. At that point you will have the ability to click an X-shaped button at the upper left corner of any preview to remove it from the page, or a push pin icon to keep the preview as part of your Top Sites. You can also drag and drop previews around the page to arrange them as you please.

To force a page to appear in Top Sites, you can go to that page and then click on the + button to the left of the address at the top of the Safari window. Then you can add the page to your bookmarks, or choose to add it to Top Sites.

Advanced Browsing Techniques

Although you can easily just use Safari by browsing, searching, and clicking, there are some pretty advanced browser features that you may want to check out as well. You can use tabs instead of windows, save copies of web pages locally, download files, and view RSS feeds.

Using Tabs

Tabs are an alternative to having multiple browser windows open. Instead, you can have multiple web pages open in different tabs of the same window. Figure 10.7 explains it a little better by showing you the top of a Safari window that has three tabs.

Tabs

Figure 10.7

The top of this Safari window shows three tabs, with the third one being the visible one.

Think of it as all three web pages are open in the same window: Apple, Wikipedia, and MacMost. But only the third one, MacMost, is visible. The other three are hidden at the moment.

To get to this state, first you would go to Apple.com's website. Then, choose File, New Tab or press Command+T. This opens up a second tab. You can use that second tab to go to another page. Then press Command+T again to create the third tab and go to another page there.

When you have these tabs open, you can click on the tab title to switch tabs. The page on the previous tab remains open, but hidden, and the new tab shows itself.

You can also use Command+Shift+[and Command+Shift+] to move between tabs.

The advantage of tabs over multiple windows is that tabs offer a way to have multiple web pages open without adding clutter to your screen.

Saving Web Pages

If you find a web page you really like, you can save the page using the File, Save As menu command. You get two choices from there: Page Source or Web Archive. The first saves the text and basic layout of the page, but not the graphics. The second attempts to save every graphic element on the page.

With some more advanced web pages, even a Web Archive can miss a few things and your saved page may not look the same as the original. The total contents of the web page are saved to a single file, which can be reopened in Safari.

You can also choose File, Mail the Contents of This Page to send a Web Archive to someone else. How the page looks to them depends on what mail program they use.

Another option is to save the page, or at least part of it, as a Web Clipping. You can do this with File, Open In Dashboard. We took a look at Web Clippings in Chapter 6, "Controlling Windows and Applications," in the section on making your own dashboard widgets.

Downloading Files

The Internet is more than just web pages. Occasionally you'll want to download files. These could be documents, applications, or installers.

An example would be if you visited the software downloads section of the Apple.com website. There you can browse and read about tons of Apple and third-party applications you can download.

> **NOTE**
>
> Sometimes when you visit a web page, a download will start automatically. Other times you need to click on a link to start a download. If a link appears to be a download link but does not work as you expect, you can also Ctrl-click on it to bring up a context menu and choose Download Linked File.

When you find one you like, and select to download it, Safari asks your permission and begins the download. It will place these files in the Downloads folder by default. You can change this location in the General Safari preferences.

After a file starts downloading, you can check its progress in the Downloads window, shown in Figure 10.8. You can see this window by choosing Window, Downloads or pressing Command+Option+L.

Figure 10.8

The Downloads window shows you the progress of the files currently being downloaded and a history of recent downloads.

After a file has been downloaded, you can click on the magnifying glass next to the file name in the Downloads window to open a new Finder window with the file selected.

You can also Ctrl-click on the file to get a context menu as in Figure 10.8. This lets you remove items from the list as well as copy the address of the download to the clipboard.

Reading RSS Feeds

RSS stands for Really Simple Syndication. You can think of it as an alternative way to view the content at a website. Instead of a fancy layout and navigation, an RSS feed is a simple list of headlines and article summaries. Almost all sites with regularly updated content, like news websites or blogs, have RSS feeds.

When you visit a site with an RSS feed in Safari, a blue box with "RSS" in it appears on the right side of the address field. Click on that box and you will switch to a view of the RSS feed, as in Figure 10.9.

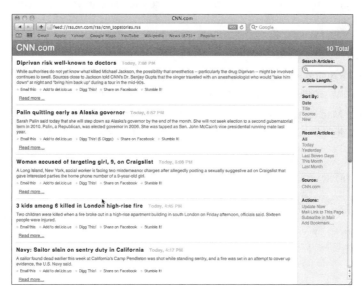

Figure 10.9

The CNN home page has an RSS feed of the most recent news stories.

Sometimes a site will have multiple RSS feeds. For instance, a newspaper website may have a feed for each of its sections. In those cases you will get a pop-up menu when you click the RSS box so that you can choose the feed you want to view. In other cases, you would need to navigate to the proper page to see the right RSS feed. For instance, the main newspaper page may link to the top story's RSS feed, and the sports page links to a sports news RSS feed.

Taking Care of Security

You can't surf the Web today without thinking about security. You have probably heard about viruses and malware. They are real and they are dangerous. Other security threats including phishing scams and fraudulent websites.

VIRUSES

The good news is that surfing the Web on Safari on your Mac is not nearly as dangerous as it is on Windows. Much of the malware out there spreads by using ActiveX controls, which are a part of the Internet Explorer browser in Windows. Other malware is spread as downloadable software that only works on Windows. Even if you accidentally download one of these files, it won't run or infect your Mac.

However, there is still a danger. Viruses can certainly be written to infect Macs, so you should be wary.

If you follow some simple rules, you will greatly reduce the risk that your Mac will become infected with a virus.

1. Don't download any software from any website unless you are sure you know what the software is.

2. If you get a dialog box asking for your permission to install something in Safari, read it carefully and only agree to it if you understand what is being installed.

3. Keep your Mac up to date using Software Update in the Apple menu. Any major virus threat to Mac OS X will likely be something that Apple will combat with an update.

> **NOTE**
>
> So how do you know whether a piece of software from a third-party software developer is legitimate? One simple thing you can do is to search the Web for references to that software followed by "virus" or "malware." If a piece of software is trouble, chances are that people are talking about it in forums and warnings are all over the Web.

SCAMS

Phishing scams and fraudulent websites are far more of a threat to Mac users because they work just as well on Macs as they do PCs. A *phishing scam* is a link or an email to a link to a website that you trust, but the link actually goes to a look-alike website. Then you enter your login information, thus giving it to someone with malicious intent.

An example may be an email that appears to be from your bank. It claims that you need to update your information or that your account balance is low. You click on that link and the web page you are taken to looks exactly like your bank's website. When you log in, you are giving your bank login information, and maybe even more, to someone looking to steal your money or identity.

The simplest way to protect yourself against phishing scams is not to follow links to critical sites like your bank. Instead, type the domain name for your bank manually to ensure that you are at the right place.

> **NOTE**
>
> But how did the phishing site know that I use such-and-such bank? How did they know my account balance was low? The answer is simple: They didn't. They simply sent out the same email to millions of email addresses. When they do this, they are bound to be right some of the time.

Safari also offers some protection against fraudulent sites. In the Security Preferences, you can check off Warn When Visiting a Fraudulent Website. Check out Figure 10.10.

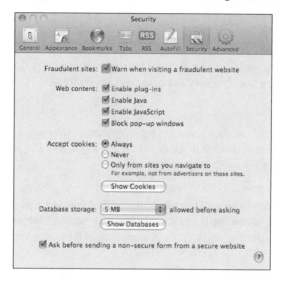

Figure 10.10

The Security panel in the Safari preferences offers some choices to make your browsing more secure.

SECURITY PREFERENCES

The rest of the Security preferences aren't as helpful as you would think. In fact, they can make your browsing experience painful. For instance, unchecking Enable Plug-Ins, Enable Java, and especially Enable JavaScript, will cripple most modern websites.

The Block Pop-up Windows option is probably one you want to leave checked as well. Otherwise, you may find yourself at a website that throws up a few, or even dozens of pop-up windows with offers or ads. Some legitimate sites earn their revenue from pop-up ads, but most have moved on to in-page ads and other ways to get by.

If you do end up at a website that displays a pop-up window that you want to see, such as a login box or some other site functionality, you will be given notice that a pop-up window has been blocked and you can choose to display that window anyway.

SECURE WEB SITE TRANSACTIONS

Another security issue is sending data securely between you and the server; for instance, when you are checking out of an online store and sending your credit card information.

In these cases, look for the padlock icon in the address field for the page you are on. If you see this, it means that the browser will be sending the data in the form to the server in encrypted format.

In the unlikely event that you do not see this, you may want to look for an alternative way to order the product or service.

Privacy

The Security panel in Figure 10.10 also includes some privacy settings. Cookies are a major topic when it comes to privacy, but they may not be as bad as you think.

COOKIES

A *cookie* is a bit of information that Safari has been instructed to remember about the relationship between you and a website. For instance, when you log in to a site, a cookie may be saved on your hard drive that stores your login information.

This information is stored on your Mac, not the server. But it is sent to the website every time you visit it. So the next time you visit the site, you may find yourself automatically logged in. Safari was simply asked by the site if it had a recent cookie saying that you were logged in. It sent this information to the site and the site acknowledged it by skipping the login for you this time around.

Where cookies ring privacy alarms is when a cookie is shared between sites. The way this works: A piece of content, like an ad, is served up by a third-party server. So you are visiting Example.com, but SomeAdServer.com is being used to display the ads. SomeAdServer.com then remembers things about you, like the fact that you clicked on an ad for a piece of video software. Then, the next time you visit a site that uses SomeAdServer.com, it may show you an ad that is of interest to video editors or photographers.

Now, whether or not this is a violation of privacy is something you need to decide for yourself. You can almost always view the privacy policy of any website by clicking on a privacy policy link on the home page of that site. This tells you what the website does with any information it gathers. Of course, although major websites and companies provide honest privacy policies, it doesn't mean that every website does.

PRIVATE BROWSING

When you browse using Safari or just about any browser, you leave behind a trail of breadcrumbs. Someone can look in your history or Downloads window to see what you have been up to. Your past use of the Google search field is also stored to make it easy for you to repeat previous searches.

But say you are searching for a birthday gift for your spouse, and they are ever so curious. They can use this trail to figure out what you got them.

If you choose Safari, Private Browsing, the trail is turned off. Pages you go to are no longer saved in the history, downloads are no longer stored in the list, and searches are no longer stored to be reused.

The Back button will still work in the Safari window, so you will also want to make sure you close that window when you are done.

Even if you are not using Private Browsing, you can always use History, Clear History to hide your tracks.

Safari Alternatives

Safari is the primary Mac browser used by most Mac users, but there are alternatives. Several open source browsers are available, and even some Mac-only browsers.

Here is a list of some of these browser alternatives you may want to try:

- **Firefox**—This cross-platform browser is popular on both Mac and Windows. It offers one huge advantage over Safari: You can get add-ons for it to add new functionality. A huge library of such add-ons exists. http://mozilla.com.

- **Opera**—The Opera browser has been around for a while and the company specializes in versions for lots of different systems. A Mac OS X version is available and has some interesting features you can check out. http://www.opera.com

- **Camino**—This is a version of the same engine that Firefox is based on. However, it has been built specifically for Mac users, so it may look a little more Mac-like. In my tests it is also very fast. http://caminobrowser.org.

- **Flock**—Flock is another customized version of the Mozilla engine, but it has added features for those using social media sites like Facebook and Twitter. http://flock.com/

- **WebKit**—If WebKit looks familiar, that's because it is actually Safari. Or, at least, it is the framework used to make Safari. The difference is that you can download "Webkit Nightly Builds," which are the most up-to-date versions of the browser engine and will have new features and speed enhancements long before they are available in the released version of Safari. http://webkit.org.

- **Chrome**—Google recently entered the browser wars with their own, called Chrome. You can check it out at http://www.google.com/chrome.

There are actually many others as well, and new ones appearing all the time. An up-to-date list appears here:

http://macmost.com/alternative-mac-web-browsers.html.

Now that you know how to surf the web, it is time to look at using another part of the Internet: email.

WHO SHOULD READ THIS CHAPTER:

If you need to know how to configure your Mac to get and send
email, this is the chapter for you. It will also go into more
advanced email techniques like setting up signatures, filtering
out junk mail, and accessing multiple email accounts.

11

Getting and Sending Email

There are two ways that people get email. The first is using a web-
based service like Gmail, Yahoo Mail, or AOL. You can access this kind
of email through the Safari web browser.

The second method is using client/server email. This usually comes
with your Internet service, a web hosting service, or from your
employer. To access this kind of email, you usually use an email client,
like the Mail program that comes with Mac OS X or Windows Mail or
Outlook. This program would be the "client" and your company or
Internet service provider would be the "server."

There is a lot of crossover between client/server email and web-
based email as well. Most client/server email has a web-based interface for accessing it while traveling. Most web-based email can be
accessed in a mail client as well.

We'll start by looking at the Mac Mail client application, and then
take a brief look at some web-based mail services that you may
already be using.

Setting Up Mail

Setting up Mail to receive your client/server email is a task that can
range from simple to mind-bogglingly frustrating. There are hundreds of different types of mail servers out there, each customizable
and with little idiosyncrasies. But the basic idea is to create a Mail
account and match the settings on that account to the settings provided by your Internet service provider (ISP) for email.

Initial Setup

If you are starting Mail for the first time, you should get a dialog box like the one in Figure 11.1. Mail recognizes that no accounts have been created yet, and concludes that you want to set one up.

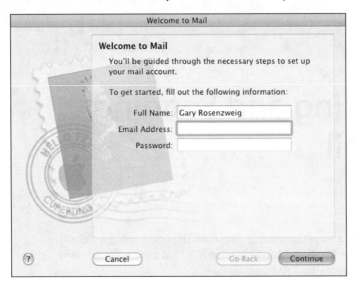

Figure 11.1

Mail attempts to walk you through the initial setup of your account.

This screen asks for your name, email address, and password. Be careful what you use as your name here, as it will be used as your name on the email that you send. So nicknames are not a good idea if you plan to use email professionally.

Your email address should be the full address, like "steve@macmost.com", not just "steve." Your password should be the password you used to set up the account, or one that was assigned to you.

> **NOTE**
>
> At this point if Mail recognizes that you have a MobileMe account, it will ask if you would like to automatically set up the account. Mail and MobileMe work together to set up this kind of account, so you don't need to worry about most of the rest of the settings.

The next screen, shown in Figure 11.2, starts to get down to the nitty-gritty details. You first need to pick an account type. Your choices are POP, IMAP, or Exchange.

A POP (Post Office Protocol) account is a standard client/server email account. Mail is sent across the Internet to your Internet service provider's server, and then stored on that server until you retrieve it with your email application.

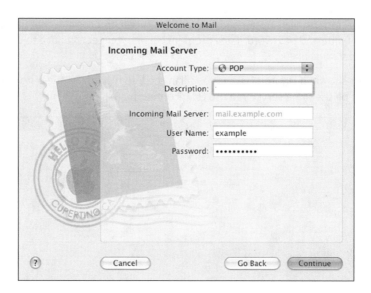

Figure 11.2
This step asks you for an account type, user name, and password.

EMAIL ACCOUNT TYPES

An IMAP (Internet Message Access Protocol) account will get messages at the server and allow you to retrieve them with your application, just like POP. But it also keeps the messages on the server, merely synchronizing your application and the server. Because messages are in both places at once, it is better for business users who access their email from several computers.

An Exchange server is a proprietary Microsoft email server that is used in business. It is a similar idea to an IMAP server.

Your ISP should tell you which types of accounts it supports. Many still only support POP email, but IMAP is becoming popular.

The Description field is for you to enter a name for this email account. For instance, you could call it "Work" or "Personal" or just use your name if it is your only email account.

The Incoming Mail Server is another item of information that your ISP should provide. If you have your own hosted website, it is probably the domain name of that site, possibly preceded by "pop." or "imap." For example: example.com, pop.example.com, or imap.example.com.

The format in which you enter your user name should also be something you are told by your ISP. Sometimes it is your full email address, like example@macmost.com. Other times the @ symbol is replaced by a plus sign (+) or percentage (%) symbol, like example+macmost.com. Sometimes it is just the first part of your email address, like "example".

The Password field should already be filled in from the information you provided on the previous screen.

When you click Continue, Mail attempts to contact the server and confirm that the server will accept the user name and password. If any problem occurs, you get a chance to change the information and try again.

The next screen, shown in Figure 11.3, lets you fill in the information for the outgoing server. This may or may not be the same server you use for incoming mail.

Figure 11.3

Outgoing mail server information may be different than incoming mail server information.

An outgoing mail server, also called an SMTP or Send Mail Transfer Protocol server, is often the same server that you use for incoming mail. Instead of pop.example.com, it may be smtp.example.com. Check the information from your ISP to make sure. Unless you are told otherwise, the user name and password are often the same as on the previous screen.

> Sometimes user authentication is not required. This can be true if the server simply allows anyone on the network to send email. In a situation where you are logged in to a company network, or hardwired to a DSL or cable modem provider, the server already knows who you are. Unlike retrieving email, where the server needs to know which account to get the mail from, each email sent already has a "from" and a "to" attached to it, so no specific account needs to be indicated.

A typical situation where your incoming and outgoing email server would be different would be in the case where you are using a company email address, but a home ISP. If your company is example.com and you get your name@example.com email at home, you need to use pop.example.com or something similar to get email.

However, your ISP at home may forbid you to use smtp.example.com to send email. It may be part of their security or anti-spam measures. Instead, they may insist that you use their special SMTP server, with a special user name, and password, or none at all because you are already logged in to their service.

In cases like this, it really doesn't matter to you because your email is still addressed "from" you. The recipient will not notice that it came from a local ISP server and not your company server.

> **NOTE**
>
> Sending email from locations like hotels or Wi-Fi hotspots can be problematic. Because spam is such a problem, many locations simply forbid any SMTP traffic at all. If you use web-based email, you are fine. But client/server email is often one-way in these situations. Advanced techniques like SSH tunneling or a Virtual Private Network (VPN) may be options if your company's IT department supports them. Find your IT guy and ask about them.

When you are done with your outgoing mail settings, Mail will again contact the server to check to make sure everything works. Then it takes you to a final screen to confirm your account settings.

Editing and Adding Accounts

After you have set up your first account, you may want to set up others as well. For instance, you may have a work email account and a personal email account. You can create another account by going to Mail, Preferences and clicking on the Accounts tab at the top of the window.

> **NOTE**
>
> Although you can use Mail to get email from multiple accounts, those accounts should belong to the same person. If you are sharing the computer, as in a family computer situation, you should create separate Mac OS X accounts. Each of these accounts would access different email, preferences, browser bookmarks, and document folders. See Chapter 22, "Customizing Your Mac," to learn how to set up multiple accounts.

Figure 11.4 shows the Accounts preferences, which lists accounts on the left and then shows information about the selected account on the right.

The account information on the right side of the window is the same information that you entered earlier in the process. You can make adjustments to those settings here.

When you click the + button at the bottom-left corner of the window, you start the same process as before, entering the basic information about each account.

In addition to this basic information, you can also examine the Mailbox Behaviors and Advanced tabs for other settings. But for most email accounts, you can leave these alone.

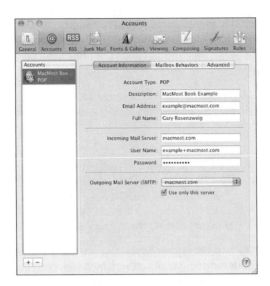

Figure 11.4
In the Accounts preferences, you can see the current accounts and add more or remove them.

Reading Your Email

After you have Mail configured to get email from your account, all you need to do to get email is to click the Get Mail button at the top of the Mail window. In fact, you don't even need to do that. By default, Mail checks for new messages every five minutes.

The Mail Window

The main Mail window is divided into three main parts: a sidebar on the left, the list of email on the top right, and a message display area below that. You can see these three parts in Figure 11.5.

The sidebar is a list of mailboxes, which are similar to folders in the Finder. The default is to have an Inbox and a Sent folder. We'll look at how to create more in a moment.

On the right at the top is the list of messages in the currently selected mailbox. There is just one message in Figure 11.5 and it is selected. So under it in the message display area is the contents of that message.

Mailbox Folders

The Inbox, Sent, Trash, and Junk email folders are present by default. But there can be several subfolders inside these. For instance, you can have two Inbox folders inside the main Inbox folder if you have two accounts.

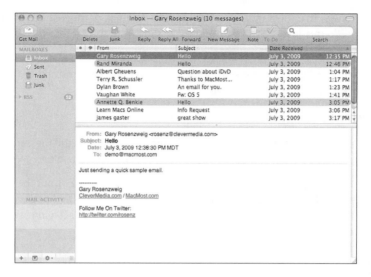

Figure 11.5
The main Mail window shows mailboxes, messages, and the currently selected message.

If you have two accounts, then selecting the overall Inbox folder shows the incoming mail for both accounts. But you can also select the individual account folders within the Inbox folder to only show mail from that account.

You can also create your own folders. To add a new mailbox folder, click the + button at the bottom-left corner of the window. You can add mailboxes simply for organizational purposes. For instance, many people create a Saved or Archived folder to put mail they no longer need in their Inbox. Or, you can create a variety of folders with different subjects, like Work, Friends, Receipts, Important, and so on.

You can nest folders inside one another. For instance, you can create a Saved folder and then Work and Friends folders. You can then drag and drop the last two into Saved.

Message List

You can click on any message in the list to view it in the viewing area below. Double-click on it and it will open a new window showing the message as well.

You can also sort messages in the message list by clicking on the column headings. For instance, to sort by Date Received, click on that column. Click again to reverse the order. In the menu bar there is an option View, Sort By, which can be used to set the sort order. View, Columns can be used to change the columns that appear.

When you are done with a message, you can choose to delete it, or move it out of the Inbox into another folder. To do this, just drag and drop the message from the list into the Trash or a folder you created in the sidebar.

Alternatively, you can select the message and press the Delete key to move it to the trash, or click the Delete button at the top of the window.

Viewing Messages

The viewing area of the window shows some basic information about the message at the top, such as who the message is from, the subject, the date it was sent, and so on.

You can expand the top portion of the viewing area to show you more about the email if you like. Just choose View, Message, Long Headers. Now you will see all of the header information for that email, including special fields added by the sender's server, your receiving server, and even servers in between.

> **NOTE**
>
> When viewing a message you can quickly and easily add the sender to your Address Book by choosing Message, Add Sender to Address Book. Even if you already have that person in your list, but perhaps without an email address or using a different email address, you will be given the opportunity to simply add this address to that person's contact information. This way you can easily build your Address Book list as you get email from your friends.

Viewing Attachments

If someone sends you a file attached to an email message, it should show up in two places in the viewing area. The first is in the header information as a short list of attachments. The second is in the body of the email itself.

Some email clients allow you to embed images into the body of the message at specific locations, whereas others will always put them at the end of the message.

If the attachment is something that Mail can display, like an image or PDF file, you'll see the attachment right in the body of the message. Otherwise, you may have to double-click on the link in the header information to launch another program to view it.

> **NOTE**
>
> Sometimes Windows users will send email attachments that you can't open on a Mac—or even other Windows machines if they don't have the right software. A .exe file is a Windows application, for instance. A .ppt file is a PowerPoint presentation file. A .doc file is a Word document, which you should be able to open in TextEdit.

You can also Ctrl-click on the attachment in either place to get more options, such as saving it or viewing it in the Finder's Quick View window.

> **NOTE**
>
> Although this is much more of a problem on Windows, you may want to be careful when opening attachments. Never open an attachment in an email from someone you don't know. And even if you do know the person who sent it, use proper judgment. Some viruses (on Windows, of course) can actually send email from a computer without the owner's knowledge. So that funny Word document from Uncle Joe might just be a malicious file that Uncle Joe didn't even know he sent.

Sending Email

To compose an email, click the New Message button at the top of the Mail window. You'll get a message composition window, as shown in Figure 11.6.

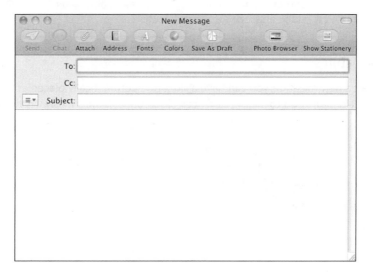

Figure 11.6
The New Message window allows you to create a new email message.

Composing Email

When you're composing an email, the first thing you need to do is to indicate the person to whom the message is being sent. You can start typing an email address or a name. If it is someone to whom you have sent email before, you'll see the address filled in by the autocomplete feature. Otherwise, you'll need to type the whole address yourself.

Another way to add a recipient to the To field is to click on the Address button at the top of the window. This brings up the list of names from your Address Book. You can select one, or several.

You can put as many email addresses as you like in the To field. If you are typing them manually, you can separate them with commas.

You can also add names to the Cc field. These recipients will also get the message, although they will see that they were not the primary recipient, just someone additional that you wanted to make sure also got the message.

The Subject field is next. Then you can type the body of your text in the main part of the window.

When you are done, click the Send button at the top of the window to send your email. A copy of the message will be stored in your Sent folder where you can see all of the messages you have sent.

If you are in the middle of composing a new message and decide to take a break, you can always save your message as a draft and get back to it later. Just click the Save As Draft button. You will then see the message in a Drafts mailbox folder in the left sidebar. Look at the Drafts folder, and then double-click on that message to reopen the composition window and work on the message some more, or send it.

Creating Signatures

When you start a new message, you can have a signature automatically placed at the bottom. To configure your signatures, go to Mail, Preferences, Signatures. Figure 11.7 shows this window.

Figure 11.7

The Signatures preferences allow you to add a variety of different signatures that you can use when composing email.

Click the + button near the bottom of the window and you'll be given a default signature that features your name and email address. You can customize this signature however you want, and change its name as well.

On the left side of Signature preferences, you'll see All Signatures and also a list of all your accounts. You can drag and drop a signature from the middle column to an account on the left. This makes that signature the default for that account.

If you drag more than one signature to an account, you get choices for that account in a Choose Signature pop-up at the bottom of the window. You can choose which signature is the default, or tell Mail to choose one at random each time, or use them one after the other in sequential order as you compose email.

If you have more than one signature, you will see a Signature pop-up menu in the New Message window that wasn't there before. This allows you to choose your signature while composing a message.

Attaching Files

You can attach files to your email message in the New Message window. There are two ways to do this. The first is to use the Attach button at the top of the window. This prompts you to find the files to attach.

The second is to use drag and drop to drag a file from the Finder into your message. When you do this, you can position the file inside your email message. More advanced email clients, like Mail, will then show the recipients that file in the proper place in the message. If it is an image file, for instance, they will see the image appear at the right spot.

You can also use the Photo Browser button at the top of the window to open a little window that shows your iPhoto library. You can drag and drop a photo from there to have it attached to your message.

You can also send files by starting with the file itself. For instance, in iPhoto you can select a photo and click an Email button in the bottom toolbar. This gives you sizing options so that you can send a smaller, more compressed image rather than a huge file. Here's another example: When you are viewing a document in Preview, you can use File, Mail Document to open Mail and start a New Message with the document automatically attached. Many other Apple and third-party applications have a mail feature similar to that.

Replying to Messages

Another way to send a message is to simply reply to one that you are reading. Click the Reply or Reply All button at the top of the window to start a new message based on the old one.

The main difference between starting a new message and replying to one is that the reply starts with the To field already filled in, directed back at whomever sent the message. The Subject field is already set as well, using "Re:" and the original subject.

The body of the message starts with the previous message quoted. Quoting simply means that the existing message is in the body of your new one, but indented in a special way to indicate that this was the old message, as opposed to new text that you type in response.

TIP

By default the entire old message is quoted in the body of your new message. But you can have only a small portion of it quoted by selecting some text in the original message before clicking the Reply button. Then only the selected text will appear as quoted. This is ideal for situations when your response only pertains to a line or two of the original and you don't want to include the entire original message in your response.

Using the Reply All button also includes other recipients of the original message, and even Cc recipients. It is generally used when you want everyone who saw the original message to see your response as well. For instance, if you get a message directed at a whole group of friends about who wants to go to lunch, you can use Reply All and all of the people who saw the original message will also see that, yes, you can go to lunch.

Another type of reply is to forward the message using the Forward button. This is basically the same as replying, except the To field is not filled in. Instead, you have to specify whom the message goes to. For instance, you could forward a lunch invitation to a friend who was left off the original list.

Other Mail Functions

There are a few other features in Mail worth mentioning. You can create notes and a to do list.

Notes

Notes are like email messages to yourself. They don't have a recipient, but they can sit in your mailbox. They are handy for reminding yourself of things to do or important bits of information.

To create a note, click the Note button at the top of the Mail window. You get a note-like window shown in Figure 11.8.

You can add and style text in a note the same way you can with a mail message. When you are done, the note appears in your Inbox alongside incoming mail. It will have a title that matches the first line of text in the note.

You view a note in the same way that you view incoming mail. To edit it, double-click on it to reopen the note-editing window.

You can turn a note into an email to send by clicking on the Send button. You'll even get a yellownotebook-like background in the email.

Notes appear in the Inbox as well as in a Notes folder that will show up in the left sidebar of the main Mail window.

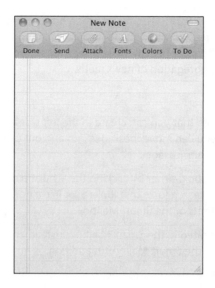

Figure 11.8
You can type or paste text into a note in Mail.

To Do Items

You can also create to do items in Mail. Click on the To Do button at the top of the main Mail window to add one. Or, you can select text in an email message and click the To Do button to instantly create a To Do item with the selected text.

All of your To Do items appear in the To Do folder in the left sidebar. When viewing the list, you can Ctrl-click on an item and set things like priority and completion date.

Items with a due date will even appear in your iCal calendars. In fact, the To Do list is shared between Mail and iCal. So you can add, delete, and edit items in both applications.

RSS Feeds

Mail can also be used as an RSS reader. We talked about RSS in the previous chapter, because Safari can read RSS feeds.

Mail reads RSS feeds in its own way—as mail messages. You can add an RSS feed by clicking on the + button at the bottom-left corner of the Mail window and selecting Add RSS Feeds. Or, you can go to File, Add RSS Feeds in the menu bar.

You can then browse through RSS feeds that may be in your Safari bookmarks, or specify the URL of a feed.

When you have RSS feeds listed under RSS in the left sidebar, you can select one and view the items in the feed in the same way that you would view a mailbox of RSS messages.

Things get really interesting when you select more than one RSS feed at a time. You see all of the items in all of those feeds, sorted accordingly. So if you are sorting the items by date, and select 10 new RSS feeds, all of the items appear in the message list sorted together by date. You can use this to create your own aggregation of news feeds.

Smart Mailboxes

Another type of mailbox folder that you can create in the left sidebar is a Smart Mailbox. This isn't the type of folder that you can move messages into and out of. Instead, it is a permanent search performed on all of your messages.

When you create a Smart Mailbox, either by clicking the + button or choosing Mailbox, New Smart Mailbox, you will get a search form that looks a lot like a normal mail search form. The results will become the contents of the Smart Mailbox.

But those messages aren't located in the Smart Mailbox. Instead, they are kept in their original locations and merely listed in the Smart Mailbox in addition.

The Smart Mailbox is kept up to date constantly. So, for instance, if you create a Smart Mailbox with all messages that include the word "special project" in the subject, any new messages that arrive meeting that criteria will automatically be added to the Smart Mailbox as well.

Advanced Mail Preferences

Mail is a pretty complex program that goes way beyond simply receiving and sending email. You can also filter email, which comes in handy if you get a lot of email. A lot of this functionality can be found by going through Mail's preferences.

General Preferences

Here are some things you can do if you look through some of the tabs of Mail's preferences. Figure 11.9 shows the Mail preferences window with General settings visible.

Here are some of the options that you will find in the General tab:

- Change how often Mail checks for new messages
- Set a sound to play when new mail arrives
- Set which folder is used when attachments are downloaded
- Decide whether Trash and Junk folders are included in searches

Options on the Accounts, Mailbox Behaviors tab are as follows:

- Whether Notes are also shown in your Inbox
- If messages you send should ever be deleted, and when
- When Junk mail messages should be deleted
- How old messages in the Trash folder should be before they are permanently deleted

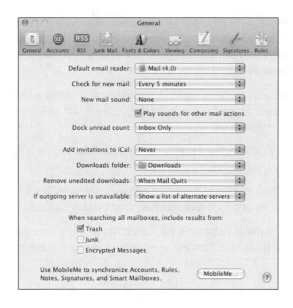

Figure 11.9

The Mail Preferences window has many tabs with different sets of settings on each.

Options on the RSS tab are as follows:

- How often RSS feeds should be updated
- If or when old articles are removed from the list

Options on the Fonts and Colors tab are:

- Choose the default fonts used to display messages
- Decide how quoted text should look

Options on the Viewing tab are as follows:

- Set the default level of detail for headers
- Decide whether images in email messages should be downloaded and displayed

Options on the Composing tab are as follows:

- Choose your default message format as plain text or rich text
- Decide whether replying to a message should automatically quote the old message

Junk Mail Filtering

Another preference tab is the Junk Mail tab. Mail has built-in junk mail filtering. It has its own secret algorithm for determining whether an incoming message is spam.

It can also use clues about spam provided by your Internet service provider. Most mail servers now employ a system like Spam Assassin for determining what messages are spam. These systems look at the message content, but they also look at where the message came from and compare it to a list of known spam servers.

The Internet service provider passes a spam "score" along as headers added to each email. Mail can then use these headers as long as you have the setting Trust Junk Mail Headers Set by My Internet Service Provider turned on.

So although Mail's junk mail filtering is pretty set and does not evolve to counter new spam attacks, your ISP's spam system does.

You can also decide to whitelist email in the Junk Mail preferences. For instance, mail from people in your address book or previous recipients list may bypass junk mail filtering.

When a message is determined to be junk, you can still find it in your Junk folder in Mail. It is a good idea to scan these items every once in a while to make sure nothing important got caught and discarded.

Rules

One way to enhance and modify your junk mail filtering is to use another Mail preference window called Rules.

A *rule* looks at each incoming email and performs an action on that email if it meets certain criteria. You can create a rule by going to Mail, Preferences, Rules and clicking the Add Rule button. You then get a form shown in Figure 11.10.

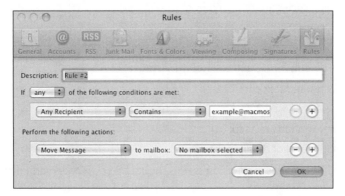

Figure 11.10

You add rules to Mail by filling out a form.

For instance, you may want to create a rule that an email with "daily report" in the subject be automatically filed away in a folder named "Reports." To do that, add a rule that "Subject Contains Daily Report" will perform the action "Move Message to Mailbox Reports."

You can select to have several criteria in a rule, and have either any of the criteria trigger the rule, or a combination of all of the criteria trigger the rule. Then you can also have multiple actions performed, such as moving the email and playing a sound.

You can use rules to further filter junk mail. For instance, if you get a lot of email from a certain address or with a certain subject that is junk, you can set a rule to look for those messages and move them to the junk folder.

Web-Based Email

An alternative to client/server email is web-based email. These services are usually free and have an advantage over client/server email from your ISP: They aren't tied to your service.

Imagine if you have an @comcast.net email address because you have a cable modem service from Comcast. But then you switch to DSL, or move to an area without Comcast. You'll lose that email address and need to update everyone with the change.

But a Gmail account doesn't care where your Internet service comes from. You can use it the same at home, work, a friend's house, on vacation, or anywhere you can access a web browser.

In addition, almost all web-based email services allow you to access your email using a POP email client, like Mail. Here are some of the more popular free services:

- **Gmail**—The free email service from Google has emerged in the last few years as the premiere web-based email service. http://mail.google.com

- **Yahoo**—Yahoo was one of the first major Internet sites to offer robust free email. They have recently updated their web-based service. The basic features are free, but some premium features are only for paying users. http://mail.yahoo.com

- **Windows Live Mail (Hotmail)**—The original and probably still the largest free email service comes from Microsoft. It is a bit weird for a Mac user to go here over the other options, but if you already have a Hotmail account you can certainly continue to use it. http://hotmail.com

- **AOL**—America Online was originally a paid Internet service provider, but now their basic email is free. You can get an account at http://webmail.aol.com/.

Of course you can also get the best of both worlds by using the Apple pay service, MobileMe. This includes a web-based email interface as well as integration with Mail.

WHO SHOULD READ THIS CHAPTER:

If you are not currently using any chat service and don't plan to, you can skip to the next chapter. But if you would like to find out how to get started using iChat, from signing up for a free service to using advanced features, read on.

12

Instant Messaging and VOIP

Some people use the Internet for web browsing and email, but others use it mostly for chatting. Instant messaging has been around as long as the Internet, and with a Mac you can participate easily with the iChat application.

iChat Setup

Just as with email, you need a service provider to chat on the Internet. MobileMe is one way to go, and there is even a free version if all you want to do is chat. There are also other free services from AOL, Google, and Jabber.

Creating an Instant Messaging Account

If you have a MobileMe account, you can use it as your chat service. Even if you don't, you can sign up for a free MobileMe-like account that gets you a mac.com address that you can use in iChat.

GETTING A FREE MAC.COM CHAT ACCOUNT

When you first launch iChat, you will be asked to set up an account. Alternatively, you can add accounts later by going to the iChat Preferences, choosing the Accounts tab, and then clicking the + button.

Figure 12.1 shows the initial setup screen with the pop-up menu for selecting a service. Notice that under the menu is a button labeled Get an iChat Account. This takes you to a web page where you can sign up for a free mac.com account.

Figure 12.1
You can choose an existing chat service provider or sign up for a free iChat account.

After you have signed up for the mac.com account, you'll have your ID and password. Even though your ID looks like an email address, you can only use it for chat.

Return to the iChat window and continue by choosing Mac.com Account from the pop-up menu and filling in your information.

GETTING A FREE AIM ACCOUNT

You can also use an AIM (AOL Instant Messenger) account in iChat. The MobileMe, Mac.com, and AIM systems are actually integrated together through a special agreement between AOL and Apple. They should work the same, although in practice it seems that people with AIM accounts sometimes have trouble with iChat, especially for audio and video chatting.

To get a free AIM account, go to http://aim.com. From there it gets a little tricky, as the website really wants you to download the AIM application for your Mac. You don't need it because iChat is everything and more.

Instead, look in the website's navigation bar for an option called Get a Screen Name. From there, you can go through the steps to get a free AIM screen name that you can use with iChat. Then return to iChat to add that account.

JABBER AND GOOGLE TALK

Jabber isn't really a chat service; it is a chat server system that is used by many services. So you don't necessarily sign up *with* Jabber—you sign up on a service that uses Jabber.

One such service is Google Talk. This is Google's chat service and it is free. If you already have a Google account that you use with Gmail, Google Docs, or any other Google service, you have a Google Talk account—they are the same.

All you need to do is enter your Google ID and password and you are connected to your Google Talk network. If you use Google Talk through a web interface, like the Gmail sidebar, you will already have buddies listed.

To use another Jabber service, you will first have to sign up with that service and then use those credentials to set up an iChat account.

BONJOUR

Another way to use iChat is to simply forget about the Internet and only chat with someone on your local network. Your Mac's Bonjour service is how your Mac finds other computers on the same network as you.

In the menu bar, go to iChat, Accounts, Bonjour. Then you will see a window that shows anyone else on your local network who is also running iChat and has his Bonjour window open. You can start a conversation, either text, audio, or video, with them by double-clicking on his name.

Bonjour connections can be tricky because it is common to have a network that specifically disallows chat traffic. A network at an office, for instance, may be locked down to only allow services that the IT department deems necessary.

Setting Up iChat

Now that you are set up with a service or services to use in iChat, you can customize your iChat experience with a custom chat icon. You will see this icon next to your lines of text in chats, and so will others with whom you are chatting.

SETTING UP A USER ICON

Changing your icon involves clicking on it in the iChat window. Figure 12.2 shows the little menu of icons that appears when you do that.

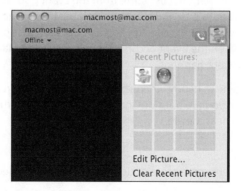

Figure 12.2
You can quickly change icons to one of the 16 most recently used icons as a way of expressing emotion while chatting.

You can select Edit Picture to add a new image. You can then take a photo using a built-in iSight camera, or select a file from your hard drive. You can also apply effects to the image to customize it further.

ALERT SOUNDS

Text chatting with iChat can be almost as noisy as audio chatting. With each message and event in iChat you get an audible alert.

To change these alert sounds, or shut some of them off, go to the iChat Preferences and look for the Alerts tab. Figure 12.3 shows this preference pane.

Figure 12.3

In the Alerts preferences you can customize each and every audible alert in iChat.

You first choose the alert you want to customize from the Event pop-up menu. Then you can choose what sound you want to play and whether the iChat icon in the Dock bounces up and down to alert you to a new incoming message. You can even run an AppleScript to make your Mac do almost anything when the event occurs. Or, you can use the Mac's speech ability to have it speak to you when this event happens.

These audible alerts do come in handy when you have iChat turned on all the time, but perhaps in the background or when you are not right in front of your Mac. If a friend shows up and sees you are logged in, you can hear the alert.

POWER USER FEATURES

If you use iChat a lot, there are some more options you will want to check out.

In the General Preferences, you can select Show Status in Menu Bar to have an iChat icon appear at the top of your Mac screen even when you don't have iChat running. You can then change your status to launch iChat.

In addition, if you deselect When I Quit iChat, Set My Status to Offline, you can quit iChat and people can still start chat sessions with you even if iChat is closed. So you can essentially be in touch all the time, whenever a friend wants to chat.

In the Messages pane of the Preferences window, you can also choose a keyboard shortcut to bring iChat to the front quickly.

Another thing you can do in this preference pane is to set chat transcripts to automatically save to a folder on your hard drive.

Buddy Lists

Now that you have iChat configured, you'll want to find people to chat with. Buddy lists are windows that show listings for people you know who also use an iChat-compatible chat system.

Your buddy list is populated with people you have chatted with before, people in your Address Book who have a chat ID field filled in, and people you have specifically added to your buddy list.

To add someone as a buddy, go to the menu Buddies, Add Buddy. You will need to then specify your friend's chat account ID. You can also put her real name if you like.

> You have a different Buddy List window for each account. So if you have a Mac.com account and a Google Talk account, you will need to bring up two separate Buddy List windows to see all of your friends.

Another way to add buddies is to simply start a conversation, and then you will find them in your Recent Buddies section of the Buddy List window. Then you can drag them up to another section, such as Buddies, Family, or Co-Workers.

Using iChat

Although we can separate text, audio, and video chatting into three separate activities, iChat's features blur the lines between these three. We'll start by looking at the capabilities of the simplest type of chat, and then build up from there.

Text Messaging

The simplest form of chatting is just to send text messages back and forth. This actually has some advantages over audio and video chatting, such as the ability to have several separate conversations at once, and the ability to carry on a conversation over a longer period while one or both parties do other things at the same time.

STARTING A TEXT CHAT

To start a text message chat, simply double-click on your friend's name or icon in your Buddy List window. Or, you can choose File, New Chat in the menu bar and enter the ID for the person you want to chat with.

This opens up a new window to contain the chat. But the session doesn't start until you type a message and press Return to send it. Figure 12.4 shows the first message about to be sent to a friend.

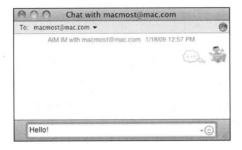

Figure 12.4
To start a chat, you must send the first message.

If your recipient is online and available to chat, he will get a message on the other end asking him if he wants to accept the chat, as in Figure 12.5.

Figure 12.5
At the other end, your friend needs to accept the chat invitation.

After your friend accepts the chat, the two of you can send messages back and forth in real time and begin to use some of iChat's other features.

SMILEYS AND FORMATTING

Just because you are using text doesn't mean you can't show emotion! You can use little graphic symbols called *smileys* mixed in with your text. While you're typing, just click on the smiling face at the bottom right and pick a graphic to insert, as in Figure 12.6.

> **NOTE**
>
> Smileys are actually text as well. For instance, the standard smiling face is a colon, a dash, and then a right parenthesis :-) . When you select a smiley, that text is actually inserted into your message. If the other party is using a chat client that only displays text, they might see these characters. If they are using iChat as well, they will probably see the same graphic that you see.

Figure 12.6

A selection of smiley graphics means you don't have to remember how to type them.

You can also format text before you send it. You can select any part of your message and use the Format menu to make it bold, italic, underlined or even change its font. You can also change its color. But this formatting may or may not show up on the other end if they are not using iChat.

CHAT ROOMS

You can include more than one person in a single chat, with all of you seeing each other's messages. The way to do this is to choose File, Go to Chat Room and then pick a name for your chat room.

This type of chat window, shown in Figure 12.7, includes a right pull-out sidebar that allows you to add people to the chat. Just click the + button at the bottom to select a friend from your buddies, or enter a chat ID.

Figure 12.7

A chat room allows you to have a whole group of friends.

After you start a chat room, you can continue to invite more people to it. Others in the room can also add their buddies.

While chatting in the room, you can still send a message directly to one of the people in the room by Ctrl-clicking on him in the sidebar and choosing one of the options. You can also just start a side chat with him in a separate window.

SMS CHAT

You can also use iChat to send messages to friends using mobile phones. In the U.S. just type the friend's ten-digit number. This starts an SMS chat session with the person through his mobile phone. Some carriers may make the receiver confirm the conversation first before accepting the message.

If one of your buddies has a mobile phone number in your Address Book and she is in your buddy list as well, you can Ctrl-click on her in the buddy list and choose Send SMS.

Audio Chat

You can start an audio chat with someone in basically the same way that you start a text chat. You choose Buddies, Invite to Audio Chat from the menu bar. If your friend is online, she will get a notice of the invitation and the chance to accept or decline.

Of course, a microphone and speakers or headphones are required for audio chatting. However, if no microphone is present, you can still participate in a one-way audio chat as a listener. That might be the case for online presentations, or if you plan on using text chat to communicate to the person speaking.

You can also add more people to an audio chat by clicking the + button at the bottom of the Audio Chat window. This same window, shown in Figure 12.8, also includes a volume control and mute button.

Figure 12.8
The Audio Chat window lets you see the volume of each person speaking through a visual meter.

> **NOTE**
>
> Using audio chat as a replacement for a telephone is a great idea, especially for international conversations. But if you plan on using audio chat a lot, you may want to invest in a good USB headset. You usually get what you pay for, so a $20 headset won't sound nearly as good as an $80 pair. But any headset is usually better than using the microphone built into the computer. At least with a headset the microphone is kept a constant distance close to your mouth.

Video Chat

Starting a video chat is like starting an audio chat, but the requirements now include a video camera like a built-in iSight or a camera plugged into your Mac.

Choose Buddies, Invite to Video Chat to start a chat, but be sure that the buddy is set up for it on his end.

To be sure you are ready for it on your end, choose Audio, Video Preview. Then you can check out how you look in the camera. You can also apply some special effects to your video image.

You can also add more than one person to a video chat in the same way you add more than one person to an audio chat—by using the + button on the sidebar.

File Transfers

While you are chatting with someone, you can send them files. If you simply choose Buddies, Send File, you will be asked to select a file on your hard drive. Then you need to complete your message and press Return.

On the other end, the friend will get the message and link to download the file. The friend must select to receive the file before it is transferred.

You can also transfer files when in a chat room or while audio or video chatting. In a chat room you can Ctrl-click on someone in the list of chat-room attendees and choose Send File from the list of options. You can do the same in an audio or video chat.

iChat Theater

If you'd rather show someone a document than send them a file, the iChat Theater function will let you do that easily.

Choose File, Share a File with iChat Theater, or File, Share iPhoto with iChat Theater. Then you will be asked to start a video chat with a buddy. This works even if you do not have a video camera. Instead of seeing you, the friend will see your presentation.

You can choose text files, PDF files, QuickTime videos, images, and even Keynote presentations.

Screen Sharing

You can also take control of your friend's Mac with Screen Sharing. This handy feature makes helping out a friend a snap. While you're chatting with them, choose Buddies, Share My Screen With, or Buddies Ask to Share, depending on which way you want to go.

Then you get to see your friend's Mac screen on your screen. Your Mac's screen appears in a small window at the bottom right. You can switch back to viewing your Mac screen by clicking on it. And then your friend's screen appears at the bottom right.

When viewing your friend's screen, you can use your mouse and control it. This allows you to show him how to do things. It can come in very handy when showing the parents (or kids) how to use their Mac.

You can also access screen sharing outside of iChat by using the Screen Sharing function of Mac OS X.

iChat Alternatives

iChat is a feature-rich text, audio, and video communication application, but it is not the only one available for the Mac. Skype, for instance, offers audio chatting with people using telephones on the other end. Some other applications offer access to networks that iChat does not.

Skype

Although you can audio chat with iChat just fine, the one thing you cannot do is talk to someone on the other end who is using a telephone, not a computer.

Skype is a program and service that does just this. It is called VOIP, or Voice Over Internet Protocol. VOIP is actually used by most telephone companies in some way for regular telephones now. But you can use it with your computer by downloading and installing Skype.

You can download the Mac Skype application at http://skype.com. There are also versions available for Windows and Linux. You can even buy Internet telephone devices that use Skype without any computer at all.

When you have the application, you can run it and sign up for a free account. The free account lets you chat with other people who are also using Skype. To talk with someone who is on a telephone line, you'll need to purchase Skype minutes or get a monthly or annual plan.

In addition, you can sign up for a Skype phone number to let people call you from a telephone using a regular phone number.

Adium

An open source alternative to iChat is Adium, a free instant messaging application that is just for Mac OS X. It is similar to iChat, but only offers text chat, not audio or video.

You can, however, connect to instant messaging services that iChat cannot, such as MSN Messenger, Yahoo! Messenger, and MySpace IM. To be fair, you can establish Jabber gateways from iChat to these services, but Adium offers a quicker and easier way to use these popular messaging services.

You can download the most current version of Adium at http://www.adiumx.com/.

Other Chat Applications

Other chat applications include the following:

- **Trillian**—A popular IM client on Windows is Trillian. As of the time of this writing, it was on its way to Mac as well, with posted beta versions available at the website: http://www.trillian.im/.

- **AIM**—If you want to only use AIM, and you want the most AOL-like experience, you can download the official AIM client for Mac. http://aim.com.

- **Yahoo Messenger**—You can also get the full Yahoo! Experience with Yahoo Messenger for Mac, from http://messenger.yahoo.com/mac/.

- **Messenger Mac**—Microsoft has a Mac-native client for their MSN chat system as well. http://www.microsoft.com/Mac/products/messenger/.

You can find an up-to-date list of Mac chat software here:

http://macmost.com/mac-chat-and-instant-messaging-software.html

Twitter and Facebook

Part instant-message environment, part social network, Twitter is redefining chat on the Internet. The idea is that you have a personal stream of short messages and people can "follow" you to see what you are up to. You can update your Twitter feed with "tweets" about important events, news, advice, or what you had for breakfast.

You can also follow other people who interest you and see all of their tweets in one chronological list. You can follow your friends, business acquaintances, newsworthy people, celebrities, enemies, or just strangers who have a good sense of humor.

Signing up for Twitter is free and can be done at http://twitter.com. You can then log on in your web browser to check on other people's tweets, or update your own feed with tweets.

You can also download Mac-specific clients that make following a lot of people and updating your feed easier.

You can see MacMost's guide to Twitter, as well as a list of clients available for the Mac, at http://macmost.com/guidetotwitter/.

Facebook, the popular social network at http://facebook.com, also has several ways for you to chat. You can update your Facebook status as a way to send a message to all your friends. You can also "write on someone's wall" to send them a message and start a wall-to-wall conversation. And you can chat in the more traditional way between friends.

If you use Facebook, you can become of fan of MacMost at http://www.facebook.com/macmost.

WHO SHOULD READ THIS CHAPTER:

If you have more than one computer at home, sooner or later you'll want to send a file from one to the other. If you are in a work environment, it is probably a necessary task. This chapter looks at file sharing between computers, both over a local network and over the Internet. We'll also look at some more advanced networking topics like File Transfer Protocol (FTP) and screen sharing.

13

Networking and File Sharing

Sending data and files between computers has always been a strangely difficult task, even for Macs. Mac OS X is a little better than most, however, with Mac-to-Mac communication being easy to set up, and even Mac-to-Windows file sharing being relatively painless.

Setting Up a Mac Network

Networking multiple computers requires a physical connection, as well as configuring the operating systems on the computers to allow for file sharing. We'll look at how to set up file sharing between two Macs first.

Establishing a Physical Connection

If you are using DSL or a cable modem at home, it may already be acting as a hub for all your computers. Whether they are wired to this router or accessing it through a wireless connection, if your Macs are both connected to the same device, you are ready to go.

The same is even more likely if you are using an independent router, such as an Apple Airport router of one model or another. If all of your Macs are connected to the Internet using the same device, they are also connected to each other.

If you don't have a router connecting your Macs, you can get one pretty inexpensively. You'll need this to set up an easy-to-use and permanent connection between more than two Macs.

However, if you only want to connect two Macs together for a short period of time, you can connect them to each other directly with an Ethernet cable or using the wireless capability of both machines. We'll look at that possibility after looking at the simpler shared-router case.

Connecting to Another Mac

Let's assume that you have two Macs both connected to the same network router, such as a DSL or cable modem, or an Airport Extreme base station. The first thing you need to do is to enable file sharing on both Macs. Launch the System Preferences and go to the Sharing preference category. Figure 13.1 shows this set of preferences.

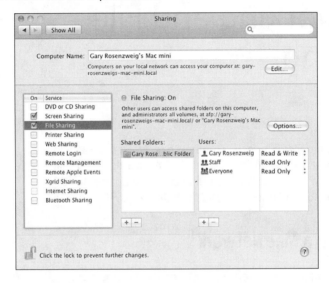

Figure 13.1

Sharing preferences allow you to turn on a number of services, including File Sharing.

Turn on File Sharing. When you do so, you'll see a number of controls appear on the right. You'll have your Public folder set to be shared by default. When that folder is selected, you can see how other users can access that folder. In this case, someone logged in to file sharing as Gary Rosenzweig can both read and write files to that folder. Anyone else can only read files—that means they can view them and copy them.

> **NOTE**
>
> Permissions for "Staff" apply to any other account on your Mac. Under Mac OS X Leopard and before, this was called "Users." Permissions for "Everyone" would include anyone on your network or accessing your Mac from the Internet.

You can view the Public folder from another Mac using the Finder. Open a new Finder window and choose Go, Network. You should see a list of other Macs on your local network that have file sharing enabled. Double-click on the Mac to which you want to go.

The next thing you see should be a password entry screen, as in Figure 13.2. You can choose to connect either as a guest or as a registered user.

Enter your user name and password to access the file server "Gary Rosenzweig's Power Mac G5".

Connect as: ○ Guest
           ● Registered User

Name: gary

Password:

☐ Remember this password in my keychain

✿,   Cancel   Connect

Figure 13.2

The password dialog lets you log in to another Mac as one of the users on that machine.

If you choose Guest, you do not need to enter a name and a password. But you will only have access to places like the Public folder that are set to be read by "Everyone."

If you log in with a name and password, it must be the same name and password as a user on that Mac. If it is your Mac, use the same name and password you use to log in when you start your Mac up.

Alternatively, you can allow any user name and password combination to work. Back in Figure 13.1 you'll notice a + and - button set under the Users list. You can use this to add user names and passwords to each Shared Folder and set whether they can read or both read and write.

After you have signed in, or have chosen to be a guest, you have access to the files on the other Mac. From here, you view, copy, and move files the same way you would with Finder windows for folders on your own Mac.

Do expect that there will be some delay when you perform actions—after all, the files are not on your hard drive; they are on another Mac's hard drive. Opening a file may take a few seconds. If you plan on working on a file, you may find it to be faster to copy that file to your own hard drive first before opening it.

Using Your Public Folder and Drop Box

Every account on a Mac is set up with a Public folder and a Drop Box folder inside it. The Public folder is the default location to put files that you want to share with others. The Drop Box is the default location for others to send files to you.

For example, say you are working on a document and you want someone on your network to take a look at it. You can move it or copy it to your Public folder and tell him to grab it from there.

He can log in as a guest to your Mac, without a password, and see all the files in your Public folder. He can grab this one file and copy it to his Mac.

Then he edits the file and wants to give it back to you. He connects to your Mac as a guest and looks in the Public folder again. The Public folder contains another folder called Drop Box. He can't see the contents of this folder, but he can drag and drop a file onto it to send it to you.

Then you look in your Drop Box, which you have full access to because it is on your machine, and pull out the file.

This is the simplest way to share a file using Mac OS X's default settings.

Sharing More Folders

You can share other folders besides the Public folder. In the Sharing preferences, shown back in Figure 13.1, you can add more Shared Folders. For each shared folder you add, you can add users to it, even creating new user names and passwords.

Say you want to share a series of documents with a colleague on your network. You can create a folder on your hard drive, say a Project A folder in your Documents folder.

Then, click the + button at the bottom of the Shared Folders list in the Sharing preferences. Add that Project A folder to it.

Then, with Project A selected, look at the Users list. You should have full read and write access. But also click on the + button below that to add your friend to the Users list. You can make up a user name for her, or select her from your Address Book. Then make up a password for her.

Now when your friend goes to connect to your machine, she can log in with that user name and password. When she does so, she will see Project A in addition to your Public folder as a folder she can share. If she selects Project A, she has access to those files over the network.

Connecting Two Machines Directly

But what if you don't have a router or hub to connect all of your Macs to? You can create a temporary wireless hub using your Mac.

Just go to the Airport icon in the upper-right portion of the menu bar and turn the Airport on. Then choose Create Network. You'll get a dialog box like the one shown in Figure 13.3.

You'll want to make sure you check Require Password to make your network secure. Then choose a password.

When you are done, you can use another Mac to connect to the first one. On that Mac, look in the same Airport menu and turn Airport on. Then look for the name of the network you just created. Select it and you will be asked for the password.

Figure 13.3

You can create a simple network to share files between Macs with Airport cards.

Now you can use the Finder and choose Go, Network and you'll see the computer appear. You can sign in with a user name and password, or as a guest, just as with a regular network.

Sharing Files with Windows

If you have just switched from Windows to Mac, you are probably looking for a way to get your Windows files over to your Mac. File sharing over a network is one such way. See "Transferring Your Documents" in Chapter 8 for other methods.

Sharing files between a Mac and PC can be tricky. The reason is that there are so many ways for Windows networking to fail. By default, file sharing may be turned on on your Windows machine, but maybe not.

Troubleshooting Windows File Sharing

Even if file sharing is on, you may have installed an antivirus software package that has locked down your system with a firewall, blocking any attempts to share files. Because there are so many different antivirus packages and configurations, it is impossible here to go through them all and describe how to set each one to allow for file sharing.

In addition, Windows XP, Vista, and Windows 7 all have built-in firewalls that may be blocking file sharing. Whatever version of Windows you have, you'll want to navigate through its Control Panel and make sure file sharing is enabled and no firewalls are blocking it.

Here are some tips to get file sharing working in Windows. The actual location of some of these items depends on what version of Windows you have:

- In the Network control panel, make sure File and Printer Sharing is one of the services for your current connection.

- Under the Advanced settings, look for Firewall settings. Make sure File Sharing is allowed as an exception.

- On your Mac, under System Preferences, Sharing select the File Sharing item on the left and then click on the Options button and make sure SMB is turned on.

- Find your Shared Documents folder in Windows XP or your Public folder in Windows Vista. Right-click on it and make sure it is set to be shared.

- Check your antivirus or Internet protection software to see if it has a firewall component. Make sure it allows for file sharing.

- Are you running more than one firewall on your Windows computer? It can be easy in Windows to run the Windows firewall and also a third-party firewall at the same time.

- On your Mac, go to System Preferences, Network. Choose your current connection, and click Advanced. Then look for the WINS tab. See if your Mac recognizes the Windows workgroup for your Windows machines, and if so, select it.

- In Vista, under the Network and Internet control panel, in the Network and Sharing Center, make sure Network discovery and File sharing are turned on.

- If you know how to use regedit.exe in Vista, try changing the LmCompatibilityLevel at HKLM/SYSTEM/CurrentControlSet/Control/Lsa from 3 to 1.

- If you are still having trouble, try disabling your Windows firewall and Windows antivirus software completely for a moment to see if they are still getting in the way.

Connecting to Windows from a Mac

When you are sure that file sharing is enabled in Windows, you can try to connect to your Windows machine through your Mac.

The first method is to do the same thing you would do to connect to another Mac: In the Finder, choose Go, Network.

If you are lucky, your Windows computer will show up in the list of network devices. In practice, it may actually take a few minutes.

If you cannot connect to your Windows machine that way, the next best thing is to determine the local IP address of your Windows machine and use the Finder's direct connection method of Go, Connect To Server. Then enter **smb://** and the IP address. You can get the IP address of a Windows computer by running Command Prompt from the Accessories set of programs, and then typing "ipconfig".

You will also want to make sure you have enabled SMB (Server Message Block) file sharing by going to the Sharing preferences window on your Mac and clicking the Options button for File Sharing.

After you have connected successfully, browsing and using the files on the Windows machine is just like browsing folders on a Mac.

Connecting to a Mac from Windows

To allow your Mac to be seen by Windows computers, turn on SMB file sharing in the Sharing preferences by clicking the Options button for File Sharing. You'll get a control as in Figure 13.4 where you can choose which accounts are allowed to share files. Make sure the account that you are going to share is checked.

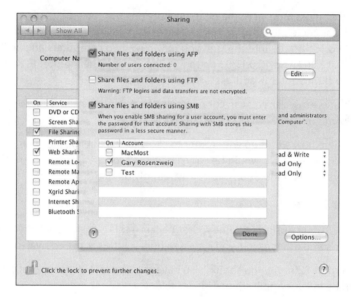

Figure 13.4

The Sharing options include AFP, or standard Mac file sharing, SMB for Windows, and FTP for one way to share files over the Internet.

Now your Mac should appear to other Windows machines under My Network Places. If not, see the previous list of Windows troubleshooting tips.

You can also try connecting to the Mac using the location information in the Mac's Sharing preferences window. For instance, it might say "Other users can access shared folders on this computer at afp://10.0.1.206/". You can try typing **10.0.1.206** in the Windows Explorer address bar, or **\\10.0.1.206\username** may work as well.

Sharing Files over the Internet

What if you want to share your files with a computer that is not on your local network? If two Macs are both connected to the Internet, it is possible to share files no matter where they are in the world.

Internet Sharing Difficulties

The tricky part is your router. You see, every device on the Internet has a specific, unique address, the IP address. It is a set of four numbers, each ranging from 0 to 255, with periods between them, like 208.77.188.166.

If you know the IP address of a Mac (can be found under Network preferences), and sharing is enabled on that Mac, you can connect to it. So if you are lucky enough to have what is called a "static IP address," you are all set.

The problem is that most Macs at home or at work are not connected directly to the Internet. Instead, they are connected to a router, which creates its own little local network. So your router may be 208.77.188.166 on the Internet, and you may have two computers and an iPhone, which are 10.0.1.201, 10.0.1.202, and 10.0.1.203 on that router. It's as if the Internet IP address is a phone number and the router IP address is the extension.

Even in this scenario, however, you can connect to a Mac over the Internet, as long as the router knows you are coming.

Now describing here how to set up your router to allow for an outside file-sharing request to be routed to your Mac is easy. Or, it would be easy if it weren't for the fact that there are hundreds of different routers and configurations, each frustratingly different.

Setting Up Your Router

So let's look at the Apple Airport Extreme router, because this is a Mac book. If you have a Linksys, D-Link, or some other router, you'll have to hunt a little for the equivalent settings.

If you have an Airport Extreme, you should also have the Airport Utility application that comes with it. It should be in your Applications/Utilities folder.

Run the Airport Utility and choose Manual Setup. This takes you right to the controls. Then click Advanced at the top. Then click the Port Mapping tab that appears.

That's what we want to do. We want to map the file-sharing port on the Airport Extreme to go to your Mac. So when you try to contact it from elsewhere, the router knows to send all file-sharing inquiries to you.

Click the + button and choose Personal File Sharing as the service. Then choose the IP address of the Mac on your network.

Now, as long as you know the IP address of your router, you can try to log in from another location.

No Ideal Solution

You'll still have two problems to deal with: First, your router's Internet IP address is likely to change if you have DSL or a cable modem. They assign your IP address from a bank of numbers and change them daily or weekly. Second, you computer's local IP address may also change. If you are using the default DHCP settings, you may get assigned a new local IP address each and every time you connect. So 10.0.1.206 now might be 10.0.1.203 next time.

So this setup only really works in two situations:

■ You and a friend are on the phone and want to connect your two machines right now. You can set everything up, look up your IP addresses, and connect to get some files transferred right now.

■ You want to transfer some files from home to your office or vice versa. You set things up and note the IP address. Then travel to the second location and connect.

If this all sounds frustrating, remember that there are situations where this will work without all these catches. For instance, if your computer at work has a static IP address, you should be able to set it up for file sharing once and then connect to it from anywhere with ease later on.

Otherwise, if you just want to transfer some files, iChat or email work well too. Another option is FTP.

FTP

FTP stands for File Transfer Protocol and has been used to send and receive files over the Internet since before you knew there was an Internet.

There are two parts to an FTP transfer—the client application on your computer and the FTP server.

GET FILES WITH THE FINDER

If someone tries to send you a file via FTP, you don't need anything special to get that file. A Finder window can be used to grab an FTP file, even if it is on a password-protected server.

In the Finder choose Go, Connect to Server and then enter the IP address or domain name of the FTP server. It should be something like **ftp://208.77.188.166** or **ftp://ftp.example.com**.

If there is password protection, a user name and password box will appear for you to enter them. After that, the server appears as a normal Finder window, though it behaves considerably slower than one showing a folder on your local hard drive.

You can copy files from here to your hard drive.

ACCESS AN FTP SERVER

Now if you want to place files on an FTP server, it gets trickier. You'll need a special piece of software called an FTP client.

Fortunately, there are plenty of these. Here is a list of some you can find easily:

■ **CyberDuck**—http://cyberduck.ch/

■ **Fetch**—http://fetchsoftworks.com/

■ **Transmit**—http://www.panic.com/transmit/

■ **FileZilla**—http://filezilla-project.org/

■ **Flow**—http://extendmac.com/flow/

■ **Interarchy**—http://www.nolobe.com/interarchy/

You can find an up-to-date list of FTP software here:

http://macmost.com/mac-ftp-software.html

All of these feature a Mac-like drag-and-drop interface. So after following their instructions to log on to an FTP server, you should be able to drag files into and out of the interface to a Finder window.

ALLOW OTHERS TO ACCESS YOUR COMPUTER

You can also set up your Mac to be an FTP server. Look back at Figure 13.4 and you'll see that FTP is a file-sharing option. Turn that on and you'll even get the address that other people can use to connect to your FTP server, such as ftp://208.77.188.166.

However, the same problem exists here as with other types of sharing over the Internet. If your computer has a local address on a router, and not a static Internet IP address, you'll need to wrestle with your router to tell it to send FTP traffic through to your Mac.

MobileMe's iDisk

Apple realizes that sharing files over the Internet is difficult because of router and IP address issues. That's why built into the very core of their MobileMe service is a file-sharing device called iDisk.

If you have MobileMe, you have an iDisk. To connect to it, choose Go, iDisk in the Finder.

You'll have three options: My iDisk, Other User's iDisk, Other User's Public Folder. The first is to connect to your own iDisk, as you might expect. The second is to connect to someone else's iDisk if you have a password. The last is to connect to the Public folder of another person's iDisk.

> **NOTE**
>
> You can also use the Other User's iDisk option to connect to your own iDisk from a Mac that isn't yours. This is handy while traveling.

So if you want to share files with another Mac user and you have MobileMe, just put the files in a Public folder on your iDisk and then instruct them how to find it.

Use the System Preferences, MobileMe settings to set up how your iDisk works. Figure 13.5 shows these preferences, which includes Public folder settings.

With the Set Password button, you can set a password for your Public folder. Then you'd have a password-protected Public directory on the Internet that you can use to share files easily.

iDisk even works with Windows. If you give out your http://public.me.com/username address to someone, and the password, he can access your Public iDisk folder regardless of which OS he uses.

Figure 13.5

Use the MobileMe System Preferences to control access to your iDisk.

Screen Sharing

Another sort of sharing between computers is screen sharing. If this sounds familiar, it is because we looked at a kind of screen sharing in Chapter 12, "Instant Messaging and VOIP." That involved iChat, but you can also share a Mac screen directly without iChat.

Setting Up Screen Sharing

If you've never seen or used screen sharing, it is quite an interesting technology. The screen of a second computer appears in a window on your computer. You can use your mouse when it is over that window to control the cursor on the other computer. You can also type on the other computer as long as the Screen Sharing application is the frontmost window.

> One of the uses for screen sharing is to simply connect to your work Mac from home or vice versa. You can also connect while traveling. Another use is to help a friend or family member troubleshoot his computer.

To do this you need both Macs to have Leopard (Mac OS X 10.5) or newer. Then you need to enable Screen Sharing in the Sharing preferences on the remote Mac.

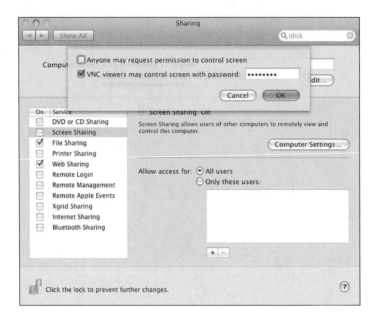

Figure 13.6

The Screen Sharing options include the ability to make up user names and passwords for people allowed to control your computer remotely.

Figure 13.6 shows the Screen Sharing options in the Sharing preferences. In addition, when you click the Computer Settings button you get even more options.

Connecting to a remote Mac with screen sharing is just like connecting for file sharing. In the Finder, choose Go, Network. Then select the computer you want to control. In addition to a Connect As button, you will also see a Share Screen button, as long as screen sharing is enabled on the other computer.

For more remote computers, you can do this with Go, Connect To Server, and then type **vnc://** in front of the IP address of the Mac. Remote screen sharing over the Internet is faced with the same difficulties as file sharing, so a router and changing IP addresses can easily get in the way.

If you connect successfully, you will be prompted for a user name and password. In addition to passwords added in the Sharing preferences, you can also log on as an account holder of that Mac. Enter those and the window with the remote computer's screen will appear.

Using Screen Sharing

While controlling another computer, you can do almost anything. But there are some limitations. Plus, it can get confusing because you are controlling both the computer in front of you and a remote one.

For instance, it is easy to move the mouse away from the screen but forget that keystrokes still get sent to the remote Mac. Pressing Command+Q, for instance, will not quit the Screen Sharing application, but instead quit whatever is running on the remote Mac. It takes some getting used to.

At the top of the Screen Sharing window are two Clipboard buttons that allow you to take the Clipboard contents from the remote machine and bring them into the Clipboard on your local machine. And the other button does the opposite.

In the menu bar of your Mac, you will find some important functions as well. For instance, the View menu lets you switch between Full Quality and Adaptive Quality. With the latter, the image of the remote computer will be a little fuzzy, but will require less bandwidth between the two machines for screen sharing to operate.

You can also turn on and off scaling in the View menu. With scaling off, you can shrink the size of the Screen Sharing application window and the remote computer's screen will be scaled down to fit. The remote computer is still set to the same screen resolution; you are just seeing it scaled down. You can also click the four-arrows button at the top of the window to switch to a mode where the screen is back to 100 percent scale, but you can now scroll horizontally and vertically to see only a portion of the screen.

Screen sharing does offer ultimate power over the remote computer. For instance, if you have nothing else but screen sharing enabled, you can go in and enable file sharing, FTP, and anything else you want remotely, later on.

WHO SHOULD READ THIS CHAPTER:

Even if you don't think you will be doing any word processing, you may be surprised at how knowledge of editing text in TextEdit can be useful. The same techniques can be used in writing email in Mail, for instance.

If you use word processing as part of your work, or you like to write as a hobby, you may want to consider getting one of the professional word processing programs reviewed in this chapter.

14

Word Processing and Printing

The first "killer app" on personal computers was word processing. Imagine the days when documents were produced on a typewriter, where you couldn't review, edit, save, or reprint!

Word processing remains one of the most important pieces of software, even though it is taken for granted now. The Mac comes with a basic word processor called TextEdit that packs some powerful features for a simple and free program. If you need more, you can always get Pages, which is part of the iWorks suite, or the popular Microsoft Word, which is part of Microsoft Office.

Basic Word Processing with TextEdit

When you run TextEdit, a new document window automatically opens. You can just start typing immediately.

It is important to know that TextEdit has two distinct modes: Plain Text and Rich Text. The first is useful for editing the simplest documents, where there is no formatting, type styles, or layout. But for word processing you want to make sure you are in Rich Text mode. If you see a toolbar with style and formatting choices at the top of the TextEdit window as in Figure 14.1, you are in Rich Text mode. If not, you can switch to it using Format, Make Rich Text.

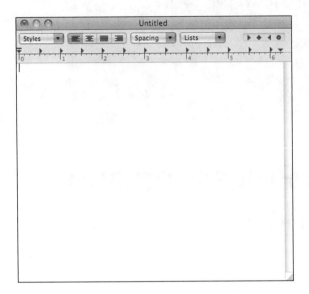

Figure 14.1
When TextEdit is in Rich Text mode, you will see a toolbar at the top of the window.

Editing Text

Typing text into TextEdit works as you would expect it to in any program. You can also use the standard cut, copy, and paste functions, all found in the Edit menu.

You can also use Undo or press Command+Z to undo your last major command, such as deleting some text. You can undo multiple times to reverse your progress.

The ultimate Undo function is on the File menu, where you can choose Revert to Saved. This undoes everything you have done before your last save.

There are a few special functions in the Edit menu as well, such as Paste and Match Style. This comes in handy when you have copied something from another document and find that the font, style, and other elements come with the Clipboard. Using Paste and Match Style pastes in just the text and forgets about the style of the text in the document where you did the copy or cut.

TextEdit also has an autocomplete function. In the Edit menu it is simply Complete. But you may want to use the keyboard shortcut Option+Esc. This brings up a list of suggestions. For instance, if you type "serend" and press Option+Esc, you get a list that includes "serendipity" and you can choose it to complete the word.

You can also use the arrow keys to move the cursor around in the text as you type. They help you move around in the document without taking your hands away from the keyboard. If your keyboard has Page Up and Page Down keys, you can use them as well. Home and End keys work too.

Fonts and Text Styles

You can change the font and style of selected text using the Format menu or the Font palette window. You can also adjust the style using the leftmost pop-up menu in the toolbar, shown earlier in Figure 14.1.

The Font menu has a variety of choices, as you can see in Figure 14.2. The first choice is to show or hide the Font window. We'll look at that soon. But the next set of choices consists of the standard styles: bold, italic, underline, and outline.

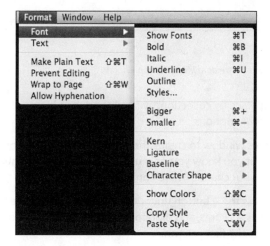

Figure 14.2

The Font submenu lets you change the font, style, size, and other text attributes.

You can choose Show Colors to bring up a color chooser window. You can use this to change the color of the selected text in your document.

To make the text larger or smaller, you can use the Bigger and Smaller options, or the keyboard shortcuts Command++ and Command+-.

If you want precision control over the way the characters are displayed, check out the Kern, Baseline, Ligature, and Character Shape options as well.

> If you have a style in use in your document already and you want to apply it to another section, just select the first section and choose Format, Font, Copy Style. Then select the second section and choose Format, Font, Paste Style. The text will remain the same, but the font and style choices from the first section will be applied to the second section.

The Fonts window you get from the Fonts, Show Fonts menu option gives you more precise control over the text style. You can see it in Figure 14.3.

Figure 14.3
The Fonts window is the same in all standard Mac OS X applications.

You can choose your typeface by collection, by family and then by specific face. You can then set the font size and a few other options.

You can also use the Fonts window to create and organize collections. For instance, if you have 100 fonts on your Mac, but you know you only use 10 or so for documents, you can create a collection of these to make your choices in the Fonts window easier.

To create a collection, press the + button under the Collection list and name it. Then, select another collection, such as All Fonts, and drag font families from the second column on to the name of your collection in the first column.

Rulers and Formatting

In addition to changing how your text looks, you can also change where it appears. There are a number of formatting options, most found as part of the ruler toolbar that appears at the top of the TextEdit window.

The ruler, which really looks like a ruler, has tab stops set at every half an inch. They look like sideways triangles, pointing right. You can drag them away to remove them, or add new ones by dragging them from a set of four tab stop types in the toolbar: left tab, center tab, right tab, and decimal tab.

If you are not familiar with tab stops from using other applications, take a look at Figure 14.4. It shows some different sections of text all using different tab stops. When you select a line of text, you'll see the tab stops in the rule that are active for that line. In the second example in Figure 14.4, you can see the left, center, and right tab stop settings being used.

You can also set the left and right margins in the ruler, as well as the indentation point. The fourth example in Figure 14.4 shows the normal margins, but with a first line indent. You set that by moving the T-like symbol in the ruler.

The fifth example in Figure 14.4 shows what happens when the two margins, the downward-pointing triangles, are moved in to make a narrow column.

Figure 14.4

Examples of using different tab stop and ruler settings in a document.

You can also set the justification of text to left, center, justify, or right.

You can also set line spacing by selecting the Spacing pop-up menu in the toolbar, which gives you Single and Double as two options, plus a third option to bring up the same selection control that you get by choosing Format, Text, Spacing. You can see it in Figure 14.5.

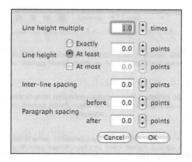

Figure 14.5

You get a lot of control over line spacing in TextEdit.

The options shown in Figure 14.5 allow you to control the height of each line in the selected text in many different ways. For instance, you can set the height of each line to an exact number of points, and then add some extra space in between paragraphs as well.

> **NOTE**
>
> You can also copy and paste formatting. Select some text and choose Format, Text, Copy Ruler. Then select some new text and choose Format, Text, Paste Ruler. The text itself remains the same, but the indentation, margins, and tabs all copy from the first section to the second.

Style Favorites

You can go even deeper into styles and formatting by adding styles to your list of favorites. Start by choosing Format, Font, Styles. You will then get a drop-down control panel in the TextEdit window as in Figure 14.6.

Figure 14.6

You can browse through all of the styles used in your document and apply new styles to sections of text.

The VCR-like controls allow you to move through your document to see all of the different types of styles used. You see the text plus some style information under it.

The Document Styles are the ones used in your document. The Favorite Styles are ones that you have added to a global list so that they can be used again in this and other documents.

Just click on the Add to Favorites button and you will be asked to give the style a name. You can also specify whether the font is part of the style and whether the ruler is part of the style. Otherwise, it would just be other attributes like size and alignment that would be included. Then click the Add button.

You can use this functionality to make a set of styles you commonly use, like title, subtitle, body text, and so on.

The control in Figure 14.6 can also be used to browse through the document, view the styles used, and assign new styles to sections.

You can also select all of the text in a document that uses the same style. Just choose Format, Font, Styles and then browse to the first use of the style. Then click the Select button. The control will go away and you'll have all of the text using that style selected. This is handy for changing commonly styled text throughout a mixed document.

When you have some favorite styles saved, they appear in the toolbar at the top of the TextEdit window in the Styles pull-down menu.

To review and delete a style from your favorites, click on the Favorite Styles radio button in Figure 14.6. You can now select the style and click Remove from Favorites.

Lists and Tables

You can also create some more complex word processing objects like bulleted and numbered lists and tables.

To create a list, type each item on a separate line and then select all of those lines. Then use the Lists pop-up menu in the toolbar, or choose Format, Text, List. You can choose from a number of bullet characters, or an ordered list using numbers, letters, or Roman numerals. You can also define your own set of characters to appear at the beginning of each line.

Figure 14.7 shows a simple bulleted list, plus the List pop-up menu with the default choices. After you use the Other option and make your own list prefix, it will be added to this list so that you can use it again.

Figure 14.7

You have a variety of options when creating a list in TextEdit.

You can further control how a list looks by adjusting the first two tabs in the ruler. The first tab is used to position the bullet or number, and the second to position the start of the line.

To create a table, position the cursor where you want to put the table and choose Format, Table. TextEdit will insert a three-column table with two rows. It will also open the Table palette window to let you alter the table more. You can see it in Figure 14.8.

Figure 14.8
You can control the size and style of a table with the Table window.

Most of the controls in Figure 14.8 apply to the cell or cells in the table that are selected. For instance, you can right-justify the text and adjust the border size and color. You can change the background color of each cell as well.

You can even adjust the width and height of cells by grabbing the borders and dragging them around.

You may want to adjust the style of all of the items in a column. But it is difficult to select multiple columns unless you hold down the Option key and click and drag to select. The cursor will change to a crosshair and you can select a rectangular area of text, such as a single column in a table. You can use the same Option-click-drag to select any rectangular area of text in TextEdit and then change its style or other property.

Spell Check

TextEdit uses the built-in Mac OS X spell check engine. When you type a word, if TextEdit does not recognize the word, it underlines that word in red. You can Ctrl-click on an underlined word to see suggestions or choose Ignore Spelling or Learn Spelling.

You can also choose Edit, Spelling and Grammar, Show Spelling and Grammar to bring up a spell check window, as in Figure 14.9.

Figure 14.9
The Spell Check window lets you move through all of the words in the document that have been flagged.

You can use the pop-up menu at the bottom of the window in Figure 14.9 to change from English to another language. You can also switch on a grammar check.

Document Properties

If you choose File, Show Properties while a TextEdit document is open, you get the window in Figure 14.10. You can add this information and it will stay in the document.

Not only is the Document Properties reference information attached to the work, but Spotlight can also use them in the Finder to help you locate the document.

In the TextEdit preferences, you can set the Author, Company, and Copyright information that is used by default when creating a new document.

You can also lock a document from within TextEdit. Choose Format, Prevent Editing. Then you can't make any more changes until you select Format, Allow Editing.

Figure 14.10

The Document Properties are saved with the document and can also be used to help find it later on.

TextEdit Preferences

A variety of preferences can be set in two tabs in the TextEdit Preferences. The first tab, New Document, defines some presets for a new document. You can see it in Figure 14.11.

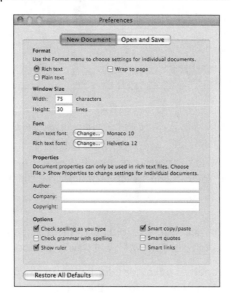

Figure 14.11

In the New Documents preferences, you can indicate whether new documents should start as Rich Text or Plain Text.

There are a lot of presets, including whether a new document starts as Rich or Plain Text. You can also set the default size of a window, what font to use for Plain Text documents, and which font to start with in Rich Text documents. There are some options that you can define as defaults for a new document as well, all of which can be changed or switched while you are working on the document later on.

The Smart Quotes option turns straight quotes into curly quotes as you type. Likewise, Smart Links recognizes when you type web addresses and turns them into clickable links in the document.

The Open and Save preferences highlight the fact that TextEdit is autosaving documents for you while you work. The autosave feature prevents you from losing your work in case of a problem. The default is that the document is saved every 30 seconds.

There are also HTML Saving Options if you are producing HTML pages using TextEdit. You can choose the exact type of HTML code to use, and whether styles are in a separate Cascading Style Sheets (CSS) file, embedded CSS, or without using CSS at all.

Now that you have a good idea of what TextEdit can do, it is worth taking a look at some word processor alternatives that you can obtain for Mac OS X.

Professional Word Processors

TextEdit is a great application for casual users looking to create some text documents. But for serious writing for personal or business reasons, you will want to get a more serious word processing application.

For years, the dominant word processor has been Microsoft Word. But recently, Apple has come out with its own competitor, Pages, that can only be found on Macs. In addition, open source word processors that mimic Word's features have gained some traction as Word can be expensive for many home users or a large office that needs to buy software for many machines at the same time.

Microsoft Word

There's no doubt that Word is the primary word processor used in business offices and by professional writers. Many people purchase it simply because it is the standard in the industry.

Microsoft Word for Mac is part of Microsoft Office 2008 for Mac, which sells for about $250, or $100 for a "Home & Student" edition.

In versions of Office prior to 2008, a Microsoft Word document is a .doc file. But with Word in Office 2008 for Mac, the new .docx file type takes over. A .docx file is smaller and will open faster in Word. But it isn't compatible with older versions of Word. So if you are sending a file to a colleague, make sure you send the right type.

One of the primary reasons that professionals use Word is for the revision-tracking features. A writer can create a document, and then several editors and the writer can trade the document back and forth, making changes and comments that each can examine.

iWork Pages

Apple's own professional word processor is Pages, which comes as part of the iWork suite of applications. You can buy that for $79 for an individual license, or $99 for a family license that can be used on five Macs.

Pages is part word processor and part publishing application. Pages has a great deal of functionality, and you can use it to design things like newsletters, brochures, business cards, posters, and so on.

Pages is a relatively new program, and was developed specifically to fit into Mac OS X. So the user interface and method of doing things are very Mac-like. For that reason long-time users of Word have trouble adjusting. But people who have never used Word or a word processor like it can learn it quickly.

OpenOffice

A third word processing alternative is OpenOffice. This is an open source project found at http://www.openoffice.org/. It is free to download and has Mac, Windows, and Linux versions that all look and work the same.

One of the main purposes of OpenOffice is to remain compatible with Microsoft Word. So if you use Word at work and have a Mac at home, OpenOffice might be a good way to use those Word files at home without buying any new software.

WHO SHOULD READ THIS CHAPTER:

If you plan to use your Mac to crunch numbers, make a presentation in front of an audience, track business data, or track your budget, this chapter will help you find the software you need to put your Mac to work.

15

Business Applications

Macs aren't just about fun, games, and expressing yourself. Some of us use Macs for work. There are plenty of serious work applications, and even an entire suite of them from Apple called iWork.

We've already looked at word processors in the previous chapter. In this chapter, let's take a look at other programs used for work, such as spreadsheets, presentations, and databases.

Spreadsheets

One of the earliest uses for personal computers was *spreadsheets*—two-dimensional grids of numbers that can be used to make lists, perform calculations, and create reports.

Numbers

The iWork suite from Apple comes with Numbers, a fairly new spreadsheet program done in the Mac style. Let's take a look at how to use Numbers for a reasonably simple task.

PERSONAL BUDGET EXAMPLE

Suppose you want to create a monthly budget so that you can see how much you are earning each month versus how much you are spending. Figure 15.1 shows a very simple spreadsheet that does just that.

Figure 15.1

This simple Numbers spreadsheet allows you to calculate your monthly expenses.

When you create a new document in Numbers, you get a set of spaces, called *cells*, in rows and columns. You can select any cell and enter some information. You can also use the arrow keys to navigate around.

> You can select a cell and then type into the space just above the column headings, or you can type directly into the cell itself.

In this example, all the data on the left side in columns B and C was typed in by hand. The section headings were made bold by selecting them and pressing Command+B.

The numbers first appeared as figures like "3500" until I selected all (Command+A) and then clicked the "$" button in the toolbar to format them as dollar values. Then they changed to figures like "$3,500."

The bold text in column E was added manually as well. However, the values under the bold headings are computed using formulas.

Instead of entering $4,100 into cell E5, I entered "=SUM(C5:C7)". This tells Numbers to calculate the sum of cells C5 to C7. The = symbol denotes that this is a formula and should be calculated.

Instead of typing C5:C7, you can use the cursor to select a range of cells. So I typed "=sum(" and then selected the cells, which added "C5:C7", and then typed ")".

So the cell shows $4,100, which is the sum of $3,500 + $500 + $100. Now here's the clever part: If you change one of those three cells, cell E5 will change automatically to show the new value.

The calculation in cell E10 is similar: =SUM(C10:C16)+SUM(C19:C21)

Then, the total in E26 is: =E27+E26

As you can imagine, you can use most simple math symbols, like +, -, * and /. You can use functions like SUM(), including AVERAGE(), MIN(), MAX(), and so on. Click the "fx" button in the toolbar while typing a formula to see all of the functions available.

CHARTS AND GRAPHS

Numbers can also incorporate graphics into your work. Suppose you want to make a bar chart using a list of numbers. Figure 15.2 shows a list of numbers representing some sort of monthly sales chart.

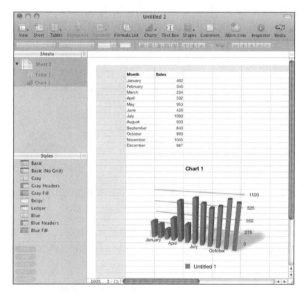

Figure 15.2

The monthly sales of something, shown in number form and with a chart.

To create the chart at the bottom of Figure 15.2, all I had to do was to select cells and then click on the Charts button in the toolbar. I selected the style of chart and Numbers automatically created it and placed it in the document. I repositioned it to be just under the rows of data.

You can also make line graphs, pie charts, and a variety of other graphics with your data. Like the formulas, the charts will update as you change the data.

BUILT-IN TEMPLATES

The two examples you just saw were started from scratch with a blank spreadsheet. But you don't need to start with a blank slate. Apple has included a set of useful templates.

In fact, when you start Numbers you will see a list of them and you will be asked to choose one, or a blank document. Topics include Personal Finance, Personal, Business, and Education. Figure 15.3 shows the Personal Budget template found in the Personal Finance category.

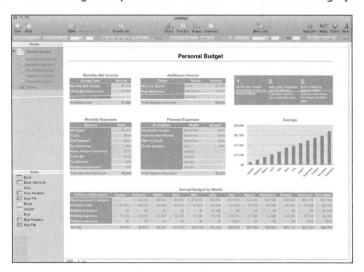

Figure 15.3

The Personal Budget template allows you to plan your savings—with a graph!

COMPATIBILITY

If you use a spreadsheet at work, on a PC, chances are it is a Microsoft Excel spreadsheet. Numbers can read Excel documents, and also export them.

In addition, Numbers handles AppleWorks spreadsheet documents. AppleWorks was a predecessor to iWork that Apple sold from 1998 to 2007, and came for free on new Macs for a number of years during that time.

You can also import other spreadsheet documents in standard formats, like .csv (Comma Separated Values).

Spreadsheet Alternatives

It seems strange to mention Microsoft Excel as an "alternative." Indeed, it dominates the spreadsheet space, even on Macs.

Excel comes with Microsoft Office for Mac, and has been around since 1985. It is the established leader in spreadsheet programs, with many books, resources, and websites dedicated to it.

Microsoft launched Excel in 1985 as a Mac-only program. It wasn't available on PCs until 1987.

The compatibility between Excel for Mac and Excel for Windows is close, but not perfect. Some styling may be different, and Visual Basic for Excel is not available in the Mac version, but is reported to be scheduled for the next version of Excel for Mac. You can only get 100% compatibility with Excel for Windows by running Windows in Boot Camp or a virtual environment.

You can also get open-source spreadsheet programs, such as Open Office for Mac. There are also some online spreadsheets, like the one that is a part of Google Docs. These are a great free alternative if you just need to produce a quick spreadsheet every once in a while.

Presentations

Whether you are in education or in business, sooner or later you have to make a presentation in front of an audience. For some people, this happens every day, depending on their job.

Keynote

iWork has a solution for this as well: Keynote. You can create snazzy presentations very easily and wow your audience with all sorts of effects and animations.

EDUCATION EXAMPLE

Presentations may bring to mind a businessperson standing in front of a meeting in a boardroom, but it is probably actually more common that a teacher or student makes a presentation in front of a classroom.

When you start Keynote, you will get the chance to choose a theme. For this example, I've chosen "Storybook." Then, you are faced with your first and only slide, with placeholder text to put your presentation title, as in Figure 15.4.

Figure 15.4

Keynote shows a list of slides on the left and the current slide on the right.

Just double-click on the text areas to edit them. For instance, the title could be "The History of Games" and the text under it could be "From Senet to Space Invaders."

To create the next slide, just click the + button at the top left on the toolbar. This creates a slide like the last one. But you probably want to have a different layout as you get into your presentation. So click on the Masters button in the toolbar and choose another slide type. I chose one with a picture on the right, title at the top, and bullet list to the left. I then filled out each one to get Figure 15.5.

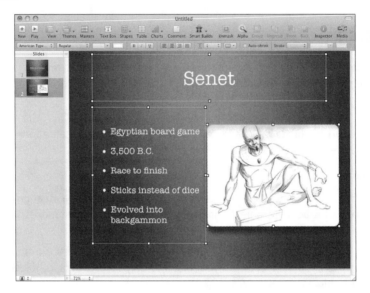

Figure 15.5

This type of slide includes a picture, title, and list.

To get the image on the slide, I replaced the default image that came with the new slide by dragging and dropping my own image file from a Finder window.

ADDING TRANSITIONS

There are basically two types of transitions in Keynote. The first is a transition between slides. The second is a transition that brings one of the elements of a slide onto the screen.

To create a transition from the current slide to the next one, you must bring up the Inspector window, shown in Figure 15.6. If you don't see it, choose View, Show Inspector to bring it up. Then click on the second tiny button at the top of the Inspector to go to the Transition/Appearance section.

In addition to choosing from a variety of transition types, you can also choose the duration of the transition, and sometimes the direction. It depends on the type of transition.

Figure 15.6

Remember that transitions act on exiting the current slide to go to the next one.

You can also create transitions based on the individual elements of the next slide. For that, choose the third tab of the Inspector. You can then select items on the slide and assign "builds" to them. For instance, the bullet list can slide in from the left and the picture can swing in from the right. You can set the order in which they appear, and have them appear automatically or wait for you to click.

PRESENTING AND RECORDING

When you are finished with your presentation, you can present it to yourself by clicking the Play button at the top of the Keynote window. There are also other playback options in the Play menu.

You can even record your presentation. This works just like presenting, except your microphone is used to record your voice, and the timing of each slide is also recorded and synchronized as you present.

> You can use Keynote to create a slideshow of your photographs. Just place different photos on each slide, or use the Smart Build feature to put a whole set of photos onto one slide. Then you can record your commentary as audio and export the whole thing as a video to share. This could be a nice alternative to simply uploading a bunch of photos to a web gallery.

You can then take this recording and export it in a variety of formats. You can even take it into iDVD and create a DVD of your presentation.

This just scratches the surface of Keynote. There are tons of themes, transitions, graphic types, and so on. You can create graphs and charts, import video, and even create picture slideshows that are embedded into a single slide.

The Help menu features documentation and a set of Apple tutorials that show off most of the Keynote features.

With Keynote 09, you can even share your presentations online. You can use iChat Theater to present your presentation to an online audience. You can even upload a video of your presentation to YouTube.

Keynote Alternatives

The standard in presentation software is, of course, PowerPoint. Keynote can open and export files in PowerPoint format. However, because presentation software relies heavily on special effects like transitions and builds, conversion is not always a smooth process.

You can get PowerPoint for Mac as part of the Microsoft Office for Mac suite. This should have a much higher, if not perfect, level of compatibility with the millions of PowerPoint presentations out in the world.

You can also use the presentation program that comes with OpenOffice. Google Docs even has an online presentation app that works for very basic presentations.

Other Business Programs

There are many other types of business programs available for the Mac. From databases to cash register software, you can usually find what you need provided by one or more third-party software companies.

Databases

A third type of business application is called a *database*. However, programs that are databases rarely call themselves that. For instance, the Address Book application that comes with your Mac is really a very specific database program.

Sometimes you need a more general database program to create your own custom solution. For instance, you may need to keep track of inventory or sales. You may want to keep records of projects and send out invoices. Or you may need to keep track of employees or students.

FILEMAKER

The granddaddy of database programs on the Mac is FileMaker. Although it was created by a third-party company for the Mac, it was owned for a time by Claris, an Apple-owned software company. It is once again an independent company.

With FileMaker, you can start off with one of many templates fitting common database tasks. Or you can build your own database from scratch. Figure 15.7 shows the Movie Library template.

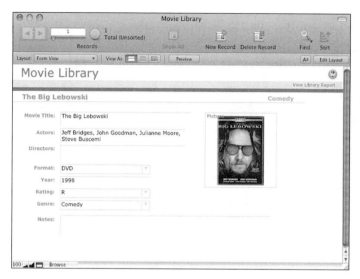

Figure 15.7

The Movie Library template allows you to quickly start a database of the movies you own.

BENTO

Now FileMaker might be a bit overkill for a lot of simple tasks. It is pretty powerful. So there is a simpler, personal database program called Bento that uses the FileMaker engine, but narrows down your choices to make it easier to create simple databases you might need.

Bento works almost like iPhoto or iTunes, but for data. As you can see in Figure 15.8, there are sidebars that make it easy to see which databases you have created. You can even access your Address Book through Bento.

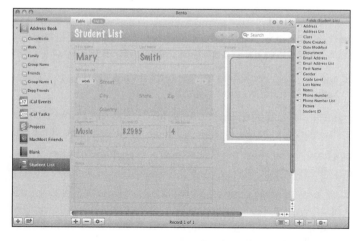

Figure 15.8

This Bento Student List template can be used by schools or tutors to keep track of students.

Organizational Software

Word processors, spreadsheets, and databases are the three standards of business software, but a new category is rapidly taking its place as the fourth: organizational software.

These are applications that help you organize your work. At the simplest, they are "to-do list" applications. But they can get more complex than that. Table 15.1 shows some examples of highly-thought-of organizational applications for the Mac.

Table 15.1   Software for Organizing Data

Software	Website	Description
OmniFocus	omnigroup.com	A personal task management program that lets you keep track of things you need to do and prioritize them.
OmniPlan	omnigroup.com	Keeps track of projects and assigns tasks to people you work with.
Evernote	evernote.com	Creates notes and lists and accesses them on your Mac, iPhone, or on the Web.
MindNode	mindnode.com	Mind-mapping software for organizing and developing ideas.
PersonalBrain	thebrain.com	Manage information visually.
Curio	zengobi.com	Link and organize information visually.
Things	culturedcode.com	Task management.
Process	jumsoft.com	Outlining software.
Pluto Pro	myownapp.com	Manage notes and tasks in the toolbar.

You can find an updated list of personal organization software here:

http://macmost.com/personal-organization-software.html

Accounting Software

Of course you can't talk about business software without talking about accounting programs. There are two main competitors here, and lots of smaller contenders as well.

Both on the Mac and PC, QuickBooks and its counterpart for personal use, Quicken, are available for Mac and compatible with the Windows versions.

In the other corner stands FirstEdge, also known as MYOB. This software has been around since the early days of the Mac, but QuickBooks has come and gone and then come back again.

Either program is a heavy hitter, ready to take on small or even medium-sized business accounting. But there are also other competitors out there, like Jumsoft's Money and Accountek's Connected.

You can also find all sorts of other business software by searching Apple.com's downloadable software area at http://www.apple.com/downloads/ or visiting an Apple Store. There are retail point-of-sale solutions, project management programs, stock market applications, and lots of software for very specific types of businesses.

WHO SHOULD READ THIS CHAPTER:

If you use a digital camera to take photos, you should get to
know iPhoto inside and out. This chapter will start you off with
the basics of the this deep and powerful photo catalog software.

16

Importing and Managing Photos

When you use a digital camera, your computer becomes your photography studio, allowing you to edit and catalog your photos. On a
Mac, iPhoto is the basic application that most people would use to
do this.

Importing Your Photos

You can get your photos from your digital camera to iPhoto in two
ways. The first is to connect your camera directly to your computer,
usually by a USB cable that comes with the camera.

The second is to remove the memory card from your camera and
plug it into a card reader that is connected to your computer. This
requires an extra piece of equipment, the card reader, but has the
advantages of being faster and not draining your camera's battery.

Either way, iPhoto should launch automatically. If it does not, you can
always launch it yourself from the dock.

The following steps describe how to import photos into iPhoto:

1. Connect your camera to your Mac with the USB cable, or plug
    your camera's memory card into a card reader attached to your
    Mac.

2. Wait for iPhoto to launch automatically. If it doesn't, launch it
    yourself.

3. Select the camera or card from the left sidebar in iPhoto. It should appear there under Devices with previews of the photos in the main space inside iPhoto, as in Figure 16.1.

4. Consider entering an event name and description.

5. Click the Import All button. Alternatively, select the photos you want to import and click Import Selected.

6. Most likely you will want to answer Yes to deleting the photos from the camera or card. Otherwise, it will be up to you to delete them using your camera's interface to make room for new pictures.

Figure 16.1
The camera is connected and appears on the left, with previews of the photos on the right.

You can also import photos into iPhoto by dragging and dropping them from a Finder window into the iPhoto library in the left sidebar. This comes in handy when you get a set of photos sent to you via email or on a USB thumb drive. You can also choose File, Import to Library.

iPhoto not only handles your still photos, but also your personal videos. Most digital cameras today have a video mode, and there are also many compact video cameras that use memory cards. You can import and manage these video clips just like photos in iPhoto.

When you have the photos inside iPhoto, your next step is to organize them.

Organizing Your Photos

Photos in iPhoto are organized in three main ways: Events, Faces, and Places. But you can also list your photos by different criteria and create albums of photos.

Events

Events are groups of photos, kind of like folders. Every photo belongs to an event. iPhoto will automatically break your photos up into events with dates as names when you import them.

When you choose Events in the left sidebar, as in Figure 16.2, you see a single picture representing each event and the event name under it.

Figure 16.2

The Events view of your photo library shows one picture representing each event.

You can roll over each event's picture and see all of the other photos in the event by moving the cursor horizontally over the picture. Ctrl-click to jump right into editing that photo, or select that photo as the new picture to represent the event in this view.

You can also edit the name of the event by clicking on the name under the picture. Or, you can click on the "i" button that appears on the picture when you select the event, and then edit the name, description, and location of the event.

If you need to merge two events into one, just drag and drop one event onto the other. This comes in handy when you want to merge pictures from two cameras into a single event—such as pictures from your iPhone with pictures from your video camera.

Faces

If you click on Faces in the left sidebar, you'll see a set of photos of people that appear in your pictures. Of course, the first time you do this you'll need to set it all up first. The following steps show you how to tag your photos with faces:

1. In the Photos or Events view, double-click on a photo with some faces visible.

2. Click the Name button.

3. You should see labels below faces asking you if the face matches a name, as in Figure 16.3. If the face is not known to iPhoto, the text "unnamed" appears.

4. Enter the name of the person in the label.

5. Repeat steps 1 through 4 several times to get things started.

6. Go to the Faces view by clicking on Faces in the left sidebar.

7. Double-click on the name of one of the people in the list.

8. Click on the Confirm Name button that will appear at the bottom of the iPhoto window.

9. Scroll through the photos, clicking once to confirm and twice to point out mistakes.

10. Click the Done button.

11. Repeat steps 8 through 10 until there are no more photos to confirm.

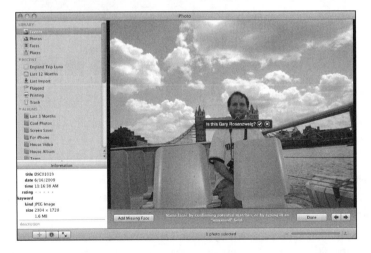

Figure 16.3

When viewing a photo you can click the Name button to see the names of people in the photo, and add names to those not identified.

> **NOTE**
>
> iPhoto is not some superintelligent face recognition system. It is simply comparing features in faces, like the distance between eyes, the hairline, and so on, to guess at which faces match. As you identify more faces as belonging to a single person, iPhoto will get a better idea of what that person looks like and it will be able to find them more often in photos in the future.

Places

Unlike Faces, Places is something that can be set by your camera, at least if you have a camera that has a built-in GPS chip. For Mac users, a common device that does this is an iPhone 3G. But some digital cameras do as well.

If you don't have a GPS chip in your camera, you can still set a location for each photo when editing it. This simply involves clicking on the "i" button while hovering the cursor over the photo, and then typing the name of a location while iPhoto attempts to look it up in its database, as in Figure 16.4.

Figure 16.4

iPhoto includes a huge database of place names to make it easy to label your photos.

To browse through your photos by location, click on Places in the left sidebar. You'll then see a map of pretty much the whole world, or at least as much of it as your photos cover. Then you can double-click on the pinpoints to zoom in on a more specific area to see more pinpoints in a close-up map. You can then dig further down to look at the photos in that location.

Albums

Linking photos together by events, people, and locations isn't always the best way to organize them. For instance, you may want to create an album of some of your best photos. These may be from multiple events and locations and may not even have people in them.

To create an album, click on the + button at the very bottom of the iPhoto window. Then you can choose what sort of entity to create, the first being a normal album.

 NOTE

You can also create a *smart album*, which is similar to a smart folder in the Finder, iTunes, or in Mail. It allows you to set some search criteria, such as date range, location, and even camera model. Then it creates the album for you and updates it as you import more photos.

If you want to quickly populate the album with photos, the best way is to select photos from the Events of Photos view first, and then click the + button to make the album. The selected photos will appear in the new album.

However, after an album is created, it will appear in the left sidebar and you can drag and drop any photo from any other view of the album onto the name of that new album in the side bar to add it.

Editing Your Photos

In almost any view in iPhoto you can select a single photo and click the pencil icon at the bottom of the screen to edit the photo.

iPhoto isn't an image editor, like Photoshop, for instance. But you can crop, straighten, rotate, retouch, adjust, and apply effects to photos.

Making Adjustments

You can manually adjust the exposure, contrast, and saturation of a photo by clicking on the Adjust button. This brings up a palette with a variety of sliders, shown in Figure 16.5.

You can play with the sliders in the Adjust palette, or click the Enhance button at the bottom of the iPhoto window to have iPhoto make some guesses as to how to set these sliders.

Removing Imperfections

You can also touch up your photos by using the Red-Eye removal tool and the Retouch tool. They can both be found at the bottom of the iPhoto window.

The Red-Eye removal tool asks you to find the center of the eyes so it can remove the red. But there is also an Auto button that appears when using this tool. Then iPhoto finds the red-eye automatically and removes it.

Figure 16.5

The Adjust palette lets you make a variety of changes to your photo.

> **NOTE**
>
> The red-eye effect is caused by the refection of the camera flash off the back of the eye. The flash occurs too fast for the pupil to close. Red-eye reduction functions in cameras will precede the actual flash with one or more flashes, giving the pupil a signal to close.

You can also remove blemishes from photos with the simpler Retouch tool. This just provides you with a circular area to indicate the location of a blemish and it samples the colors around the area to remove it.

Rotating and Resizing

Three buttons at the bottom of the iPhoto window allow you to adjust the orientation and size of your photo.

The first, Rotate, simply allows you to rotate your photo 90 degrees counterclockwise with each click. This is handy if you have taken a vertical picture with your camera and want it to look right in iPhoto. Some cameras recognize when you turn them, but others play dumb and send the photo to iPhoto as-is.

The Straighten button lets you rotate your image in small increments, to compensate for pictures that aren't quite straight. You get to move a slider left and right to adjust. You are also given a grid of vertical and horizontal lines so you can align the ground, walls, or other elements more easily.

The Crop button lets you cut off the edges of a photo. You can set the crop area manually with the cursor, or use a popup menu with some common photo preset sizes.

Adding Effects

You also have a small set of special effects available that you can apply to a photo. For instance, you can pull out all of the color to make a black-and-white photo, or apply a sepia filter to make it look old-fashioned.

You can try these out by clicking on the Effects button at the bottom of the iPhoto window.

When you apply any of these effects, you must click the Done button at the bottom of the window for them to take effect. After that, you can revert to the original by choosing Photos, Revert to Original while editing the photo again.

Printing Your Photos

Now that you have all your photos in iPhoto, you can view them whenever you are in front of your computer. If you have an iPhone or iPod, you can also sync them to that device and carry copies of those photos with you. Your iPhoto collection can even be accessed on an Apple TV.

But, if you still prefer paper, you can print out your photos in a variety of ways.

Using Your Home Printer

The obvious way is to use a color inkjet printer that you might have. If it is connected to your Mac and working as it should, you can choose from a variety of printing options in iPhoto.

Figure 16.6 shows the initial print screen that you get when you choose File, Print. You can add a border or mat, or print a sheet with several selected photos, called a *contact sheet*.

Figure 16.6

iPhoto offers a variety of print options.

If you click the Customize button, you get even more options. You can change the border and background, and even set iPhoto to print a set of two or four on a page. You can also select the photo and zoom in on it, printing only a section.

Ordering Prints

You can also choose File, Order Prints to send your photos to the Kodak Print Service. The prices have varied over time, so I won't mention them here as they may be even more affordable by the time you read this.

But I can report that not only is the quality decent, but there are many nonstandard options as well.

For instance, instead of just ordering plain prints, you can order books, calendars, and cards. Just click on the Keepsakes button at the bottom of iPhoto. It is usually a good idea to create an album with all the photos you want, select that album and all photos in it, and then click Keepsakes, Book to print a book.

You'll get the chance to make some design decisions. Or, with books, you can just let the photos flow into the pages. It is a lot more convenient to order a book than to get prints and put them into a photo album yourself.

The following steps explain how to order a photo book:

1. Create a new album by clicking on the + button at the bottom of the iPhoto window.
2. Using the Events, Photo, Faces, or Places view, drag and drop photos from the main viewing area onto the new album in the left sidebar.
3. You may want to then review all the photos in the new album. You can drag and drop them inside the album to set their order, and click on their titles in the bottom-left Information pane to name them. You can also set descriptions that can then be used in the book.
4. Select the album in the left sidebar. Make sure either all photos in the album are selected, or none. If some are selected, it will only use those selected photos.
5. Click on the Keepsakes button at the bottom of iPhoto. Then select Book.
6. Choose the type of book and style.
7. Use the editor that will appear to drag and drop photos onto pages of the book. Set text areas with titles and descriptions. Experiment with layouts and features.
8. Click the Buy Book button to bring up the ordering window.

Sharing Your Photos

iPhoto provides many ways to share your photos with your friends in addition to printing photo books and showing them around.

Creating Online Photo Galleries

You can share your iPhoto photos easily with services like MobileMe, Facebook, and Flickr. Buttons for each of these appear at the bottom of iPhoto as you browse through your images.

To use any one of these, you first have to sign up for that service. MobileMe is a paid service from Apple, and Facebook and Flickr are free. Flickr also has a premium paid service.

Flickr, in particular, is a good way to share your photos with anyone, as it doesn't require others to have an account in order to view your photos. You can sign up at http://flickr.com.

Facebook is a social network, of which photo sharing is just one piece. Typically, others will have to have a Facebook account and be a "friend" of yours to see your photos. But the advantage is that when you post new photos, your friends will get a notice of the fact without you having to email everyone. You can sign up for a Facebook account at http://www.facebook.com/.

You can also send a selection of photos to iWeb if you prefer to use that website tool that comes with iLife. Just choose Share, Send to iWeb.

Emailing Photos

The quickest and easiest way to get someone else to see one of your photos is to send them an email. If you use Mac OS X's Mail program, this couldn't be any easier.

Use the following steps to email photos to a friend:

1. Select the photo or photos you want to send using any view in iPhoto.
2. Choose Share, Email.
3. Select the size of the photos in the dialog box that appears.
4. Click Compose Message.
5. Mail will open and a new message will appear already populated with the photo(s).
6. Add and edit the subject and body text of the email.
7. Set the "To:" field to the person you want to get the email.
8. Click Send.

Remember to be mindful of the person on the other end and not send them full-resolution photos if they are on a slow Internet connection.

Creating CDs and DVDs

If you want to give someone a collection of photos on a piece of media, you have two main options.

You can choose Share, Send to iDVD to create a DVD slideshow of the photos. You can also opt to include the original photos on the DVD as well. They can be read when the DVD is inserted into the drive of another Mac or PC.

Another option is to choose Share, Burn. This allows you to create a CD-ROM or DVD-ROM of the photos. You can then give them to someone else to view with their Mac and iPhoto. This is also handy if you want to take the photos to a kiosk that makes prints from photos on CD.

> **NOTE**
>
> You may be able to take a CD or DVD burned from iPhoto to one of the photo-printing kiosks. But it may be safer to use the Finder to burn copies of your photos onto a plain CD or DVD instead. To do this, you will probably want to select the photos you want and use the File, Export function to export them to a folder. Then use the Finder to burn a CD from this folder.

You may also, from time to time, want to archive your photos onto a CD or DVD this way. See Chapter 24, "Backing Up and Archiving Your Files," for more suggestions about how to back up or archive photos and other files.

Managing Your Music and Video

Computers, especially Macs, are becoming media centers for your personal music and video. You can store audio and video content, play back content, organize content, and even buy content. At the center of all this for a Mac user is the iTunes application.

Importing Music into iTunes

You can get music into iTunes in several ways. You will learn about purchasing music from the iTunes music store in the next section. But for now, let's see how to import music from CDs you already own.

Before you follow the steps for importing music, you may want to change one of the preferences in iTunes. From within iTunes, choose iTunes, Preferences, General, and then click on the Import Settings button.

Figure 17.1 shows the Import Settings. The two settings that would make sense for most uses are AAC Encoder and MP3 Encoder. The first is Apple's own encoding, which is great quality and slightly smaller files than MP3. But MP3 is more standard, meaning that you will be able to transfer it to non-Apple devices and burn MP3 CDs, which hold more music than regular audio CDs, to listen to in your car.

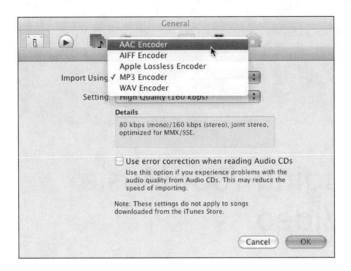

Figure 17.1

The Import Settings are hidden in iTunes preferences, but you may want to change these before you run iTunes for the first time.

You'll also see other formats listed in Figure 17.1, but MP3 or AAC are what you would want to use for building an iTunes music collection. After you have decided between AAC or MP3, you can import your first music CD.

Follow these steps to import music from a CD:

1. Run iTunes.

2. Insert the CD into your optical drive.

3. iTunes will check an online database to see if it can identify the artist, title, and track names of the CD.

4. iTunes should automatically ask you if you want to import the music. If not, wait until the CD and tracks appear in iTunes and look for an Import CD button to click.

5. Wait for iTunes to import and convert each track to AAC or MP3 format and add them to your music library.

You can now eject the CD using either the Eject button on your keyboard or the Eject menu in the menu bar. You can then continue importing more CDs from your collection.

Importing music that is already in MP3 format and is on your hard drive is even easier. You can drag and drop MP3 (or AAC) files from the Finder into the iTunes library. You can either drag them to the Music item in the Library on the left sidebar, or into the main area of iTunes if the music library is being viewed. iTunes reads the data in the files and applies artist, album, and track names if they are embedded in the file.

> **NOTE**
>
> Another setting in the iTunes Preferences is under the Advanced tab, and it's a check box labeled Keep iTunes Music Folder Organized. When this setting is checked, songs will be copied and stored in the iTunes Music folder by artist and album automatically. You can turn off this setting, and the accompanying setting Copy Files to iTunes Music Folder When Adding to Library, if you'd rather have iTunes leave the files where you want to keep them.

Viewing and Playing Your Music

When you have some music in your collection, you can click on the Music item in the left sidebar to view it. There are several views: list, grid, and cover flow. Figure 17.2 shows the list view.

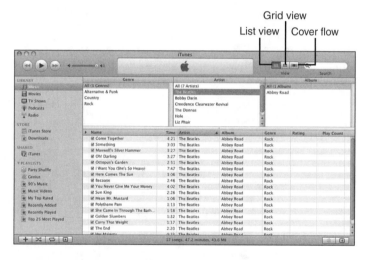

Figure 17.2

This list view also includes the artist/album "browser" at the top, which can be turned on or off in the View menu.

You can play any song by double-clicking on it. With the browser turned on, as in Figure 17.2, you can also double-click on a genre, artist, or album to start to play the entire set of songs.

In list mode, the iTunes window is similar to the Finder, allowing you to re-sort the songs by clicking on one of the column headings.

The other two views allow you to see more artwork than text. The grid view shows everything by album, using the album cover as an identifier with the album name and artist under it. The cover flow view combines both the list view and a look at the album covers in a 3D view above the list.

> **NOTE**
>
> If an album doesn't have artwork, you can get iTunes to find the artwork online in most cases. Just Ctrl-click on the missing artwork and choose Get Album Artwork. You'll need to have an iTunes account and may need to be signed into it, but the album doesn't need to have been bought from iTunes. There is also a preference under the Store tab in iTunes preferences to "Automatically download missing album artwork."
>
> Alternatively, you can choose one song from the album, Ctrl-click and choose Get Info. Then you will see under the Artwork tab an interface for adding your own image. You can get album artwork from online stores or an Internet image search.

Using the iTunes Music Store

Another way to get music into iTunes is to purchase it. With iTunes, you have the world's largest music store right there in your Mac.

To get to the store, click on the iTunes Store item in the left sidebar. Your eyes will be assaulted with colorful pictures and thumbnails from music albums, TV shows, and movies. Figure 17.3 shows a typical iTunes front page.

Figure 17.3

The iTunes Store front page changes constantly to promote new content.

The iTunes Store, despite being available from the iTunes application, works like a set of web pages. Click on pictures and text to view more information about music albums, TV shows, movies, and podcasts.

When you dig down to the song, episode, or movie level, you can click on the Buy buttons to download content. Of course, you will need an iTunes Music Store account to do that. If you already have a MobileMe account, you can use that. If not, you will be asked to sign in, and alternatively sign up for an account.

> **NOTE**
>
> What music is available in the iTunes store depends on what country you are in. Different agreements between different music companies and Apple mean that some music is available only in some places.

Using the content you buy from iTunes has restrictions—and these have changed over the years. Initially, all music purchased on iTunes was protected using digital rights management (DRM). You were only allowed to play the music on your computer and up to four others that were linked to your iTunes account. You could only transfer the music to iPod devices that were also linked to your account. You couldn't play these AAC files on other MP3 players or by using other music-playing software on your computer.

But Apple introduced iTunes Plus, music of slightly higher quality with no DRM, in 2006. iTunes Plus was only available for some songs. In 2009, iTunes Plus was slowly extended to the entire iTunes music catalog. In addition, people who had previously purchased some copy-protected music were allowed to upgrade to DRM-free versions for a small price.

So music is now DRM-free in iTunes, but TV shows and movies still have DRM. So video content that you purchase can only be played on computers registered to your account, or devices like the iPhone, iPod, and Apple TV.

Organizing Your Music

You can organize your iTunes content using playlists. A playlist is like a photo album in iPhoto. Content added to a playlist is still in its original location, such as a music album, but it also exists in one or more playlists.

So you could simply create a playlist of some of your favorite songs.

To create a playlist, click on the + button in the bottom-left corner of iTunes. Then it will appear under Playlists on the left. Give it a name as well. You can now drop any piece of content from your library into the new playlist.

Playlists are handy for things like parties, where you want to set up your Mac or iPod with a set of songs to play for the occasion. Playlists sync to your iPod and iPhone, so you can have them there as well. You can also use playlists to organize a group of songs to burn to a CD.

You can also create a smart playlist. This is like a smart folder in the Finder. Choose File, New Smart Playlist and you will be asked to provide criteria, as in Figure 17.4.

Figure 17.4

This playlist will contain music that you've added in the last three months and update automatically.

Smart playlists can help you find things in a crowded iTunes library. For instance, you could have a smart playlist of music you have added in the last three months. As you add new music and time marches on, the playlist will stay up-to-date.

You can also use ratings to make smart playlists. You can apply a rating of one to five stars to any song by Ctrl-clicking on the song or choosing File, Rating with the song selected. So you can then make a playlist with all your four- and five-star songs.

Subscribing to Podcasts

The first three categories of content in the iTunes Music Store are Music, Movies, and TV Shows. The fourth is Podcasts. This category is very different.

Podcasts are episodic audio and video shows produced by a variety of companies and individuals. They are almost always free and cover just about any topic you can possibly imagine.

For instance, there are podcasts about news and politics, music and science, art and pop culture. Some podcasts are daily, others weekly, and some whenever the podcaster decides to create a new episode.

You can browse the podcasts at the iTunes Music Store by going into the store, making sure you are on the Home page of the store, and then looking for the Podcasts item on the left.

To subscribe to a podcast, follow these steps:

1. Browse the podcasts section of the iTunes Music Store and find a podcast you want to try. You can also use the search box at the upper-right corner of iTunes to search for topics and titles. The results will show from all sections of the store, so look for podcasts in your results.

2. Select a podcast to read more about it. There is a description and reviews for each show, as in Figure 17.5, and you can view the website for most podcasts to find out more.

3. Click on the Subscribe button to add the podcast to your podcast subscription list.

4. In your iTunes Library, under Podcasts, you can view the shows you are subscribed to and which episodes you have downloaded.

5. iTunes will automatically download new episodes of each show you subscribe to.

6. You can set your iPod and iPhone sync preferences to automatically transfer all recent podcasts so that you get new episodes of your shows each time you sync.

Figure 17.5

You can read reviews of each podcast in iTunes before subscribing, but podcasts are free, so it usually doesn't hurt to try it out and form your own opinion.

Sometimes, particularly with video, you will find that a podcast will not sync to your iPod or iPhone. This is because a very specific type of video file is needed for video to play back on those devices. However, if you Ctrl-click on the item in iTunes, you will usually see an option like Convert for Playback on Your iPod. You can use that to make a new version of the video that will sync.

You are said to "subscribe" to podcasts because it is similar to getting a magazine subscription. New episodes are automatically sought out and downloaded by iTunes. You don't have to go into the iTunes store or look on a website to get the latest episode; it just appears in your iTunes Library.

Some people have totally converted from listening to the radio while driving to listening to podcasts. They have a whole set of shows they like, and iTunes gets the new episodes and puts them on their iPod automatically. So all they need to do is plug their iPod into their car stereo and listen to fresh new content during their commute.

> You can also produce your own podcasts. Most shows are made by people just like you. And your Mac comes with almost everything you need to start: GarageBand is the tool used by many podcasters to produce their shows. Even iMovie can be enough to produce a simple video podcast. The Web is full of podcasting tutorials and advice for beginners.

Syncing with Your iPod and iPhone

Syncing your iPod or iPhone to your iTunes music library can be very easy or extremely complex. It all depends on what level of control you want over the synchronization.

If you simply want all the music you own to be both on your Mac and on your iPod, the default settings to sync everything make it very easy. All you need to do then is to connect your device to your Mac with iTunes running. Then you need to remember to do this each and every time you add some new music to your library.

If you subscribe to podcasts, this could be every day as new episodes will automatically be added to your library. But you plug your iPod or iPhone in every day anyway to recharge it, right?

> Your iPod or iPhone will sync more than just music. It will also grab your contacts and calendar events. Even iPod Nanos, which aren't as complex as the iPhone or iPod touch, will store this information in case you need it while on the go. Alarms will sync, allowing your iPod to remind you of events. Photos will sync: iTunes makes smaller versions of some of the photos from iPhoto and stores them on your iPod or iPhone. It comes in handy when you want to show someone your new baby, dog, car, or Battlestar Galactica action figure.

If you want to have more control over what you sync, things get complex very fast. Figure 17.6, for instance, shows the iTunes screen when an iPhone is connected. Notice that when the iPhone is selected on the left, a whole set of tabbed pages appears on the right. You have decisions to make about syncing information, ringtones, music, photos, podcasts, video, and applications.

As shown in Figure 17.6, you can opt to sync all songs and playlists. However, if you don't select that option, you now need to select playlists to sync. So, to sync your music collection selectively, you'd need to put the music you want on the iPhone into at least one playlist. Then select it here for syncing.

Of course if you happen to have more music than will fit on your iPod, you will not be able to sync everything and will need to manually manage your music using this method.

Figure 17.6

iTunes lets you customize your synchronization preferences, with a lot of details to be filled in by you.

Similar options are available for ringtones, photos, podcasts, and video. Typically, you have to commit to syncing all, or specifically pick out the content you want.

Playlists work in a strange way, however. For instance, if you add a podcast episode to a playlist, and that playlist is set to sync, you will get that podcast episode whether it is set to sync in the Podcasts screen or not.

You can use smart playlists to help you sync content to your iPod. For instance, you can create a smart playlist in iTunes that shows the 25 most recent podcast episodes. It will automatically update as new episodes are added. Then set that playlist to sync with your iPod. Now, every time you sync, you will get the 25 most recent podcast episodes and have a handy playlist on your iPod to help you find them.

Front Row

Although iTunes might seem the end-all and be-all of media content on your Mac, there are other programs that play back media as well. The DVD Player application that launches when you insert a DVD is one example. The QuickTime player can be used to play back almost any audio or video content. And then there is Front Row, an application that turns your Mac into a media center.

Front Row actually accesses your iTunes content. It is not an organizational tool, but a playback tool. It takes over your entire Mac screen, as in Figure 17.7.

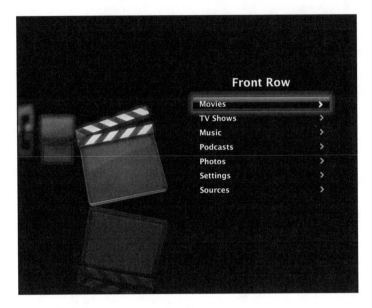

Figure 17.7

If you own an Apple TV, Front Row looks familiar. It is basically the same thing.

With Front Row you can browse though your content using the arrow keys and spacebar to select and Esc key to go back. Or, use the Apple remote control that comes with some Macs, or can be purchased separately from Apple.

iTunes Tutorials

In a way iTunes is not just a single application, but a whole collection of utilities that allow you to control and enjoy your audio and video content. Here are some tutorials on how to use various aspects of iTunes.

Create an Audio CD

You can burn your own audio CDs using DRM-free music from your collection. It is sort of like making a "mix tape" in the 80s.

Follow these steps to create an audio CD:

1. Create a playlist with the songs you want. Select the playlist and check to make sure it will fit on an audio CD. For instance, if the writable audio CDs you have claim to hold 80 minutes, make sure the status bar at the bottom of iTunes shows 80 minutes or less for the playlist.

2. With the playlist selected, click the Burn Disc button at the bottom of the iTunes window.

3. Next, you'll see a dialog box as shown in Figure 17.8. Choose Audio CD.

4. Select your options. You can add a gap between songs, add Sound Check to force the average volume of all the sounds to be about the same, and check the Include CD Text option to include the names of songs for advanced CD players to display.

5. Click Burn.

6. Insert the writable audio CD into your optical drive.

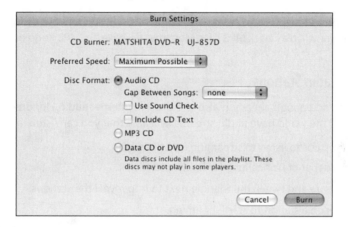

Figure 17.8

You can burn your music in a variety of ways to writable media.

An audio CD should play in just about any CD player in the world. There are some that might be finicky about playing writable CDs, which differ slightly from factory-printed CDs.

Create an MP3 CD

It is a shame to only be able to fit 80 minutes of music onto a disc. After all, as data, you can fit hours and hours of music. But audio CDs follow an old standard from the 80s, before clever things like MP3 files were invented.

Some CD players, however, can play back both plain old audio CDs and "MP3 CDs." These are simply discs with a series of MP3 files on them. You can create these discs with iTunes as well.

Follow these steps to create an MP3 CD:

1. Make sure all the music you want to use is in MP3 format. View your music in a list and press Command+J to add "Kind" as a column. The songs you want to use should show "MPEG audio file."

2. If you need to convert some music to MP3, do that by choosing iTunes, Preferences, General, Import Settings and changing the Import Encoder to MP3. Then go back to the list of songs and Ctrl-click on a song and choose Create MP3 Version.

3. Create a playlist, just as you would to make an audio CD. However, you can put a ton of music in it. Instead of looking at the time at the bottom of iTunes, look at the size. Most CD-ROMs hold 650 MB of MP3 files.

4. With the playlist selected, click the Burn Disc button at the bottom of the iTunes window.

5. Next, you'll see a dialog box as shown in Figure 17.8. This time choose MP3 CD.

6. Click Burn.

7. Insert the writable audio CD into your optical drive.

The most common use for this is to create a killer music collection for your car on a single disc. Not every CD player will play back MP3 CDs. Most that do have an "MP3" logo on the front display somewhere.

Listen to Free Radio Stations

As if iTunes didn't do enough already, it also streams live Internet audio. Hundreds of radio stations from around the world have audio streams available that you can listen in on.

Use the following steps to listen to streaming Internet radio:

1. In the left sidebar of iTunes, look for Radio and click it.

2. Choose a Genre and tweak the triangle next to it to reveal the stations.

3. Double-click on a station to start streaming.

4. Wait. Sometimes it takes a minute to start streaming. Don't get too frustrated if it doesn't work on the first try. Sometimes stations only stream at certain times of the day, and sometimes keeping the streaming service going is not a top priority.

You can also stream stations that are not listed. Any station that uses standard MP3 streaming should be playable through iTunes. However, some stations use a Windows-only format or an older format that iTunes doesn't handle.

Create a Genius Playlist

You can make your own playlists by selecting individual songs, or you can make a smart playlist using search terms. A third way to make a playlist is to use the Genius feature in iTunes.

The Genius feature takes a song and then builds a playlist around it from other songs in your music collection. It does this by communicating with the iTunes server at Apple and comparing data about the songs.

To turn on Genius, if it is not already on, choose Store, Turn On Genius. You will get a warning that this means Apple will receive information about your iTunes library.

The following steps explain how to create a genius Playlist:

1. Select a single song in your music library.

2. Ctrl-click on the song and select Start Genius.

3. You'll now see a list of songs based on that one starting point.

4. Change the number of songs at the top right of the iTunes window, or click Refresh to get a new set of songs.

Using iTunes DJ

So you feel like listening to some tunes. You don't want to listen to any song in particular, you just want to start some music and keep it going.

Select iTunes DJ from the left sidebar, under Playlists. What you'll get is a random list of your music. Press the spacebar or the play button at the top of iTunes to start the music.

But you don't need to settle for the random list of songs. While the music is playing, you can start browsing for the next song to play. Once you find the perfect one you can Ctrl-click it and choose Play Next in iTunes DJ to insert it as the next song in the list.

Click on the iTunes DJ item in the left sidebar at any time to see the list of songs recently played and new ones that are queued up. You can drag songs up and down the list as well.

iTunes DJ is not just for personal musical journeys, either. It can be used to create a musical backdrop for your next party. It constantly adds new songs to the bottom of the list, so you will never run out of music.

And if you've got a few party-goers with iPhones you can invite them to join your wifi network where they will be able to use Apple's Remote app to suggest and even vote on songs to be played in iTunes DJ.

Back Up Your iTunes Content

After you've made a few purchases, your iTunes music collection can be worth quite a bit. Then add in the time it took for you to rip your CD collection. You'd hate to have to do all that again.

So it is wise to back up your iTunes collection every once in a while. Here's how.

Here's how to back up your music:

1. Choose File, Library, Backup to Disc.
2. Choose to back up the entire library or just purchases. You can also choose to only back up items never backed up before.
3. Click the Next button.
4. You'll be asked to insert a blank disk, either CD or DVD.

Using Time Machine also creates a backup of your iTunes content. But this technique from within iTunes not only creates a backup, but also an archive, which is useful in case you decide to trim down your collection at some point, and then find you miss an old album.

Share Your iTunes Library

Your Mac can be the center of all media content for your house if you let it. To this end, iTunes lets you share your entire library with other Macs and devices in your house.

Go to the Sharing preferences pane in the iTunes preferences. Here, you can turn on library sharing for your local network. This means that other Macs on your network can see your music and play it. Figure 17.9 shows the Sharing preferences pane.

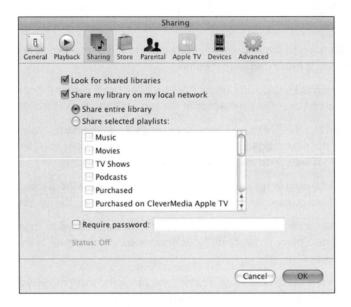

Figure 17.9

The Sharing preferences pane lets you share all or only some of your music with other Macs on your network.

You can only share the items in certain playlists if you like. And if you are at work and don't want just anyone to see your music, you can require a password as well.

Another Mac user on the network will then see your music show up in the left sidebar, as long as she has Look for Shared Libraries checked.

You can also sync your Mac with an Apple TV on your network using the Apple TV preference pane. Apple TV will see shared iTunes libraries, but will only sync directly with one Mac.

Under the Devices preferences pane, you can also set your iTunes application to look for and use AirTunes speakers—these are speakers connected to Airport Express devices hooked up to your network. They allow you to play music from your Mac to a stereo somewhere else in your house.

So now all your hard work of creating an iTunes music library, organizing it, subscribing to podcasts, and creating playlists can pay off as you share your collection with all the Apple devices in your house.

WHO SHOULD READ THIS CHAPTER:

If you need to run Windows on your Mac, this chapter looks at the methods and software you need to get the best of both worlds.

18

Running Windows on Your Mac

What if you just can't leave Windows behind? Perhaps there is some critical program you need that only runs in Windows. Or, maybe there is a website you need that only works with Internet Explorer.

Well, there are two ways to run Windows on your Mac. The first is to use something from Apple called Boot Camp that allows you to reboot your computer using a separate hard drive partition with Windows installed. The second method is to use one of the virtual machine applications out there that allow you to boot and run Windows while still running Mac OS X.

Boot Camp

Boot Camp isn't really an application. It is more like a name given to a feature of your Intel-based Mac. It allows you to choose from a variety of bootup options when you start your computer. Typically, this choice is between booting into Mac OS X or Windows.

> **NOTE**
>
> Macs and PCs use essentially the same hardware ever since Apple moved to Intel processors. But Macs are built specifically to run Mac OS X, not Windows. However, after Windows is enticed to install itself on your Mac, it runs on it just as it would on a PC. No hardware emulation is required, so you have Windows running at full speed and power.

Installing Windows

Mac OS X is already installed and working, of course. So all you need to do is install Windows as well.

First, you need to get a copy of Windows. You can buy one online or in a store. But it must be a full version of Windows, not an upgrade version.

When you have your Windows installation disk, complete with a registration code, you are ready to start.

Run a program called Boot Camp Assistant found in your Applications/Utilities folder. This program walks you through the steps needed to create a new partition on your main hard drive and install Windows on it.

One decision you have to make is which file format to use for this Windows partition. If at all possible, use FAT32. This format allows you to easily move files to and from your Windows partition while you are running Mac OS X. The only major disadvantage is that you can't have a Boot Camp Windows drive partition greater than 32GB. This also only works with Windows XP. With Windows Vista, you're forced to use the other format, NTFS.

The start of the process involves creating a new hard disk partition to hold your Windows install. You can either choose to take a chunk of space from your one and only internal drive, or use a second drive if you have a Mac Pro. Either way, Boot Camp must install to an internal hard disk.

When you have a second partition ready, you can proceed to install Windows onto it. Boot Camp Assistant prompts you when it is time for that.

You'll need that disk you just bought. You'll be asked to choose a partition to install Windows to, and that would be the one with "bootcamp" in its name. In some cases, you may need to select the drive and click the Format button during the Windows install. Otherwise, Windows will not let you proceed.

After the initial Windows installation, you've got to insert your Mac OS X installation disk again. This could be a boxed Mac OS X disk, or the disks that came with your computer. This disk will then spring into action to install all the drivers that Windows needs to talk to your Mac hardware.

When that is complete, you'll probably want to reach for that Start menu and run Windows Update. Chances are there are plenty of updates you'll need to get right away to bring Windows up to speed.

Then, before too long, you'll want to look into Windows antivirus software. Your Windows-on-a-Mac is just as susceptible to viruses as any Windows machine.

Rebooting into Windows

Now that you have the ability to boot into Windows, you'll need to become skilled in switching from Mac to Windows and back.

The easiest way is to reboot your computer and hold down the Option key. Hold it down until you see a simple choice appear between your Mac and your Windows partitions. Use the arrow keys and the Return key to select which one you want.

You can also go into the System Preferences and look for the Startup Disk preferences. You can select which operating system you want to boot into by default. The special drivers that you installed on the Windows side included a matching Control Panel for Windows that allows you to make the same choices.

> Looking for a quick escape from Windows back into Mac? There should be a little Boot Camp icon in the Windows taskbar, all the way over in the bottom right. Click it and you'll see a Reboot into Mac option there. This beats having to wait around holding the Option key while Windows shuts down.

Boot Camp Control Panel

This Boot Camp control panel, seen in Figure 18.1, has a few settings that would otherwise be difficult to control running Windows on your Mac.

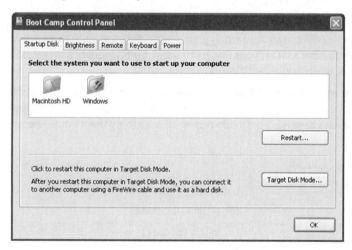

Figure 18.1

The Boot Camp control panel allows you to choose to reboot back into OS X, and control some minor hardware functions.

The options that show up in the Boot Camp control panel will vary depending on which Mac you are using. MacBooks, for instance, have Brightness and Keyboard panes that won't show up in the Mac Pro or Mac Mini because they don't have attached keyboards and displays.

In general, the control panel gives you access to a few settings that are Mac hardware specific, and not handled by Windows. The contents of this control panel will change as Boot Camp evolves in the future.

Right-Clicking

One issue with some Macs is how to right-click. Now that the Mighty Mouse comes standard with desktops, it isn't such a big deal. The right side of the Mighty Mouse works just like the right mouse button of a Windows mouse.

On newer MacBooks, however, there is only one button. In fact, there are no buttons because the trackpad itself doubles as a button. But these newer MacBooks allow for alternate button presses depending on how the trackpad is configured.

If you are stuck with a one-button mouse or an older MacBook, you will have to resort to the Apple Mouse Utility, found at http://rhdesigns.tk/. This allows you to press the Control key and click to simulate a right-click in Windows. This is Windows software, so you'll need to install it after booting into Windows.

Special Keys

A long time back, Macs and PCs were very different computers inside. Today, they are more or less the same, and it is the operating system that is the real difference. That, and the keyboard.

Mac and Windows keyboards have some minor differences that could cause problems unless you know how to handle them. The biggest difference is between the Command and Control keys on a Mac and the Ctrl key on a PC.

In Windows, you use the Ctrl key as you would use the Command key on a Mac. So Command+V for paste is Ctrl+V on Windows. And when you're using Boot Camp, the Ctrl key maps to the Control key. So you have to train your fingers to speak both languages. When booted into Mac, use Command+V, when booted into Windows, use Ctrl+V.

In addition, there are some special keys on Windows keyboards that are not available on a Mac keyboard. Table 18.1 shows how to type them. Because Apple keyboards vary slightly depending on the model, some keys have multiple mappings. You'll have to try them out to see which one fits your keyboard.

Table 18.1   Special Keys

Ctrl+Alt+Delete	Control-Option-Delete (second key)
PrintScreen	F14, F11, fn-F11, fn-Shift-F11
Scroll Lock	F15, fn-Shift-Option-F11
Pause	F16, fn-Shift-F12, none
Backspace	Delete (next to = key)
Insert	Help, fn-Enter
Num Lock	Clear, fn-F6
Alt	Option
Enter	Return
Right-side Alt key	Option-Control
Delete	Delete (above arrows), fn-Delete
Windows key	Command

Virtual Machines

The main problem with Boot Camp is right there in the name—you have to boot your computer to choose a new OS to run. However, there is another way. You can run Windows on top of Mac OS X using a virtual environment provided by one of three main applications: Parallels, VMWare Fusion, and VirtualBox.

Choosing a Virtual Machine Application

All three applications do basically the same thing, offering a way to install Windows on a virtual hard drive that appears as a large file to the Mac. Then you can boot Windows on the virtual drive and run it in one of three modes: in a window, full screen, and with Windows windows intermingling with Mac windows.

Parallels and VMWare Fusion cost about $80. VirtualBox is free, as it is open source software.

- **Parallels**—http://www.parallels.com/
- **VMWare Fusion**—http://www.vmware.com/products/fusion/
- **VirtualBox**—http://www.virtualbox.org/

One of the features that you get with Parallels and VMWare Fusion is the ability to use your Boot Camp partition in the virtual environment. So you install Windows once, and then use it for both Boot Camp and Parallels or VMWare. Otherwise, you'd need to install two separate copies of Windows, one for Boot Camp as a partition and one for the virtualization software as a virtual drive. That can get expensive, not to mention that any Windows software you install would also need to be put in both places.

Virtual Machine Modes

When working with a virtual machine, there are several modes to choose from. The old-fashioned way of thinking about virtual machines is to have them run in a window as in Figure 18.2. So you have a single window that acts as the display for the virtual machine.

The advantages to this are that everything is in one place and it is easy to distinguish what is running in Windows from everything else running on your Mac. This also is the best mode for any full-screen Windows applications, like games.

Similar to running in a window is the idea of the Windows virtual machine taking up the entire screen. This would be similar to running Windows by itself, with Boot Camp, but it would allow you to quickly switch back and forth between Windows and Mac. You can even use Spaces to get Windows running in one space and Mac running in all of the others. Or, if you have two monitors, you can get Windows running full screen in one of them.

Another mode, called *coherence* in Parallels, is to have the Mac and Windows interfaces intermingled. So you will see windows for virtual machine applications and documents mixed in with windows for your Mac (see Figure 18.3). This is best when you need to access websites using Internet Explorer, or work with Windows-based business applications and such.

Figure 18.2

Windows Vista running as a window using Parallels.

Figure 18.3

Windows running in Parallels coherence mode, with Mac and Windows apps intermingled.

Virtual machines are not just for Windows. You can also run other operating systems in them as well. The popular and free Ubuntu operating system can be downloaded and installed easily on any of the virtual machine solutions.

You can have multiple virtual machines if you want. You can have a Windows XP one, a Windows Vista one, an Ubuntu one, and so on. You can run them one at a time, or all together. This makes the Mac a great testing environment if you develop software or websites.

WHO SHOULD READ THIS CHAPTER:

If you plan on using your Mac to work with graphics, this chapter will fill you in on what software is available for you, where to get it, and how to get started.

19

Creating with Images

Editing images and creating illustrations is the primary use of computers for some people. The Mac has many professional-level applications for this, like Adobe Photoshop and Illustrator. There are also professional photo-editing and management tools for those who want to go beyond iPhoto.

But beginner-level and free tools are harder to find. Mac OS X does not come with any basic image program like MS Paint in Windows or the MacPaint program that shipped with older versions of the Mac. But there are many free and inexpensive programs out there for you to use.

Making Image Adjustments

Although no true image-editing programs come with Mac OS X, two of the programs we have already looked at have some image-changing capabilities. Both iPhoto and Preview allow you to open images and adjust attributes of the entire image. You can also crop and resize images.

We looked closely at iPhoto in Chapter 16, "Importing and Managing Photos," so let's look at Preview here. iPhoto also tends to want everything to exist in your iPhoto library, something that may get in the way if you simply want to edit one image.

Making Adjustments with Preview

The same Adjust Color tool palette that appears in iPhoto also comes up in Preview when you choose Tools, Adjust Colors. Figure 19.1 shows this palette above a Preview window with an open JPG image.

Figure 19.1

The Preview application allows you to adjust the color in an image.

Most of the color controls assume that you are editing a photograph, rather than an illustration. But Preview still gives you decent control over the image in either case.

For instance, you could create a washed-out version of the image by bringing down the contrast while increasing the exposure. That might make for a nice website or Pages document background.

Cropping and Resizing in Preview

You have a variety of ways to crop and resize an image with Preview.

To crop an image:

1. Choose the Select tool at the top of the window and select the type of selection tool you want to use.

2. Select an area of the image.

3. Choose Tools, Crop or press Command+K.

4. Save the new cropped version of the image.

If you want more control over the size of the image, use the Tools, Adjust Size option instead. You'll get a set of controls like the ones shown in Figure 19.2.

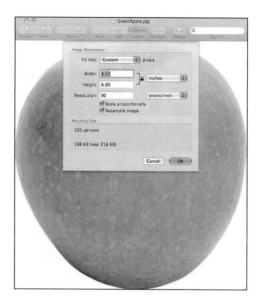

Figure 19.2

The resize controls give you the ability to change the dimensions of the image, scaling it down if necessary.

The Fit Into pop-up menu has a variety of common options, such as a 320×240 size that is handy for emailing a photo to a friend.

You can also decide whether you want to scale the image proportionally, or stretch it to fit the next size exactly.

Free Drawing Tools

Although Mac OS X doesn't come with any real drawing tools, there are some open source tools available for free that you can download.

Paintbrush

Paintbrush is a very simple drawing tool. You can start with a blank image or open an existing one. Then you can paint on it using a brush tool, eraser, bucket fill, selection, and so on.

Figure 19.3 shows some of this basic capability. You can select the Text tool and add some text in any font on your machine, and then place it exactly where you want on the image.

There is also a simple brush stroke under the text. You can adjust the brush size and color, and draw freehand or using a line or curve.

Figure 19.3

Some text and a brush stroke have been added to this image.

Here's how to create an image to use for an email party invitation:

1. Find a picture of yourself. Open it in Paintbrush.

2. Choose the Oval tool from the tool palette. Set it to a Fill Only oval instead of an oval out-line by clicking on the solid rectangle that appears in the tool palette. You can see it in Figure 19.4. Select a color as well if you like by clicking on the large color chip at the bot-tom of the tools palette.

3. Draw an oval over one eye in the image. If it doesn't look right, use Command+Z to undo and try again.

4. Select the Line tool.

5. Draw a line across to complete an eye patch, like in Figure 19.4.

6. Select the Text tool. Click on the image and a text entry box will appear.

7. Type your invitation text, and also click the Font button to change the font to something bigger and more fun. You can even add a drop shadow with one of the buttons at the top of the standard Fonts control.

8. Click Place and then place the text on the image.

9. Choose File, Save As and select the file format JPEG for a more compact image to use in an email.

You can download Paintbrush here: http://paintbrush.sourceforge.net

Figure 19.4

A simple party invitation image created in Paintbrush. Arrrgh!

Seashore

At first glance, Seashore, another open source Mac application, seems to have some of the same functionality as Paintbrush. But Seashore goes a little deeper.

There are more tools, like a clone tool, a lasso, and gradient. But the tools themselves have more depth as well. There are many options for the selection and brush tools, including support for pressure-sensitive tablets. Just about every tool has a full set of adjustments.

Figure 19.5 shows the use of the clone tool to make a second stem to the Apple, as well as a brush that uses the Fade Out feature to create a more realistic stroke.

Seashore also allows you to export in a variety of formats. This can come in handy if you need to alter an image and then compress it into a JPG file for use on a website or sending to a friend.

You can download Seashore here: http://seashore.sourceforge.net

GIMP

If you are looking for something a little closer to Photoshop, but without the price tag, look no further than GIMP, the GNU Image Manipulation Program.

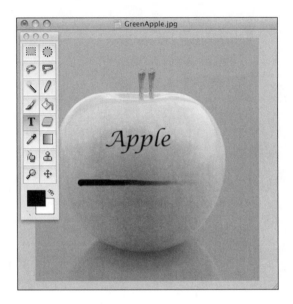

Figure 19.5

The Seashore drawing application contains some pretty sophisticated features for a free program.

NOTE

So, the power of Photoshop for free? What's the catch? Well, GIMP isn't a Mac program. It only runs on your Mac by using the X11 application environment, which is an optional install on the Mac OS X disk, and X11 is probably not on your Mac unless you have installed it yourself. So if you really want to use GIMP, you need to find the Mac OS X CD that came with your computer, insert it into your Mac, and navigate through the menus to install just X11.

When you do that, your Mac will be able to run programs that require X11, including GIMP. But don't expect the nice Mac interface you've come to expect from other Mac programs.

GIMP is a powerhouse image-editing tool. Just look at Figure 19.6 and you can see how complex it is. On the left are the tools, with options changing depending on the tool. On the right are even more options, including layers for creating professional graphics.

The tools in GIMP are so complex that you almost need a graphic arts degree to use it. So if you need the power, but can't afford anything else, GIMP is for you. You can find out more and download it at http://www.gimp.org/.

Figure 19.6

The GIMP image editing tool is powerful, but not for the casual user.

More Graphics Tools

If you want to invest a little money into creating graphics, there are a variety of downloadable tools you can purchase.

- **GraphicConverter**—This is a tool that may have had its roots in converting one file format to another, but has picked up a plethora of functions over the years to become a pretty comprehensive image-editing tool. http://www.lemkesoft.com/

- **Pixelmator**—A powerhouse image-editing tool at a reasonable price, this application strives to work well with every aspect of Mac OS X. You can use your iSight camera, integrate with iPhoto, and even automate tasks with Automator. It has Photoshop-like features and lots of control over every tool. http://www.pixelmator.com/

- **VectorDesigner**—This program focuses more on drawing and the use of lines and shapes (vectors) that illustrators use to create art. http://www.tweakersoft.com/vectordesigner/

- **ArtRage**—This drawing application concentrates on painting tools for artists. http://www.ambientdesign.com/

- **Rainbow Painter**—This is another painting tool with a full set of tools, effects, and features. http://www.rainbowpainter.com/

- **Photoshop Elements**—Photoshop's little brother is meant for casual users but still includes many of the powerful features found in the full version. It usually sells for under $100 in stores and online.

You can find an updated list of Mac image-editing and drawing applications here:

http://macmost.com/mac-image-editing-and-drawing-applications.html

Of course if you are a professional, you probably already know that Adobe Photoshop is the most-used image-editing software, and Adobe Illustration the most-used illustration software. Adobe also makes a tool called Fireworks, which is somewhere in between and specializes in graphics for the Web and other computer applications. Corel Painter is another professional option.

WHO SHOULD READ THIS CHAPTER:

If you want to use your Mac for any sort of audio recording, whether music or speech, you should learn the ins and outs of GarageBand.

20

Creating with GarageBand

Part of the iLife suite is GarageBand, an audio-editing and music creation tool that can be used for a variety of tasks. Let's look at how to use GarageBand for some of them.

Creating Music

The most basic use for GarageBand is to use the built-in music loops to make a piece of music. You'll do this by overlaying different loops: drums, bass, guitar, and so on.

When you first launch GarageBand, you will be given some choices as to how to start, as shown in Figure 20.1.

Simple Looping Music

Now let's go ahead and create a simple looping piece of music. We'll just use the built-in loops.

The following steps demonstrate how to create music from loops:

1. Choose Loops in the project window shown in Figure 20.1.
2. Look on the right for the loop browser. It should be a collection of buttons as in Figure 20.2. If you don't see it, choose Control, Show Loop Browser.

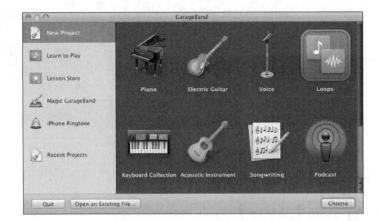

Figure 20.1

When you start GarageBand or go to create a new project, you'll be given a few choices as to how to get started.

Figure 20.2

The Loop Browser lets you browse through all of the different kinds of music loops that are built into GarageBand.

3. Click on All Drums to narrow it down a bit. A list will now appear under the buttons. Scroll down to find "Jazzy Rock Drums 07." Click on it once to preview it.

4. Click and drag "Jazzy Rock Drums 07" to the center area of GarageBand. This creates a track and places the music loop in it. Drag the loop so that it is all the way to the left.

5. In the bottom toolbar, click on the Turn Cycle Region On or Off button. It is to the right of the Play and Move Ahead buttons and has a symbol that looks like a circle with two arrows. Now you should see a yellow bar appear at the top of the center area. This represents the

area that will loop. You can drag the end of the cycle region to make it larger or smaller. The window should now look like Figure 20.3.

Figure 20.3

You now have a single track with a music loop, plus a cycle region set to match the music loop's length.

6. Back in the Loop Browser, click the Reset button. Then click the Bass button. You will now see a list of bass loops.

7. Click the large Play button at the bottom of the window, or click the spacebar to start the music playing. You should hear the drum loop play over and over.

8. Select any bass loop in the list to hear it against the drum loop. Continue to try different bass loops.

9. Select "Cool Upright Bass 13." Click the spacebar or the Play button again to stop the music. Drag "Cool Upright Bass 13" into the center area, just under the drum loop. It should create a second track and look like Figure 20.4.

Figure 20.4

The second track is a loop that is only half the length of the first track.

10. Hover your cursor over the upper-right corner of the "Cool Upright Bass 13" loop in track 2. You should see the cursor change to a circle arrow. Now you can click and drag the end of the loop to extend it. Double its length so that it is the same length as the first track.

11. Reset the Loop Browser again and this time click the Guitars button to see a list of guitar loops. Narrow it down further by clicking the Relaxed button as well.

12. You can click Play or the spacebar and sample the guitar loops over your current song. When you are done with that, click and drag "Classic Rock Steel 01" to the center area below the second track to create a third track.

13. Now, let's adjust the sound levels of each track. Use the small volume controls in each track to raise or lower the sound. Lower the sound of the drums slightly and the bass about half way. It should look like Figure 20.5 now.

Figure 20.5
The third track is in place and volume levels are adjusted.

You can continue to add more tracks if you like, but you get the idea. You can also get more music loops from purchasing a collection from Apple or some third-party vendors.

Altering Your Song

You can go much deeper with loops than just putting them together. You can alter the instrument in many cases, and even the notes that are being played.

First, let's try playing with instruments. Say you like the song we just created, but aren't crazy about the steel guitar. You can change the instrument used to play that loop because it is a software instrument loop. In other words, the notes are recorded as data, and any instrument can be used to play them. These loops appear with a green music-note icon in the Loop Browser.

The other type of loop is a real instrument loop. These are sound recordings. You can't alter the instrument used to play those because they are actual recordings.

To change the instrument being used to play the guitar part of the song, follow these steps:

1. Select the Acoustic Guitar track by clicking on the part of the track under the Tracks column in the GarageBand window.

2. Choose Track, Show Track Info. You'll now see the Loop Browser replaced by a list of instrument types.

3. Click Play or the spacebar to start the music looping again.

4. Choose an instrument category and then an instrument. The guitar part will change instruments while the music is playing.

If you want to get down and dirty with the settings that make one instrument different from the other, click the Edit tab at the top of the Software Instrument controls. Now you have access to a bunch of different settings, all of which control the exact synthetic sound of the instrument. You can make your own version of any instrument this way and save it for future use.

Altering the Notes

Software instrument tracks are ultimately just a collection of notes. Double-click on any software instrument loop in one of your tracks and you will see these notes below the tracks, as shown in Figure 20.6.

Figure 20.6

The Editor allows you to control the notes directly.

Not only can you view the notes, but you can also make changes to them. If you don't like the "piano roll" view, you can switch to a more traditional musical score view by clicking Score in Figure 20.6.

If you want to go further, you can compose music on GarageBand using a MIDI instrument, like a keyboard hooked up to your Mac via USB. This allows you to record directly into a software instrument track. All you need to do is select the track and click the round red record button.

If you don't have a MIDI instrument handy, you can fake it using an on-screen keyboard, or even your computer keyboard. You can turn either option on from the Window menu: Window, Keyboard, or Window Musical Typing.

Recording Audio

Software instruments are synthetic computer data, but real instruments are… actual recordings of real instruments being played. And there's no more real instrument than the human voice.

Recording from a Microphone

You can record your voice, or whatever is going on in earshot of a microphone, using GarageBand.

You can record from a microphone using the following steps:

1. Start GarageBand again and choose Voice as the type of project you want to create. You could also choose Podcast, Acoustic Instrument, or Loops. The latter would mean that you would need to add your own real instrument track before beginning.

2. With the Voice project option, you'll be started off with two tracks: Male Basic and Female Basic. Remove the one you don't need by selecting the track and pressing Command+Delete.

3. Next, check your recording input. Choose GarageBand, Preferences, and the Audio/MIDI tab. Look at the Audio Input setting to make sure your microphone is selected, as shown in Figure 20.7.

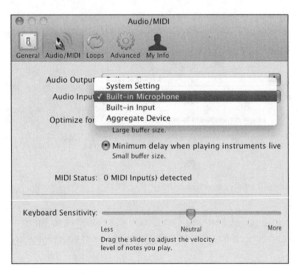

Figure 20.7

Make sure the microphone you want to use is selected in the preferences.

NOTE

The worst possible microphone you can use for recording your voice is probably the one internal to your Mac. It is an adequate microphone, but as part of the Mac's case, it picks up vibration and fan noise. Plus, it is probably too far from your mouth at most times. Better to spend at least a little money and buy a headset or decent desktop microphone if you want better quality.

4. Make sure GarageBand's metronome is turned off (check the menu Control, Metronome). Also, make sure that unwanted sound interruptions, like your incoming Mail sound, are turned off.

   Click the red round record button and speak into the microphone. You should test it first, recording a little bit, testing playback, and then deleting the contents of the track to start again.

Editing a Recording

After recording audio, you can use GarageBand to edit that audio. Simply double-click on the content in the track that represents the audio you recorded and an editor appears below the tracks, as in Figure 20.8.

Figure 20.8
The audio editor allows you to cut, copy, paste, and delete segments from a recording.

When you move your cursor over the audio waveform in the editor, it changes to a cross. You can select a portion of the audio just as you would select text in a word processor. Then you can use the Delete key to remove a section.

This breaks up the audio recording into two parts: the part before the deleted area and the part after it. You can then go up to the tracks area and drag the later part to the left to fill the gap. You may want to turn off Control, Snap to Grid to make it easier to match up the ends.

You can also copy a section of audio and paste it elsewhere in the editor. Or, you could create a new track by clicking the + button at the bottom left of the GarageBand window and pasting the audio in there.

You can also split and join segments in the tracks area by using Edit, Split and Edit, Join (Command+T and Command+J). So another way to delete a segment would be to split the track at the start and end of the segment in the track and then select it and press Delete.

Exporting from GarageBand

When you are done recording, you have to decide how to save it. You can simply save it as a GarageBand file. This means you can only play it back by opening it in GarageBand again.

You can also export your recording in a variety of other ways. They can all be found in the Share menu. The first such option is Send Song to iTunes. With this, the recording is exported in the current settings used by iTunes to import music from audio CDs. You can find this setting in the iTunes preferences, under Advanced.

Using Share, Send Song to iTunes exports a copy of the song, places it in your iTunes library, and opens iTunes to start playing the recording.

Another option is to use Share, Export Song to Disk. This allows you to create either a compressed or uncompressed version of the song. The control that appears after selecting this choice is shown in Figure 20.9.

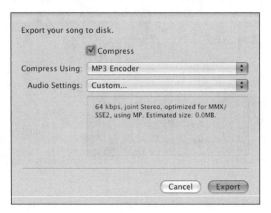

Figure 20.9

You can export songs directly from GarageBand with a few options.

If you choose to export the song uncompressed, you get a raw AIFF file. This is ideal if you want the highest quality or simply want to use the recording in another audio editing program.

Otherwise, you get to choose AAC or MP3 format, and tweak the settings as much as you like.

If you are exporting some audio to send to a friend via email, you probably want to choose MP3 format, and "Good Quality" to create a reasonably sized file. If you are exporting something to listen to on your iPod or burn to an audio CD, you may want to consider "Higher Quality."

A lot depends on the type of song you are exporting as well. Spoken word doesn't need to be as high quality as multi-instrument music, for instance.

Making a Ringtone

You can use GarageBand to create a ringtone for your iPhone. To start, select the iPhone Ringtone category from the left side of the GarageBand project chooser. You'll get three choices: Example Ringtone, Loops, and Voice.

The first choice gives you a single track with a sample recording. The second choice gives you a four-track example. The third choice gives you two tracks, one for each gender, but with no recording.

Regardless of which one you choose, you can remove the existing tracks and use the Loop Browser to create your own ringtone from scratch. Or, you can record your voice over your microphone. Or both.

The only real difference between a normal song and a ringtone is that the cycle region has been turned on and set to 13 and a half measures at 120 beats per minute and 4/4 signature. This is a 25-second loop, in other words.

You can now dump in as many loops or recordings as you want, and alter them to make the perfect ringtone.

When you are done, you can export the ringtone by choosing Share, Send Ringtone to iTunes.

This creates an .m4r version of the song. That's really an .aac file with a different extension so that iTunes knows to use it as a ringtone.

To get this ringtone to your iPhone, you need to first connect your iPhone and then launch iTunes. Then go to the Ringtones tab of the iPhone sync controls and make sure it is set to sync to your phone. You may need to re-sync to actually get it there, though.

> You can make as many ringtones as you want. A ringtone can be associated with a specific contact, so you can make individual ringtones that tell you exactly who is calling without having to even look at your phone.

You may also be able to make ringtones for other phones besides the iPhone. But GarageBand's built-in ringtone projects won't help you with that. If your phone can accept an MP3 file as a ringtone, you can simply share your song as a compressed MP3 file and follow your phone's instructions on how to get the file onto the phone and use it as a ringtone.

This chapter only scratches the surface of what you can do with GarageBand. For instance, you could hook up several instruments: microphones, guitars, MIDI keyboards, and so on. Then you could record them all at the same time into their own tracks. Then, you could play back that song and record new tracks to coexist with the old. GarageBand can be a whole multitrack recording studio.

WHO SHOULD READ THIS CHAPTER:

If you want to experiment with digital video, this chapter will get you started. Even inexpensive digital still cameras have a movie mode today, so you may be closer to editing your own video and burning DVDs than you think.

21

Creating with Video

Not too long ago it took a high-powered computer to edit video. But now even the lowly Mac Mini and the lightweight MacBook Air have enough power to do it. But editing video doesn't just take power; it also requires software. Fortunately, your Mac comes with iMovie, part of the iLife suite.

Recording Video with iMovie

Recording some video with iMovie is easy if you have your iSight camera hooked up. If you have a separate video camera, you can also easily import video from that as well.

Recording from iSight

If you have a MacBook or iMac, you have a built-in iSight video camera. You can use that to easily record video of yourself into iMovie.

Here's how to record from your iSight camera:

1. Run iMovie and choose File, New Project. The dialog box in Figure 21.1 appears. Choose "None" as the theme for now and, if you prefer, give the project a name other than the default. Click Create.

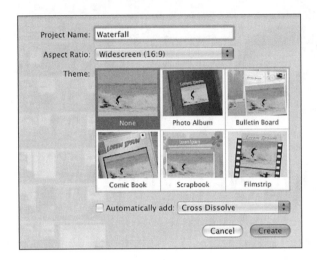

Figure 21.1

Choosing an aspect ratio is important and depends on the type of camera you have.

   2. Choose File, Import from Camera. This opens a video preview window. Make sure your iSight camera is working. If you see yourself, it is.

   3. Click the Capture button. You'll be asked to name a new "Event." Events are collections of video clips.

   4. When you are ready, continue by clicking the Capture button in the next dialog box and make a short recording. Smile!

   5. When you are finished, click the Stop button and then click Done.

   6. The recording appears in the event that you named. If it doesn't appear at the bottom of the iMovie window as in Figure 21.2, make sure the event is selected on the left.

   7. You've now got a recording of yourself. To do something with it, click to select a portion of it, signified by the yellow outline. You can adjust the start and end of the selected portion. Then drag the selection from the event portion of the iMovie window to the project portion above it.

You now have a simple movie project with one clip. You can use the Share menu to export it in a variety of formats, or send it directly to services like MobileMe or YouTube.

Importing Video from a Video Camera

How you import video from a camera depends a lot on the type of camera. Older cameras that use MiniDV tapes or something similar require that you hook them up to the Mac via Firewire or USB. Then iSight will let you import the video from the tape by choosing File, Import from Camera.

Figure 21.2

The typical iMovie window shows the project, a preview, and the event at the bottom.

But newer cameras record video directly to computer files. In this case, you may already have imported the video using iPhoto. Or, you can hook the camera or media card up to your computer and see the files as they would appear on an external hard drive.

> If you have video files on a media card or the internal memory or drive of a camera, you should copy them to your local hard drive before using them in iMovie. This will speed up processing a great deal and prevent disaster if your camera comes unplugged while you are editing.

You can choose File, Import, Movies to grab video files of almost any format and bring them into iMovie as part of an event.

When you have several clips in an event, you can drag them up to the project part of iMovie to add them to the project.

Editing Video in iMovie

You don't have to settle for just using your video clips as-is. You can also trim them and make other modifications.

In Figure 21.3, there are three clips in the event window, and all are used in the project above it. Notice that they are not in the same order. Each was dragged and dropped in the order in which they should play in the finished movie.

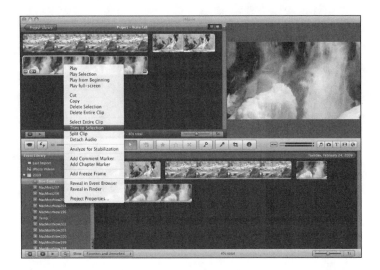

Figure 21.3

An iMovie project in progress.

You can drag and drop clips into any space inside the project—before or after any existing clip or even in the middle of one.

You can also select only a portion of a clip in the event space and drag that portion to the project space. Or, in the project space, you can trim a clip by selecting only the portion you want and Ctrl-clicking to get a context menu with a variety of choices, as in Figure 21.3.

> **NOTE**
>
> Working with clip selections is at the very heart of iMovie. You've got to get used to selecting the beginning and end of a clip's yellow selection area. When you master that, you can perform all sorts of tasks by selecting an area and choosing the appropriate menu item.

So you have a variety of ways to edit your movie:

- Select only a portion of a clip in the event area and drag that portion to the project area.
- Select a portion of a clip in the project area and choose Edit, Trim to Selection.
- Select a portion of a clip in the project area and choose Edit, Split Clip. This cuts the clip into two parts, or three parts if you have selected a portion in the middle of a clip.
- Drag and drop a clip from the event area into the middle of another clip in the project area. This splits the second clip and inserts the new clip between the two parts.
- Drag and drop clips before and after each other in the project area to rearrange them.

The project area can be a clumsy place to operate if you want to make a precision edit. There are two other modes for editing clips. The first is the Clip Trimmer.

Select a clip in the project space and choose Window, Clip Trimmer. The event space is replaced by a closer view of the clip as in Figure 21.4. You can move the beginning and end selection to trim the clip more precisely. You can also adjust the viewing scale at the bottom right so that you can get an even more accurate cut. Then click Done when you are finished.

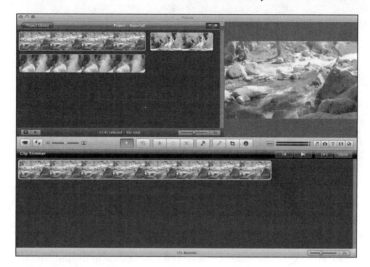

Figure 21.4
The Clip Trimmer lets you make precise cuts.

A similar view is the Precision Editor. You can go to that view by choosing Window, Precision Editor. But this only works well if you are using transitions between the clips.

Modifying Video in iMovie

When you have a project going that has several clips, you'll want to start using things like transitions, effects, and even titles.

Using Transitions

Think of transitions as special clips that only fit between regular video clips. This is exactly how you add them to your movie.

Follow these steps to add transitions to a video:

1. View the transitions by clicking on the Transitions button in the middle toolbar, over to the right. You can also choose Window, Transitions. You will see a grid of transition icons appear to the right of the event clips as in Figure 21.5.

Transitions button

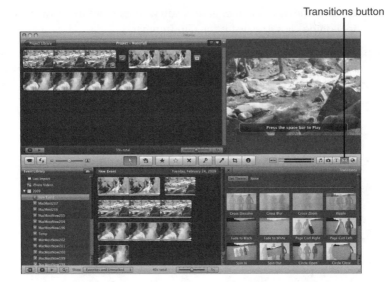

Figure 21.5

Transitions appear at the bottom right and are simply dragged and dropped into your project.

2. Roll over the transitions to get the basic idea.

3. Drag a transition to your project area between two clips and drop it there. Figure 21.5 has a ripple transition between the first two clips and a Cross Zoom between the second and third.

4. Preview the transition by clicking on the first clip, just before the transition, and then clicking the Play button to see it play out in the preview area on the right.

5. Select the transition in the project and choose Window, Precision Editor to further hone the transition.

To replace an existing transition, simply drag another transition to take its place. To remove a transition, just select it and press the Delete key.

Using Effects

You can also easily apply a variety of video effects to any clip in your movie.

You can apply video effects by following these steps:

1. Select the clip to which you want to apply the effect.

2. Choose Window, Clip Adjustments to bring up the Inspector window.

3. Look for the Video Effect setting in that window. It should read "None." Click on that space.

4. Look through the video effects and preview them right in the window, as in Figure 21.6.

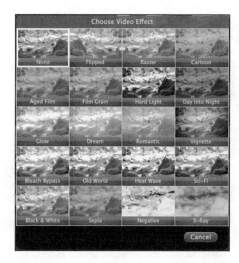

Figure 21.6

There are many video effects to choose from.

The effects are applied dynamically. That means that your original clip is still there and the effect is on top of that. So you can always change an effect or remove it without losing anything. To remove an effect, just change the effect to the first one, labeled "None."

Using Titles

There are two types of titles. The first is a title sequence that appears front and center, usually by itself, but it can be over a background.

Then there are titles that appear under or alongside other video. For instance, text may appear along the bottom like the name of the person speaking or the location of the video being shown.

Most of the titles in iMovie can be used either way but make more sense when used one way or the other. Let's look at a standalone title sequence.

STANDALONE TITLES

As an example, let's create an opening title for the movie we are making. We'll choose the Drifting title sequence.

Here's how to add a standalone title:

1. Click on the T button in the middle toolbar, or choose Window, Titles. Then you can roll over each of the title types to get the general idea of what each one does.

2. Click and drag the Drifting title to the front of your project.

3. Next, you'll be asked to choose a background. Choose Retro.

4. You now should see something like what you see in Figure 21.7. The title has been added as a clip before the rest of the clips in the project. In the preview space, you'll see the title with some sample text.

Figure 21.7

An opening title has been added to the project.

5. You can edit the text right in the preview space. If you can't, simply double-click on the preview space and you should see the text become editable. You can also click on the Show Fonts button to change the font, size, and style.

6. You can also double-click on the title clip in the project space to change the background and also the duration.

You can create a variety of opening, closing, and transitional titles this way. The titles in the project act just like video clips, so you can drag and drop them to move them around in the project.

OVERLAY TITLES

Sometimes it is useful to put text over the video to add more information. Commonly, this is done along the bottom of the video. iMovie has a variety of these kinds of titles as well. Let's add one to the example.

The following steps explain how to add an overlay:

1. Look for the "Torn Edge - Tan" title.

2. Drag and drop that on top of a video clip in the project—not between clips, but right on top of one.

3. You'll now see a title appear over the top of the clip, like in Figure 21.8.

Figure 21.8

Titles appear in the project just over each clip, as they do with the initial title sequence and the overlay title here.

4. You can double-click on the preview space to edit the text in the title.

5. You can double-click on the title above the clip in the project space to edit duration, background, and the fade in and out.

6. You can also grab the edges of the title above the clip in the project space to stretch or shrink it. This way, you can have the title appear over only part of a clip instead of the whole thing.

Adding a Soundtrack

You can mix sound and music with your video very easily in iMovie. You can use music from iMovie, GarageBand, your iTunes collection, or any other sound file.

You can add a soundtrack by using the following steps:

1. Select the music browser in iMovie by clicking on the musical notes button in the middle toolbar, or choosing Window, Music and Sound Effects.

2. Browse through all of the music. You can search as well. Select the Piano Ballad from the iLife Sound Effects, Jingles category.

3. Drag that to the project space. You have two options here: Drag it into the general area of the project space and it will become the background music for the entire movie. Or, drag it on top of a video clip and it appears under the clips as in Figure 21.9.

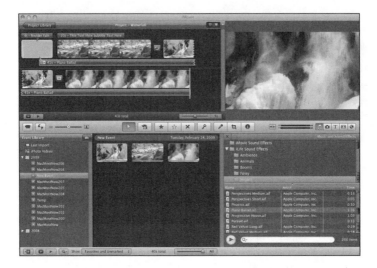

Figure 21.9

Some music has been added to the project, appearing as a green bar under the clips.

4. You can drag the music track in the project space to adjust where it begins. You can also pull the end of the clip to have it fade out earlier.

5. Double-click on the music track in the project space to adjust its duration, volume, and other audio controls.

You can add multiple audio tracks to your iMovie project by repeating the steps. The tracks simply stack under the video clips.

 NOTE

If you have sound in the video and you want to get rid of it so that it doesn't compete with the music, just select the clip and choose Edit, Detach Audio. The audio separates from the video and appears as another audio track under it. You can then double-click it to lower the volume, or delete it by selecting it and pressing the Delete key.

You can add sound effects, voice over narration, music, and so on.

Creating a Photo Slideshow

Although photographs aren't the first thing that comes to mind when you think of making videos, iMovie is a great tool for stitching together photos in a lively slideshow. Doing this is as easy as you would expect.

You can create a slideshow as follows:

1. Create a new iMovie project.

2. Click on the camera icon in the middle toolbar, or choose Window, Photos. This brings up a photo browser with your iPhoto collection.

3. Drag and drop a photo in the project space from the photo browser. You can also drag and drop an image file from the Finder into the project space.

4. Double-click on the photo in the project space to adjust the duration that the photo will appear in the video, or to add a video effect.

5. Click on the photo in the project space and use the tool pop-up menu to bring up a context menu allowing you to enter either the Precision Editor, Clip Adjustments, Video Adjustments or the Cropping, Ken Burns & Rotation controls (see Figure 21.10). Select the last one.

Figure 21.10

The tools pop-up menu in any clip allows you to adjust all of the options for that clip.

6. The preview space will now allow you to adjust the fit, crop, rotation, and the Ken Burns effect.

> The Ken Burns effect is simply an animation that moves and zooms in slightly on the photo rather than just having it stand still. The name comes from the award-winning documentary director who uses this visual effect often to bring old photos to life.

Continue to add more photos. You can add transitions between them, apply video effects, put titles over them or between them, and also add some music.

Making DVDs with iDVD

After you've created an iMovie masterpiece, you might like to show it to some friends. Instead of having them gather around your computer, you could burn a DVD and watch it in the family room on the big screen TV.

iDVD comes with iLife and your new Mac and makes it fairly painless to create a quick DVD, as shown in the following steps.

1. Launch iDVD and choose File, New to create a new project. Make sure you select a Widescreen (16:9) ratio.

2. Choose Center Stage as your theme.

3. You should now see a screen like Figure 21.11. Anything labeled as a Drop Zone means that you can drag and drop a photo or video onto it. This will merely act as special effect for your DVD menu, and not as the main content of the DVD.

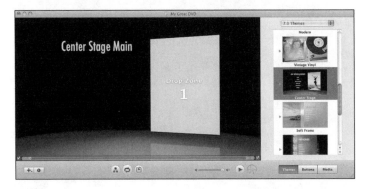

Figure 21.11

The Center Stage Main theme is a good simple one to get you started.

4. On the right side of the iDVD window, choose the Media button at the bottom. Then look at the top and choose Movies.

5. Browse through your movies to select one you want to put into Drop Zone 1. Drag and drop it there. You now have a short video loop on your DVD's menu, just like a movie DVD you would buy at the store!

6. At the bottom of the iDVD window, there are three circular buttons: Show the DVD Map, Start or Stop Motion, and Edit Drop Zones. Click the first one, or choose View, Show Map.

7. The map view looks like Figure 21.12. The third piece of content shown was created by clicking the + button on the bottom left, and selecting Add Movie. This added a third box to the diagram. Then, a new movie was dragged from the right on to the box. The movie can be something you exported from iMovie, or a raw clip from iPhoto.

Figure 21.12

The Map view allows you to add more content to your DVD.

8. Double-click on the second box in the diagram to go back to the main view. You will now see a button there. It is the button to take the viewer to the video you just added. Select it, wait, and then click on it to edit the name of this button.

You should also click on and edit the title in Figure 21.11. You can continue to repeat steps 6, 7, and 8 to add more buttons leading to more videos. You can also choose to add another menu screen instead of a video, to create even more branches.

You can preview your DVD by clicking the Play button at the bottom of the window. Then, when you are ready to burn the DVD to a physical disk, click the Burn button next to the Play button or choose File, Burn DVD.

You can also go directly from iMovie to iDVD by choosing Share, iDVD in iMovie. Or, you can export the movie to be made available for iDVD by choosing Share, Media Browser.

This just scratches the surface of what you can do with iDVD. You can even use it to create slideshows. You can combine movies that you edit in iMovie with photo slideshows, background music, and so on.

WHO SHOULD READ THIS CHAPTER:

If you want to learn how to get your Mac to look and behave differently than the default settings, this is the chapter for you. You may discover that there are plenty of things that you can easily change to personalize your Mac and get it to work the way you want it to.

22

Customizing Your Mac

It is time to start learning things about your Mac and have your Mac start learning things about you. You can make a variety of choices about how you want your Mac to look, act, and react to your commands.

Let's examine how to customize your account and set up new ones, how to change the way the desktop and Finder look, and how to customize OS X for your location. We'll also look at third-party utilities to customize your Mac even beyond the basics.

Finder Appearance

The System Preferences Appearance pane includes a number of small items that can be used to change how windows in the Finder, and almost all other applications, work. Figure 22.1 shows the preferences.

Many of the settings here are truly minor. For instance, the Appearance choice of Blue or Graphite only affects minor colors and design of windows. The font-smoothing options, likewise, may be hard to even notice.

But the default highlight color can be useful if you have trouble noticing what text is selected in your applications.

You can also change the number of recent items that appear in the Recent Items submenu of the Apple menu at the upper left. The default for applications, documents, and servers is 10. Power users may want to have more than 10. If you find yourself using the recent items menus often, and also often find that items you want are just beyond the previous 10, you can set this as high as 50.

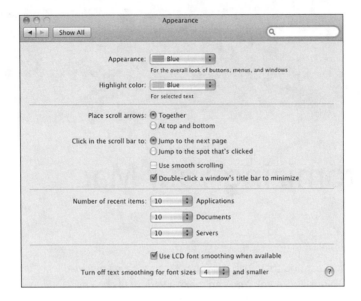

Figure 22.1

The Appearance preferences allow you to control how scroll bars work.

A large number of the Appearance preferences deal with scroll bars. You can choose to have the arrows together at the bottom of the bar. Figure 22.2 illustrates the difference.

Figure 22.2

The left window has the scroll arrows placed together, and the right has them at the top and bottom.

You can also switch between two behaviors for the scroll bar. This setting affects what happens when you click on space above or below the scroll bar indicator. The default behavior is to jump forward one page when you click below and back one page when you click above.

You can also have your scroll bar clicks simply jump the window contents to that location. Try out both modes with a long Finder window, like your Applications window, to see how they work and which one you prefer.

> **NOTE**
>
> You can test out all of the Appearance preferences live. Just have the Preferences window open and a Finder window or some other window, and those windows will react to your preference changes as you make them.

The smooth scrolling option creates a smoother visual when scrolling up and down large pages. But the benefit is hard to see because turning this setting off seems to make scrolling more responsive.

One more gem in the Appearance preferences is Double-Click a Window's Title Bar to Minimize. I actually prefer to keep this turned off, as I find it is easy to minimize a window already with the Minimize button, and sometimes a mistaken double-click can trigger this when it is most annoying.

User Accounts

At the heart of customization in Mac OS X is the idea of user accounts. This enables multiple people to use the same Mac, and each person keeps different preferences and settings.

So, if your spouse likes the Dock on the left and a picture of outer space as a desktop background, he or she can have that set up in his or her account. Meanwhile, you can have the Dock at the bottom and a picture of a waterfall in the background. And that's only scratching the surface.

Administering Your Account

In the Accounts pane of the System Preferences, you can administer your user accounts. Figure 22.3 shows what the pane may look like initially, with one account set up with your name as an admin.

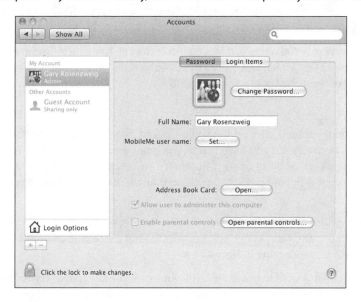

Figure 22.3

The System Preferences Accounts pane allows you to add, remove, and edit user accounts on your Mac.

On the left you will see a list of accounts. You'll have your own account, plus a Guest Account that represents what a user who logs in as a guest to your machine can do.

Notice the little padlock icon at the bottom left? In order to make many changes to your account, you need to unlock your account preferences by clicking on this padlock and entering your password.

CHANGING YOUR USER ICON

Let's look at what you can do to customize your own account. First, you can change your user icon. You can select from a set of premade icons, choose any image file, or take a photo right this second with a built-in iSight camera.

When you click on the icon, you are presented with a selection of icons and an Edit Picture option. Click one of the icons to use it, or choose the Edit Picture option to use an image you have on your computer or use your iSight camera.

> **NOTE**
>
> There are lots of other ways to get an image to be your account icon. After you choose Edit Picture, you can copy and paste images from other applications as well as drag and drop image files from the Finder onto the icon in the Edit Picture viewing area.

CHANGING YOUR USER NAME

You can change your full user name. This differs from your account ID or short user name that you specified when creating your account. For instance, if your full user name is "John Smith," your short user name may be "john" or "jsmith" or even "johnsmith." The short name is used to name your user folder in the Users directory. Therefore, it cannot be easily changed.

But you can change your full name just by clicking in the Full Name text field in Figure 22.3. You have to authenticate first, which just means you need to enter your account password. You have to do that to make most changes to your account.

LOGIN OPTIONS

To change your login options, click on the Login Options item at the bottom-left side of the same window as Figure 22.3. If you haven't unlocked your account preferences yet, then you won't be able to edit any of these options. But then if you click on the padlock below and authenticate yourself with your password, you can then see a new set of options, as shown in Figure 22.4.

If you are the only user of your Mac, and no one else can get access to your computer at all, you may want to turn on Automatic Login, and assign it to your user name using the pop-up menu at the top of the preference pane in Figure 22.4.

This means that when your Mac boots up, it will automatically log you in to your account. You can see how this would be dangerous if someone else you didn't trust could get physically in front of your computer. Definitely not something you want to turn on for a MacBook.

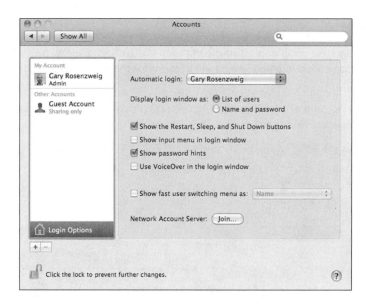

Figure 22.4

The Login Options preferences allow you to change how you log in to your Mac.

The next option could make your Mac a little safer, if someone else gets his hands on it. If you turn on the setting Display Login Window as Name and Password, someone logging in will need to know both your user name and the password. Otherwise, they can just select a user from the list.

The options Show Input Menu in Login Window and Use VoiceOver in the Login Window make logging in more accessible. The first allows the user to select a language, and the second will speak the text in the login window. You can also opt to show password hints, which could be useful for someone who could easily forget their login password.

Fast User Switching

One powerful feature of accounts is the ability to switch between them quickly and easily. To do this, enable fast user switching in the Login Options shown in Figure 22.4.

Basically, you can now have more than one user logged in at the same time. But only one user's account is active at any moment. However, you can use a drop-down menu on the right side of the menu bar to switch between users.

Then you can easily switch between users by just selecting that user in the drop-down menu.

This is useful if you have multiple people on the same Mac, and need to switch between them often. For instance, if the other person always wants to "jump on and quickly check email."

This saves all the time of logging off and logging back on again. All running applications stay active and Finder and document windows stay open. So you are essentially pausing your work to move to another account temporarily.

Guest Accounts

If you occasionally have people using your computer, say to check their web email or perform a quick task, you don't need to create a separate account for them. Instead, you can enable guest accounts.

Select the Guest Account entry in the Account preferences pane, shown in Figure 22.5. Then you need to check off Allow Guests to Log In to This Computer.

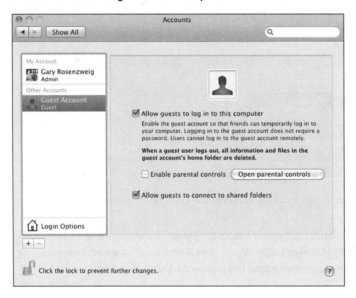

Figure 22.5

Guest accounts are a great way to let a friend "borrow" your computer for a few minutes without giving them access to all of your stuff.

When a user logs in as a guest, they don't need a password. They have their own little account space, with no access to your account, documents, settings, and so on. They can only access your shared folder if you have selected "Allow guests to connect to shared folders" in Figure 22.5. When they log off, everything they have done is deleted and the guest account is restored to its initial state for the next person to use it.

You can also only enable parental controls for guest accounts, which is handy if it is a little one borrowing your Mac.

Adding New Accounts

To create a new account, go to the main Account preferences pane, and click the + button at the bottom left. You will get a form like the one in Figure 22.6.

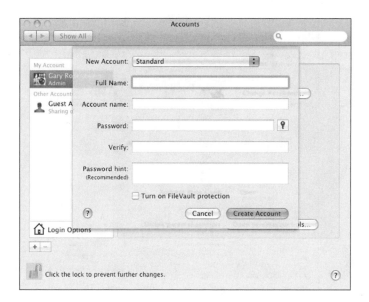

Figure 22.6

To create a new account, you basically need to supply an account name and password.

The full name of an account can be easily changed, but pick your account name with great care. This will be the name of the user folder and it is difficult to change. Keep it short, but unique. A first name is usually good in a family situation. At work, you may want to use first initial and last name or something similar.

You need to choose between a Standard account and an Administrator. The later can control other accounts and things at the main level of your computer, like the contents of the Applications and Library folders. A Standard account works for most purposes for secondary users, as long as they don't need administrative access for anything.

If you plan on setting up the account with parental controls, you can skip the standard account and choose Managed with Parental Controls. This enables parental controls by default. You can also enable parental controls in a standard account.

A Sharing Only account is just for remote Macs to be able to log on and transfer files. You can't actually log on to a sharing-only account on the Mac and run applications or do anything else.

Parental Controls

When you have an account that is either Standard or Managed with Parental Controls, you can go to the Parental Controls preferences to take charge of it. You must go there using an administrator account, and then you will see a list of non-administrator accounts on the left. Select one and click Enable Parental Controls to go to the next step.

Figure 22.7 shows the initial part of the parental controls preferences. There are several tabs, including System, Content, Mail & iChat, Time Limits, and Logs. There are tons of options in each category.

Figure 22.7

The Parental Controls preferences are extensive with tons of options.

SYSTEM CONTROLS

In the System Controls preferences, you can choose whether the user gets to use the regular Finder, or a simplified version of the Finder. You can also choose to allow the user to run only certain applications. For instance, you can allow only non-Internet applications, or allow everything except for iChat.

You can also select from a variety of controls at the bottom, like whether they can burn CDs or change their password.

CONTENT CONTROLS

Under Content, you can choose one of three settings for Safari. The first is to allow everything. The second is to use built-in filters to try to stop the user from visiting adult websites. When you choose this, you can add specific sites to the list, and also set some sites to be allowed.

The third option is to allow access only to specific websites and that's it. This could be useful for the youngest users, or children who are supposed to only use the computer to access sites for homework.

MAIL AND CHAT CONTROLS

You can use this category to allow the user to send or receive email only from people in a specific list. You can do the same for iChat.

Of course, if they can access a web-based email site like Yahoo or Gmail, they may be able to get around this easily. At the same time, with chat, if they can install and run their own chat application, they can get around the restrictions placed on iChat. They can even visit a website that lets them chat without a specific application. So you want to make sure you have all of the other options locked down.

TIME LIMITS

If you need to limit the amount of time your child spends on the computer, you can set separate weekday and weekend time limits.

You can also set a specific bedtime so the Mac can't be used during certain hours.

> There are ways to get around all of these restrictions for enterprising young minds. So it is probably best to use a combination of parental controls and other parenting techniques if you really want to control your child's computer and Internet access.

LOGS

Another option, besides control, is to set up logging for the account. This logs every website visited, application run, and each chat session.

The child with the account may not even know he or she is being logged, so this is a good option if you want to monitor, but not control.

Desktop Backgrounds and Screen Savers

You can customize the look of your desktop with the Desktop & Screen Saver preference pane, shown in Figure 22.8. It has two categories, one for desktop background and the other for screen saver choices.

Desktop Backgrounds

Apple gives you a collection of background images to use in several categories. You can also pick out images from your iPhoto collection and folders on your hard drive. By default, the Picture folder is listed, but by using the + button at the bottom of the list on the left allows you to add more folders to the list.

You can then select an image on the right to be your desktop background. Or you can select a folder on the left and then click the Change Picture option at the bottom and set a time. This rotates the images between the pictures in the selected folder.

If you want to set up your own group of images to use for a rotation like this, just create a special folder in your Documents or Pictures folder and load that new folder up with images. Then, in the preferences, click the + button to add it to the list on the left. Then select that folder in the list and the Change Picture option at the bottom. Also choose Random if you want the images to be shown in random rather than sequential order.

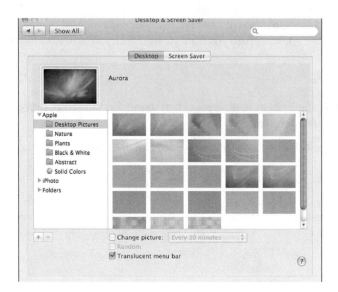

Figure 22.8

You can select different backgrounds or pictures to use as your desktop.

Screen Saver

Displays today don't have to deal with screen burn like the old CRT displays of the past. But people still like screen savers.

You can select from a variety of odd and unusual screen savers, and set a time for the screen saver to kick in. Most of the screen savers have options to choose from as well. And you can add a clock to any screen saver as a bonus.

You can even choose Use Random Screen Saver to get a variety.

> Most screen savers are useless fun, just something to color up your cubicle or home office when someone walks by and you aren't there. But the RSS Visualizer under the Apple category takes headlines from RSS feeds from some predefined locations, or one that you specify, and displays them. So your screen saver could be showing you interesting tidbits of world news, blog postings, or someone's Twitter feed.

Common Customizations

The System Preferences have a number of common customizations hidden in different panels. Let's take a look at several of them.

Languages

In the Language tab of the Language & Text preferences you get to choose which languages are available on your Mac. You can see this pane in Figure 22.9.

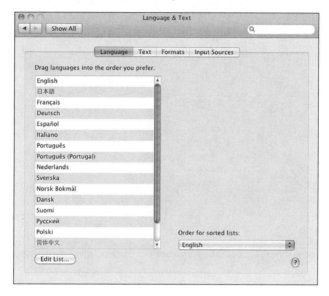

Figure 22.9

In Mac OS X 10.6 (Snow Leopard) this is the Language & Text preferences, but in earlier versions of Mac OS X it was the International preferences.

Other languages will sometimes come into play when you are using applications that have interfaces designed for multiple languages. For instance, all of the menu items and button labels might be available in several languages and automatically display the one that is first in your list.

In this pane you get to choose which languages are active on your Mac. You also get to order them so that if an application supports more than one language, it knows which one you prefer.

Number and Date Formatting

Does "3/8/2009" mean March 8th, 2009 or August 3rd, 2009? Different countries order their dates differently and Mac OS X allows you to go either way. In the Language & Text preferences, under Formats, you have choices you can make about dates, times, and numbers. Figure 22.10 shows the Formats preferences.

This window gives you a lot of control through the Customize buttons on the right. For instance, you can come up with your own custom way to display the date or time. Changes will be reflected in a variety of Mac programs and controls.

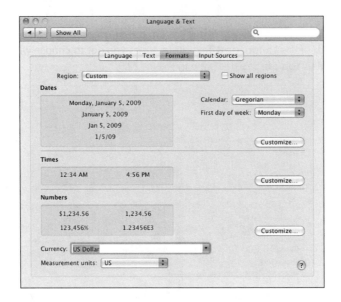

Figure 22.10

The Formats preference pane is the solution to frustration when your dates and numbers don't seem to be shown correctly.

Security

You can further lock down your Mac with the Security preference pane. Under the General category, you can require the password for your account when the computer wakes from sleep or the screen saver.

If you are using an administrator account, there are also other steps you can take. For instance, you can disable automatic login for all accounts, require a password to change any system preferences, and automatically log out accounts after a period of inactivity.

FileVault

Another selection under Security preferences is FileVault. What this does is to encrypt the entire home directory for that user. So every file, preference, library item, email, and other bits of information are stored on the hard drive completely scrambled and unable to be read by anyone who is not logged in to that account with the password.

This is an extreme measure of security, and it has its drawbacks. Decrypting each file as you need it can slow down your Mac, especially for things like watching or editing videos, or anything that needs to access large files fast.

> **NOTE**
>
> If you have a regular account and you forget your password, there are ways a Mac expert can get to your files. It's not easy, but it can be done. But if you turn on FileVault, your files are encrypted and no one can get to them without the password. So it is critical that you don't forget your password. Use a secure password, by all means, but consider writing it down or storing it somewhere that is secure as a backup plan.

But if you are in a situation where you have very sensitive and important data, and your Mac is vulnerable to being stolen, you may want to consider this.

Spotlight

In Chapter 5, "Working With Files and Folders," in the section "Searching for Files," you learned how to use Spotlight to search for anything and everything on your Mac. Well, you can customize your Spotlight experience with the Spotlight pane in the system preferences.

Here, you can specify where Spotlight should restrict its searches. For instance, you can tell it to never search for music, movies, or fonts if you have a lot of those but never need to see them in a Spotlight search.

You can also specify locations where Spotlight should not look in the Privacy section of the Spotlight preferences. This can be useful for privacy, but you can also use it to speed up searches. For instance, if you have a folder with a million data files for a business project, you can add that to the list so that Spotlight will ignore those files.

CDs and DVDs

So when you insert a blank disk into the optical drive, your Mac will automatically react. You can pick your default reaction in this preference pane. You can set it to open the disk in the Finder, open iTunes, or open the Disk Utility program. You can also select another application or even run a script.

My favorite choice, however, is "Ignore." That way you can insert a blank disk and then run a program to handle it yourself.

You can also make choices here about what to do when music CDs or video DVDs are inserted. For instance, you can have it launch the DVD player automatically.

Display and Computer Sleeping Habits

Using the Energy Saver control panel, you can set how long your computer will wait without any action before it shuts off the monitor and goes to sleep.

If you are using a MacBook, you can customize your settings according to whether the battery is being used, or if the computer is plugged in.

Putting the display to sleep is different than using a screen saver, and it is really why screen savers are just eye candy now. It is better to turn your screen off completely and save energy and the light inside the screen. The LCD screens in all iMacs and MacBooks today turn on just as fast as they can wake from sleep.

Mouse and Trackpad

In the Keyboard & Mouse pane, in the Mouse or Trackpad category, you've got settings that determine how fast the mouse tracks, the time between clicks for two clicks to be considered a "double click," and a few other things.

This pane changes depending on what type of pointing device you have connected. You could have a single-button mouse, a multi-button mouse, a Mighty Mouse with a scroll ball in it, a MacBook trackpad, and so on. Even the trackpads come in all sorts of different flavors, with the most recent MacBooks able to recognize multi-touch gestures.

This is definitely one preference pane you want to visit and experiment with to see which setting would optimize your personal style.

Keyboard Shortcuts

Another pane to be aware of is the Keyboard Shortcuts pane, also in the Keyboard & Mouse preferences. This is where you can set up your own keyboard shortcuts for a variety of tasks.

NOTE

Sometimes, as with Adobe software, there are conflicts between keyboard shortcuts. F5 might be used for one thing by Mac OS X and another by the application. In those cases, you can usually remap the shortcut in the application in its own preferences window. Or, you can remap the keyboard shortcut here in the system preferences if the application's shortcut is more important to you.

Date and Time

The Date & Time preference pane, shown in Figure 22.11, contains a variety of options as to how the time is displayed on your Mac, the current time and date, and even how the time can be set automatically.

Unless your Mac isn't hooked up to the Internet at all, you should select a time server to use to make sure your clock stays in sync with reality. The digital clocks inside computers tend to run a little fast or slow if left alone.

You can also go to the Time Zone category and choose your local town so your Mac knows its time zone.

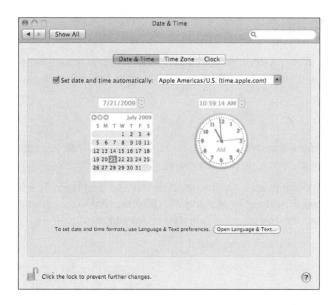

Figure 22.11

The Date & Time preferences allow you to choose to set the time using an Internet server.

The third category, Clock, lets you determine how the clock will appear in the menu bar at the top of your desktop. You can use a digital or analog clock, and a variety of options, like whether it shows AM and PM. You can even choose to have time announced every so often by a computerized voice.

Universal Access

The Universal Access preference pane is really meant to help people who have sight or hearing issues. You can zoom in on the screen, turn on VoiceOver to have text on the screen read to you, and make a variety of screen adjustments.

But some of these items can also be used by those with perfect sight to simply make using your Mac easier.

For instance, the screen zoom functionality can be useful for artists to be able to close in on pixels for exact editing. It can also be useful for giving over-the-shoulder presentations to people at your desk.

In the Hearing category, you can turn on Flash the Screen When an Alert Sound Occurs if you often find yourself turning down the volume to zero while at work or in a public space.

In the Mouse category, you can turn on Mouse Keys, which allows you to use the numeric keypad to move the cursor. This could come in handy in situations where your mouse is malfunctioning.

Third-Party Utilities

In addition to all of the ways in which you can customize your Mac with built-in Mac OS X preferences and settings, there are some third-party utilities and modifications you might like to check out.

iStat

If you like to know more about everything going on inside your Mac, you can monitor temperature sensors, fan speeds, and even processor usage with something called iStat.

It comes in three different flavors: iStat Menus, iStat Pro, and iStat Nano. The first one puts all the information you need in the menu bar, along with a System preferences pane to customize which bits of info you see. The other two are dashboard widgets.

They are all free, but a donation is requested.

> http://islayer.com

smcFanControl

If you are using a MacBook, you probably know that they can get hot. If you want to cool it down more, it is just a matter of telling the internal fans to spin up a little faster.

You can take control of these fans with smcFanControl, another free menu bar addition that you can download.

> http://homepage.mac.com/holtmann/eidac/

Jumpcut and ClipMenu

Cut, copy, and paste have been around since the dawn of the Mac and they work essentially the same way. But with Jumpcut or ClipMenu you can super-charge the process by storing multiple clipboard items.

You just cut and copy as you would normally, and the last 10 or so items will appear in a menu bar pull-down. So, for instance, you could copy three items, and then recall each one of those to paste them in later on. ClipMenu is a more advanced utility with some more advanced features like the ability to use images as well as text, and you can create some permanent items that will always be available to paste from ClipMenu's menu.

These are both free and open source Mac OS X extensions to the Finder.

> http://jumpcut.sourceforge.net/
>
> http://www.clipmenu.com/

TypeIt4Me

Another productivity enhancer is TypeIt4Me, a system extension that will monitor your keystrokes and replace what you type with something else.

For instance, I can set it to replace "mgsm" with "The MacMost.com Guide to Switching to the Mac," which could save me a lot of time because I need to type that pretty often.

> http://ettoresoftware.com/

Spirited Away

A very simple free system extension is Spirited Away. The concept is that when you are not using an application, it will automatically hide it for you.

This is great for people like me who use a lot of applications at once, so much so that my displays always look cluttered. It makes it easier to concentrate on the task at hand if you are only viewing the application you are currently using.

> http://drikin.com/spiritedaway/

Choosy

If you like to use both Safari and Firebox browsers, you may have trouble deciding which should be your default. Choosy allows you to choose which browser you want to use each time the decision needs to be made.

For instance, if you get a link in email that takes you to a PDF file on the Web, you can choose to open that file in Safari because it handles PDF files so well.

> http://www.choosyosx.com

More Dashboard Widgets

Of course, talk of customizing your Mac with third-party programs will eventually lead to Dashboard widgets. Thousands of them are available, from useless eye candy to useful gadgets. And they are pretty much all free.

You can browse through a directory of Dashboard widgets at the Apple website:

> http://www.apple.com/downloads/dashboard/

At MacMost.com there is a page with recommended Mac applications, utilities, and extensions with new items added every week:

> http://macmost.com/recommendations/

WHO SHOULD READ THIS CHAPTER:

Unless you already feel that you know enough to keep your
Mac's OS, software, and hardware updated, read on to find out
more about keeping your Mac current.

23

Keeping Your Mac Up to Date

Caring for your Mac means keeping it up to date. You need to keep
your copy of Mac OS X current with free software updates from
Apple. You also need to check for free updates of any other software
you buy from other companies.

Sometimes these updates offer new features, but usually they are
bug fixes. Occasionally they are critical updates that prevent viruses
or fix flaws in the software.

You can also update your Mac itself, with new hardware such as
memory or larger hard disks.

Using Software Update

The primary way to keep your Mac and its software updated is to use
the built-in Software Update feature. Just choose Software Update
from the Apple menu at the upper-left corner of your screen.

Running Software Update

Immediately Software Update connects to Apple's servers and looks
for new updates to download. This may take a few minutes because
it needs to check through your system for all software that you have
installed, such as iWork, Final Cut, or any other Apple-made software.
Then it asks the server to compare your versions of the software with
the updates it has in its database.

There are no acceptable excuses when it comes to software updates. You really need to do them to keep your Mac secure and working properly. If you don't have a permanent Internet connection, make sure you take opportunities to connect to the net in some way to run Software Update whenever you can. One of the reasons that Windows computers are so unreliable and virus-infected is that so many Windows users ignore their system updates. Apple has done a better job of getting their users to do the right thing. Be a part of it!

The primary thing that Software Update does, however, is look for Mac OS X updates. These could be major updates, like version 10.6.1 to 10.6.2, or they can be component-specific updates like a new sub-version of QuickTime or new printer drivers.

Figure 23.1 shows the Software Update window when it has finished searching.

Sometimes you will get more information about the update. In Figure 23.1, for example, the QuickTime update includes more information as well as links to documents online that you can read if you are interested.

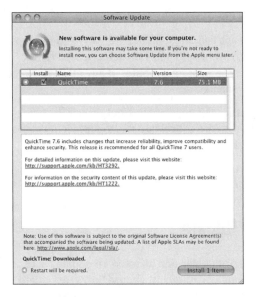

Figure 23.1

This update includes some information and links.

Installing Updates

The good news is that Software Update pretty much takes care of everything for you. You just have to allow its actions. So in Figure 23.1 it is essentially asking you if it is okay for you to install this update.

Answer yes by clicking the Install 1 Item button. If you are too busy at the moment, click the Not Now button to return to Software Update later.

In most cases you will be asked for your account password to continue. This is an extra security measure, as no software is allowed to make changes to your system without asking first.

> If you are having trouble with Software Update, check to make sure you are logged in as an administrator. If you are the only user and this is the only account, you should be. Otherwise, if there are multiple accounts, make sure you log in as one of the administrator accounts occasionally to run Software Update.

Next, you will get a progress bar followed by a message that the update was installed successfully.

Sometimes you will be required to restart your computer, as in Figure 23.1. There is a little message on the bottom of the window that reads "Restart will be required."

This happens if the update has affected core operating system tasks. In these situations the update needs to basically shut down your system to complete the update. Sometimes you will even notice your Mac restarting twice in succession—the first time to install the update and the second time to reboot so that you can use your Mac with the changes in place.

When Software Update is done, it will usually run a second check for new software. This is because some updates rely on other updates being installed first.

Software Update Preferences

When Software Update is done running, it remains open with some menu choices. This is how you can change the Software Update options.

Figure 23.2 shows the first pane of the Software Update preferences that you get by choosing Software Update, Preferences. Alternatively, you can change these settings without running Software Update at all, but instead looking for the preferences in the System Preferences application.

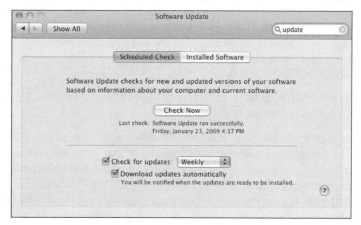

Figure 23.2

You can set how often you want Software Update to automatically check for updates in the Software Updates preferences.

In addition to being able to set the check time to Daily, Weekly, or Monthly, you can also set it to download updates automatically. This means that they will be downloaded in the background so that they will be ready to install when Software Update notifies you. If you are on a slow or nonpermanent connection, you may want to turn this setting off.

You can also see on this screen when Software Update last ran. And you can force it to run again by clicking the button.

The second tab, labeled Installed Software, will give you a list of things that you have recently installed.

Update Options

When you see the list of software to install, as in Figure 23.1, you don't have to just accept and install all software right at that moment. You can uncheck any piece of software that you want to hold until next time.

For instance, if you are desperately awaiting an iTunes update, and you see that a large printer driver update is available at the same time, you can uncheck the printer driver and just do the iTunes update.

In addition, you can select an item in the list and choose Update, Ignore Update. This permanently holds off on that update. It puts the item in a list that you can return to later if you change your mind.

> **NOTE**
>
> Why would you want to ignore a software update? Usually, you wouldn't. But users of some advanced software such as Final Cut Studio may hear that some of their third-party extensions are not quite ready for the new version of Final Cut, so they may want to hold off on that update until later. Another reason might be that the update really doesn't affect you and the bandwidth is at a premium. For instance, the Samsung printer update in Figure 23.1 doesn't really apply to you if you don't have a Samsung printer. However, if you have the time and bandwidth you should install all relevant updates even if you don't think you need them right now. You never know what other things a seemly useless printer update could improve on your Mac.

If you choose to ignore some updates and you later regret it, you can choose Reset Ignored Updates from the Software Update menu.

In the Update menu you can also choose Download Only, Install, and Install and Keep Package. You would use the first option, Download Only, if you have time to download the update now, but don't want to install it until you are done with some of your current computing tasks. You would use the second option, Install, if the update has already been downloaded, and you now want to install it. The last option, Install and Keep Package, keeps the installers for the software around. This is handy if you have more than one Mac. You can then take these installers and run them on another Mac. The files are shown to you in a Finder window by Software Update after they are downloaded.

Third-Party Software Updates

Software Update will keep your OS X and your Apple software up to date, but it does nothing for your third-party software. Some third-party programs, like applications from Adobe and Google, feature their own software update functions, always on the lookout and notifying you when new versions are available.

But other software only checks when you launch it, prompting you to download the update when it finds something new.

And then some software won't check at all, leaving it up to you to remember to go to the website and see if your version is still current.

Almost any software you install on your Mac has an About menu item in the application menu. Figure 23.3 shows one example.

Figure 23.3

The About box for Panic's Transmit FTP software shows the version number and has a link to the website.

In the About box is usually also a link to the website for the software. If not, you can usually find the website for the software by searching or looking at the documentation.

At the website, you should be able to find the current version number for the software. You may want to bookmark these pages for software you own.

> **NOTE**
>
> Just because you didn't update to the latest version of the software doesn't mean there isn't a new sub-version for you to download. For instance, you may be using version 2.0 while paid upgrade 3.0 comes and goes. (You didn't think it was worth the upgrade price). But there could possibly still be a version 2.1 released if a major flaw in 2.0 is uncovered. It is unlikely, but worth looking out for.

Sometimes software also has a Check for Updates menu choice in the application menu. This will do some of the work for you by checking online for an update. Figure 23.4 shows an example.

An updated version of Transmit is available!

Transmit 3.6.7 fixes a number of little things to polish Transmit even further. This update is recommended for all users, and is free for Transmit 3 owners. To upgrade, download the new version and replace your existing copy with it.

Would you like to download the new version?

Ignore   Remind Later   Go To Download Site

Figure 23.4
When you go to Transmit, Check for Updates, the software checks its own server for the current version and gives you some instructions to update the software.

Some software goes as far as downloading the update and installing it for you, restarting itself as part of the process. Other software just downloads an updater and lets you run it at your own leisure.

 NOTE

There is also a website you can go to that all Mac experts have been using for years. It is Version Tracker: http://www.versiontracker.com/.

This site, originally built specifically for Macs, lists just about every piece of software ever available for the Mac. You can find out what the most recent version of the application is, and visit the company's home page. It is also a great site for finding new Mac software.

Upgrading Mac OS X

Apple gives you free updates for the version of Mac OS X that came with your Mac. For instance, if you bought your Mac with Mac OS X 10.6, you will be able to use Software Update to get 10.6.1, 10.6.2, and so on.

But eventually a whole new major version of Mac OS X will come out and Apple will expect you to pay for it. Since version 10.2 Apple hasn't offered upgrade pricing either, meaning that a new version costs the same no matter what version of OS X you are currently running.

This makes sense since all Macs come with Mac OS X installed, so technically any purchase of an OS X box is an upgrade.

Determining when a new version of Mac OS X has been released is usually not a problem, as Apple's marketing department's job is to make sure everyone knows. But you will also get occasional emails from Apple to the email address you used to register your Mac. Visiting http://www.apple.com/macosx/ also gives you the low-down.

When a new version does arrive, it's hard to say what the upgrade process will be like any more than predicting anything else in the future. But past upgrades have included several options.

The first is to leave your applications and data intact and simply update your OS. If all goes well, you'll find everything just as before, except that the Finder and other parts of Mac OS X will be new. However, it is possible that older software that you haven't updated, or software that third-party developers have not yet updated, will cease to function properly.

If you have some critical software that you absolutely must be able to use, be sure to check the developer's website to see if it is compatible with the new Mac OS X.

> Adobe, in particular, has been bad about supporting new versions of Mac OS X. Usually the software works anyway, but they will not claim official support for the new OS until they release the next version of that software. You may want to check user groups and forums to see if any one has reported having problems with software like this using the new Mac OS X.

Similar to the upgrade option is an Archive and Install option, though it may be called something else in future versions of Mac OS X. This type of upgrade takes your existing Mac OS X system folder and renames it. Then it installs a clean new version of Mac OS X. It also leaves your applications and documents alone.

Another option is to wipe your hard drive clean and start from scratch. You will, of course, need to back up or archive any data you have first. Then, after starting from scratch you need to reinstall your applications and restore your data.

Some users do prefer this method, however, as it gives them a clean start with the new version of the OS.

So far, each Mac OS X install disk is a bootable DVD-ROM that comes with a copy of Disk Utility. When you first boot up using that DVD, you can skip out of the installation at the start and go to Disk Utility instead.

From there, you can erase, verify, repair, and even repartition your hard drive if you want. This would usually be the first step to starting from scratch with a new version of Mac OS X.

Most people will probably want to simply follow the upgrade path.

Upgrading Your Hardware

You can keep the same Mac, and the same OS and all your files, but still make your Mac a little better by upgrading some of your hardware. You can upgrade memory, for instance, as well as your hard drive. Let's look at some of the most common hardware upgrades.

Upgrading Your Memory

This is the most common type of upgrade. You can buy more memory from various sources, including the Apple Store. Chances are that your Mac came with only about half the maximum amount of memory it can use.

DO YOU NEED MORE?

One way to see if more memory will help your Mac's performance is to run the Activity Monitor application, found in your Utilities folder. Select the System Memory tab at the bottom and see how much of your current memory is being used. It should look like Figure 23.5.

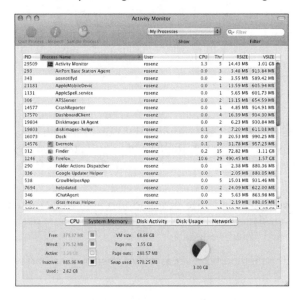

Figure 23.5

The red and yellow (free and wired) indicators show you how much memory is being used.

Make sure you have your typical applications open when looking at the Activity Monitor results. For instance, if you use Photoshop all the time, have Photoshop open and use it while testing.

If you think that more memory is in order, the next step is to find out what type of memory your Mac uses. Run another utility that comes with your Mac, called System Profiler. Click on the Hardware tab in the left sidebar and then select Memory. You should see a display like the one in Figure 23.6.

This look through System Profiler tells you two things. First, it shows you what type of memory you have and at what speed it runs. You'll need these bits of data when shopping for more memory.

Second, it tells you how many slots you have and what is in them now.

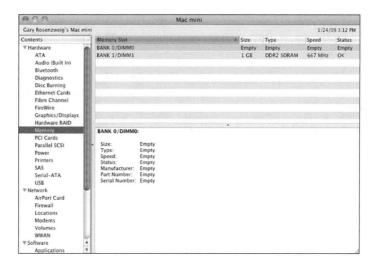

Figure 23.6

The System Profiler indicates that one memory slot is empty and the other has a 1GB stick of DDR SDRAM running at 667 MHz.

For instance, if you have two slots and they both contain 1GB of memory, to get any more you will have to remove one and replace it with a new stick with more memory. For instance, you could replace the first 1GB stick with a 2GB one for a total of 3GB, including the other 1GB stick you are leaving in place. Or you could replace both 1GB sticks with two new 2GB sticks for a total of 4GB.

> Remember that there is a difference between memory and hard drive storage. Your hard drive stores all of your data, programs, and Mac OS X. When running, your Mac temporarily loads required data from storage into memory for faster access.

WHERE TO BUY

You may not need to worry so much about what type of memory your Mac needs because some websites that discuss Mac memory will advise you based on your Mac model.

Apple.com, for instance, starts you out by asking which model of Mac you have. Then it displays only memory that works in that computer.

After you know which type of memory you need and how much you would like, the next step is to hit the Web and determine how much memory you can get for your Mac, and how expensive it is.

For instance, you may want to replace both sticks of your Mac Mini with 8GB each. But in reality, the Mac Mini you have may only be able to handle 2GB sticks.

Apple.com's site only seems to sell memory for the most recent Macs. In addition, it doesn't do a very good job of telling you what you can get for your Mac. To top it off, it is often the most expensive place to buy memory.

There are several other places where you can buy Mac memory and get advice on the maximum amount you can have. Check out this special page that will be updated regularly with links to Mac memory vendors:

> http://macmost.com/buying-more-memory-for-your-mac.html

INSTALLING NEW MEMORY

There are almost as many ways to install new memory as there have been different models of Macs. Apple includes some tutorials at Apple.com, but only for some machines. Other tutorials are done by third-party websites.

You can check out this page for links to many tutorials on upgrading your Mac's memory:

> http://macmost.com/installing-memory-in-your-mac.html

Of course the other option is to have new memory installed for you by a computer repair shop or Apple store that is certified at Mac repairs. If the tutorial online looks a little bit scary, you may want to consider this. Some local shops will put the memory in your Mac for free as long as you purchase it from them.

Upgrading Your Hard Drive

Memory is one of the few internal parts of your Mac that you can upgrade with Apple's blessing. Anything else is at your own risk, and, as the saying goes, will void your warranty.

But Macs do use standard hard drives that can be replaced with one you purchase online or in a store. As your Mac gets older, the hard drive is likely to be the part that gives out first, as it has the most moving parts.

Of course if you are still covered by AppleCare, you should have Apple replace the drive. Otherwise, look for a repair shop that specializes in Mac repairs.

Another reason to replace the hard drive is to get a larger one. In the case of a Mac Pro, you might not even want to replace the original drive but simply add a second one instead. There is plenty of room in the box for that.

Installing your own new hard drive definitely takes some skill. So only do it if you feel you are experienced enough with computer hardware, or the Mac is old enough that you don't mind losing it completely if you mess up.

Here is a web page with updated information and links to tutorials on how to install your own hard drive, and services that will do it for you.

> http://macmost.com/upgrading-your-mac-hard-drive.html

If you are replacing a hard drive, you need to get your data from the old drive to the new one. Mac OS X's backup tool, Time Machine, is the perfect tool for this. Make sure your backup is complete and up to date before removing the old drive. Then after installing the new one, you can boot with your Mac OS X installation disk and choose to use a Time Machine backup to restore your system. See Chapter 24, "Backing Up and Archiving Your Files," for more information on using Time Machine.

If it works, it is a perfect situation. You get all of your applications and documents back, just the way you left them.

Video Cards and Other Upgrades

If you have a Mac Pro, you have several ways to upgrade your Mac that are not easily available to other Mac owners. The most obvious one is the video card.

Whereas on other Mac systems the video card is actually a part of the Mac hardware—the motherboard is the old-fashioned term—on the Mac Pro the video card is actually a card. You can open your Mac Pro and pull out the card and swap it with another. You can also add a second, third, or fourth video card. In fact, with cards that can drive two monitors at once, you can have up to eight monitors hooked up to your Mac Pro if you fill all the card slots.

Apple usually lists the video cards that they sell with the Mac Pro as separate purchases that you can buy. So if you bought your Mac Pro with the default card and want to upgrade to something faster and more powerful, you can find it there. The price may not always be the best, though, so you may want to shop around.

To install a new video card in a Mac Pro is just a matter of opening the case and inserting the new card in place of the old one.

You can also add other PCI-compatible cards to your Mac Pro, providing there are software drives for Mac OS X. One example would be a professional audio card.

Anything other than memory or a video card can be a difficult install. Unless you really know what you are doing, you want to leave other upgrades to professional repair shops that know Macs well.

Some companies will upgrade your Mac's processor, for instance.

WHO SHOULD READ THIS CHAPTER:

Every Mac user should have a backup plan. Unless you are already using Time Machine or something else to back up all your data, you should definitely read this chapter. It could be the most important one.

24

Backing Up and Archiving Your Files

Imagine what it would mean to you right now if you suddenly lost all your files on your Mac's hard drive. Everything. All your files, contacts, emails, browser bookmarks, word processing documents, spreadsheets, iMovie projects, photos, and music.

It could happen. Something as simple as a minor defect in your hard drive could do it. Not to mention a catastrophe like a fire or theft. Having a good backup plan can turn these disasters into merely minor annoyances.

Using Time Machine

There are two types of backups: local and remote. Time Machine is the backup software that comes with your Mac, and it does local backups to an external hard drive.

Backing Up with Time Machine

To use Time Machine, you will first need to acquire an external hard drive. This can be a simple USB2 hard drive, as long as it is larger in size than your internal drive. So if you have a 320GB internal drive, look for at least a 500GB external drive for Time Machine backups, if not something larger. Fortunately, these can now be found for less than $100 and, as a backup solution, they are worth every penny.

> **NOTE**
>
> You can go with a smaller hard drive if you are more selective about what you back up. For instance, if you only back up your user folder, and you are not playing with huge media files like videos all the time, your backup will be significantly smaller. However, you will not be able to use some of the features of a Time Machine backup, like a total hard drive restoration.

Another option is to use a Time Capsule. This is a product from Apple that is a combination of an Airport Extreme base station and a hard drive. The hard drive is meant specifically for Time Machine backups. However, it will take much longer to back up over a wireless network to a Time Capsule than it will to a USB2 drive.

To set up Time Machine to start making backups to a new USB2 drive, follow these steps:

1. Plug the drive into your Mac and make sure it comes up in the Finder. Don't worry about the name or contents of the drive—we'll be erasing it shortly.

2. If you have never configured Time Machine before, you may instantly get the dialog shown in Figure 24.1. If so, and you are ready to erase that drive and commit it to being a dedicated Time Machine backup, do it and skip to step 5.

Figure 24.1

Attaching a hard drive for the first time should bring up this message.

3. Go to the System Preferences, Time Machine. If you have never configured Time Machine before, you will be asked to connect and select an external hard drive, as in Figure 24.2.

4. Click the Select Backup Disk button and pick a drive. Remember, whatever drive you choose will be erased and used 100% from now on as only a backup drive.

5. Back in the Time Machine preferences, select Options. The only real options you have are to select drives, folders, or files to not back up.

> **NOTE**
>
> The first time Time Machine backs up your data, prepare for a long wait. It can take hours or even all night to back up gigs of data to a drive. You can always use the Time Machine menu bar pull-down to stop a backup if it is getting in the way of your work. Time Machine will simply try again an hour later.

Figure 24.2

You've got to select a hard disk for Time Machine to be able to do anything.

Time Machine works best when you tell it to simply back up your entire internal hard drive. This way, you can completely restore your drive if anything goes wrong.

Recovering with Time Machine

Imagine that your hard drive crashes. You go to the local computer store and buy another one. You can have it installed, or install it yourself.

Then you insert your Mac OS X install disk in the optical drive and boot the Mac with that. One of your very first options is to restore the contents of the drive from a Time Machine backup. You select that, hook up your external drive with the backup, and you can get your entire computer back: data, applications, mail, photos, preferences, everything!

The other way to use Time Machine is simply to recover an older copy of a file you are working on. For instance, say you are preparing a presentation. You're working on it in Keynote over several days.

Yesterday you got inspired to make everything hot pink and use a font called Racecar Deluxe, along with pictures of snakes. Then you wake up today and realize that this is the wrong direction to go for a presentation on life insurance.

Reverting to the file you used the day before yesterday is fairly easy if you have been running Time Machine.

Start by going to the folder on your drive with the presentation file. Then choose the Time Machine icon in the upper right, in the menu bar. Choose Enter Time Machine.

You'll next get a complete makeover of your entire screen. Sit back and enjoy the show. The end result will look something like Figure 24.3.

Figure 24.3
The Time Machine browser is definitely the most bizarre interface in Mac OS X.

The way you navigate in Time Machine is to use the two 3D arrows to the right of the center window. You can go back and forth in time to look at older versions of the folder. You'll need to go back for anything to really work, because you start off looking at the current state of the folder, with the current versions of the file in it. You can also click on the timeline on the right to jump right to a specific backup.

When you find a file you want to restore, select it. Then you will be able to click the Restore button all the way at the bottom-right corner.

If the file exists in your current folder, you will be asked if you want to replace the newer one, keep both, or keep the original. If the file doesn't exist currently, Time Machine places the old file back into your current folder.

You can, of course, choose multiple files and even whole folders to restore.

Backing Up with MobileMe

Having a local backup is a great way to protect against hard drive failure or user error like accidentally throwing a file away. But only a remote backup protects you from things like fire or theft.

Of course, you could simply make Time Machine backups to multiple drives and store one in another location, like a friend or relative's house. But you could also back up some of your data to an online service like MobileMe.

When you subscribe to the MobileMe service, you get some remote storage space called your iDisk. You can use this as another drive by connecting to it in the Finder by choosing Go, iDisk.

Another benefit of MobileMe is that you also get access to a program called Backup. This can be found on your iDisk in a folder named "Software." Download it to your Mac by dragging it to your Applications folder.

NOTE

In a way, Backup has been replaced by Time Machine. As of this writing, it hasn't been updated since 2007. It may be on its way out. The fact that it has so many customizable options that Time Machine doesn't have is probably the reason it is still around at all.

There are some third-party applications like EMC Retrospect for Macintosh that have similar functions.

Backup allows you to make backups of specific folders, files, and settings on your Mac. You can back up to an internal or external drive, CD or DVD, or to your iDisk.

When you start Backup, you will be asked to create a new backup process. To back up files to your MobileMe iDisk, choose to use a "Custom" template when Backup starts. Now you've got a lot of say on what you want backed up, when you want the backups to occur, and where the data goes. For instance, Figure 24.4 shows a backup that includes a variety of user data, plus the contents of some folders.

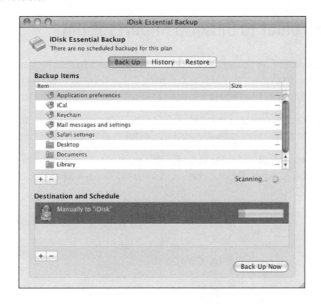

Figure 24.4

This custom backup contains a variety of content to be saved to the iDisk only when requested manually.

You can even have a search used to determine what files get backed up. For instance, you could specify that all .doc files are backed up.

One problem with backing up to both CD/DVD and iDisk is the lack of space for many users. You don't need to be a video editor to run out of space—if you take a lot of photos or store a lot of music, you'll soon find that you simply can't fit it all on a DVD or even your iDisk.

Another issue for an iDisk backup is speed. A super-fast Internet connection is still very slow when compared to USB2 speeds. So getting your files up to your iDisk may take a while.

The good news is that Backup will back up your data incrementally. For instance, if you have 1,000 files to back up, then it backs up 1,000 files the first time you run the backup process. But the second time you run it, it will only add files that have changed. That might just be a fraction of the 1,000 files.

Backup is also a good solution for those who think Time Machine is too much, taking up an entire external drive and running every hour. If you have a small amount of data and want to back up using iDisk or a CD every few days, this is a decent option.

The bad news about Backup is that its future is uncertain. Apple rarely mentions its Time Machine predecessor, so one could theorize that it will eventually be discontinued. If that happens, hopefully some other MobileMe functionality will replace it.

MobileMe already acts as a sort of backup for critical data like contacts and calendar events, since it keeps a copy of these on the server and syncs them to other Macs or devices you have, assuming you use that feature of Mobile Me.

Using a Burn Folder to Back Up Important Data

Burn folders are special Finder folders that contain only aliases to real files and folders on your hard drive. In addition to aliases, you can also burn a CD or DVD of the linked contents of the burn folder by selecting it in the Finder window and clicking the Burn button.

You can use burn folders to create quick data CDs or DVDs for any purpose. But because burn folders contain aliases, not actual files, they are also useful for making periodic backups or archives.

Figure 24.5 shows a typical burn folder used for this purpose. At the bottom of the window you can see the size of disk needed. This example could easily fit on a CD-ROM, but a larger burn folder may require a DVD.

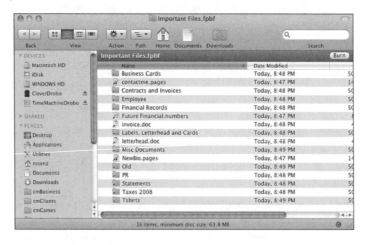

Figure 24.5

This burn folder contains aliases to important files and folders that should be backed up to CD on a regular basis.

For instance, say you had some important documents, like financial spreadsheets, ongoing research papers, and presentations that you are constantly updating. You could create a burn folder and drag and drop these items into it. Aliases linking to these items would be created in the burn folder and you could burn a CD with those files on it.

But then later, as you update those files, the burn folder links to the updated versions of those files. So you can make a CD from that burn folder again and get the new files on the CD. It becomes a quick and easy way to back up important data files.

You can also, of course, use the same technique to burn and reburn CDs with any files that are regularly updated. Say you have a set of spreadsheets that get updated every so often. You could have a burn folder with links to those files and then quickly and easily make CD-ROMs for everyone who needs them, whenever they need them. No need to create a new burn folder every time.

Creating Archives with Disk Utility

Backups are for emergencies. But what about when you want to get rid of something off your hard drive, but want to keep a copy around just in case?

For those who create lots of content—whether it is audio, video, programming, writing, or anything—it is occasionally necessary to archive some old content to make room on your hard drive.

You can do this by burning a CD or DVD. The Disk Utility program that comes with Mac OS X is ideal for archiving. You can find it in the Applications, Utilities folder.

Creating a Disk Image

One way to use Disk Utility is to create disk images. A disk image is a virtual CD or DVD that exists as a single file on your hard drive. It usually has a .dmg extension and can be opened and mounted as if it were a real CD or DVD.

Use the following steps to create a disk image:

1. Run Disk Utility.

2. Click on the New Image button at the top of the window, or choose File, New, Blank Disk Image.

3. Figure 24.6 shows Disk Utility as it is asking for information about the disk image you are about to create. You need to do several things before clicking the Create button.

4. Name the file. Something like MyDisk.dmg will do. Also, choose where it will be saved, just as you would do when saving any document for the first time.

5. Also name the volume. This is what you will see in the Finder once the disk is mounted. You might even want to name it the same thing as the .dmg file, like MyDisk.

6. Choose the volume size. You may want to choose the size of a CD or DVD if you plan on using the disk image to burn one of these. They are both options in the pop-up menu.

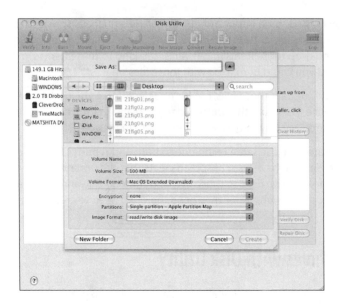

Figure 24.6

Make sure you name both the .dmg file and the volume before creating a disk image.

7. Leave the rest as defaults for now, and click the Create button.

8. It may take a while, but the .dmg file is saved and mounted and an image of it appears on your desktop.

When you have a disk image mounted, you can drag and drop files into it. The actual files are copied to the disk image, just as if you were copying them to an external drive.

When you fill the disk image up, you can unmount it in a number of ways, such as dragging the disk to the trash. Don't drag the .dmg file to the trash—just drag the disk image that appears on your desktop. The .dmg should stay where it is.

Now you have a disk image that contains many files, all existing as one file on your hard drive. This is handy for organizing old projects. For instance, if you have a project that consisted of 500 files of different types, you could store them all in one disk image and they would exist inside that one file, easy to move around and archive by burning it to a CD or DVD.

Burning a Disk Image

A disk image can be burned to CD or DVD from within Disk Utility. It only takes a few steps:

1. Get the disk image to appear inside Disk Utility. The easiest way is to choose File, Open Disk Image from inside Disk Utility.

2. Select the .dmg or the disk image inside it on the left sidebar of Disk Utility.

3. Click the Burn button at the top of Disk Utility, or choose Images, Burn.

4. You'll be asked to insert a disk. Insert one of the proper size to begin.

Disk images are kind of the opposite of burn folders as they never update. The content inside them is an actual copy of the original, so if the original changes, the copy in the disk image stays the same.

For this reason they are good at archiving content, not backing it up.

They are also useful when you are not sure how many copies of a CD-ROM you will need. For instance, if you want to prepare a CD for a meeting, and know you need to burn five copies, but may need more later, create a disk image and burn five copies of it. Keep the disk image around in case you are asked for more later. You can then just reopen the disk image in Disk Utility and burn another copy.

WHO SHOULD READ THIS CHAPTER:

It is easy to not worry about problems until they occur. But problems seem to happen just at the worst possible moment. Read this chapter to familiarize yourself with what can be done when you are having trouble. So if trouble strikes, you are prepared and ready to find a solution.

25

Getting Help

Macs are like any other device, appliance, or tool. From time to time, there are problems. With millions of machines produced each year as efficiently as possible, there are bound to be hardware issues here and there. And with the thousands of ways you can configure, update, and alter your Mac, there are bound to be software issues as well.

So it is important to know what to do when something goes wrong. Much of the time you can find a quick solution online. Other times you'll simply have to take your Mac to an expert for help.

Finding Help Online

The Apple.com website is packed with "how-to" and troubleshooting articles, as well as large and heavily trafficked discussion forums. When you have a specific problem, this should be your very first stop.

Apple.com Knowledgebase

The place to go for support at Apple.com is http://www.apple.com/support/. Figure 25.1 shows this main support page, though its appearance will change and evolve.

Figure 25.1

The Apple.com support homepage at http://www.apple.com/support/ is a place every Mac user should check out for help.

You can divide Apple.com's support sections into two parts: articles and forums. The articles range from short web pages with quick tips and solutions to tutorial videos. They are broken up into different sections, and no longer referred to directly as a "knowledgebase."

Your first step in finding information at the site is to figure out in which category you need help. In most cases this is easy, such as if you are having trouble in a specific application, like Mail, iMovie, or Pages.

But sometimes a problem could be harder to pin down. For instance, if you are having trouble typing in Mail, it could be a problem in Mail, a problem in OS X, or a problem with your keyboard. A good strategy is to look for the list of products in the support section and make a list in your head of all of the categories that could apply. Then start with the most likely candidate.

> **NOTE**
>
> Did you remember to check the Help documentation that is part of every Mac OS X application and the Finder? Those documents represent some of the most common questions that people ask. A lot of searches and support requests are for questions that could be answered in the Help documents. Just go to the Help menu at the top of the screen.

When you drill down into a topic, you will usually see three categories of articles: Troubleshooting, How To, and Top Support Topics. Browse though these to see if your issue is mentioned.

But because the article database is huge, you may want to go right to searching. You can start a search by going to http://www.apple.com/support/ and using the search box at the far upper-right corner of the page. When you type in a term and press Return, you'll get results listed like those in Figure 25.2.

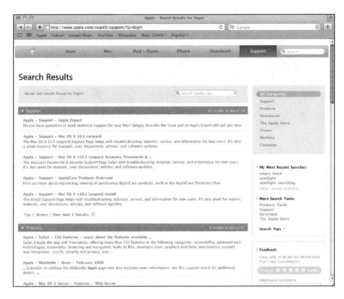

Figure 25.2

Search results appear from all over Apple.com, but Support is listed first if you are already in the support section.

The search results might not all be shown on the page. For instance, in Figure 25.2, you can see "10 results of about 19" in the bar at the top of the support results. You can click on "View next 5 results" to see more.

The support articles are arranged in a variety of ways inside the support site, so sometimes you will end up with an article as a search result, and other times you will end up at a page with a list of more articles. So it might take some detective work to find what you need.

Here is a list of some key pages at Apple.com:

- http://www.apple.com/support/—Main support page
- http://www.apple.com/support/snowleopard/—Snow Leopard general issues and Snow Leopard applications
- http://www.apple.com/support/hardware/—Mac hardware support pages
- http://www.apple.com/support/contact/—Ways to contact Apple for help
- http://discussions.apple.com/ —The discussion forums
- http://www.apple.com/support/contact/phone_contacts.html—List of international Mac support phone numbers

As numerous and as complex as Apple's support pages are, the best information comes from the other part of the site, the discussion forums.

Apple.com Discussions

Discussions can be found at http://discussions.apple.com/. Right away you can see in Figure 25.3 that there is a much more basic, easy-to-use design that makes it quick to find the right forum.

Figure 25.3

The Apple Discussions website is the ultimate Mac community, at least for people having trouble with their Mac.

But you don't need to select a discussion to search. You can just use the Search Discussions box on the upper right to search through all forums.

> You should consider creating a login ID for the forums. You can use the same Apple ID that you use for iTunes, the Apple Store, and other Apple services. Not only can you create a profile, but you can also get alerts when people add replies to topics you are interested in or have contributed to. You can also specify your Mac in your profile so that when you post with an issue, everyone can see which machine you have and tailor their answer to meet your needs.

Discussions are where you will get help for most of your pressing problems. Just be sure to search thoroughly first to see if anyone else has reported the same issue and a solution has already been posted.

The forums are frequented by both Apple personnel and very helpful individuals from all over the world. You can sometimes get a response in minutes, if not hours.

> If you find a genuine bug in Apple software, the Apple discussion lists are a great place to report it. Additionally, you can also go to http://bugreport.apple.com to file a report after you create a free Apple ID or use your MobileMe account ID.

Just be sure to state your problem very clearly. For instance, if you are getting an error message, mention the steps that led up to the error message appearing.

Other Sites and Forums

Apple.com isn't the only place to search for answers to problems. Of course you can always look at MacMost.com to see if there is a video tutorial on the subject. Here are some other sites that can be helpful:

- http://forums.macrumors.com
- http://www.mac-forums.com
- http://forums.macnn.com/
- http://www.insanelymac.com/forum/
- http://forum.maccast.com/

Sometimes the best way to find an answer is to search the whole Internet. A Google search can quickly find the solution to a Mac problem.

AppleCare and the Genius Bar

If you need more help than can be provided online, you'll need to take your Mac to an Apple Store or someone else who can help. For the first year after buying your Mac, you have a service warranty. You can also extend that with AppleCare.

AppleCare

The initial support you get is one year of service coverage. This will help you if your Mac breaks down. Any hardware issue that is a defect you should be able to get repaired for free. There are a lot of reports on the Internet of people getting Macs completely replaced, though Apple is a little more vague about exactly what they will do if you have a problem.

> Thinking of getting AppleCare just in case you drop your MacBook and it breaks? Your initial warranty and AppleCare do not cover accidents. You may want to see if you can add such coverage to your homeowner's or renter's insurance. Or, you can purchase computer accident insurance from a variety of companies.

You also get 90 days of phone support. So you can call Apple if you have a question or a problem.

Beyond that initial period, you can get two additional years of service support and extend your phone support to the same length with the purchase of an AppleCare plan.

You can buy it online at Apple.com or at an Apple store.

> Your initial support and AppleCare covers your Mac hardware, Mac OS X, iLife, and iWork. Any other applications that you purchase from other companies and from Apple will have various levels of support from those companies.

If your Mac stops working, or you have a problem and suspect that the only way to fix it is by having it repaired, you've got several options. The first is to make an appointment at the Apple Store to go to the Genius Bar. You can do that online, assuming you've still got a way to access the Internet. Or, you can drop by the store and make a reservation right on the spot. Then, if the employee can't fix your problem he or she can send it in for repairs.

If you don't live close to an Apple Store you should call the Apple support number. You may be asked to go to a certified Mac repair shop near you, or send your Mac in to Apple through the mail.

The Genius Bar

Taking your Mac in to the nearest Apple Store is the last resort if you are far away, but can be more convenient than other types of support if you are close.

> Genius Bar employees are not your typical computer support staff. They are usually people who had a love of Macs even before coming to work for Apple. Then they get sent to Apple headquarters in Cupertino, California to get two weeks of training and testing. The vast majority of geniuses really know their stuff.

The Genius Bar is Apple's main form of customer support. If you are lucky enough to live close to an Apple Store, you can go to the Genius Bar anytime you want, though you probably want to make an appointment online first.

When it is your turn, you'll be called up to the Genius Bar and an Apple employee will try to help you.

If you are having trouble with your Mac, bring it with you so the genius can work with you on your Mac to solve the problem. That's easy for MacBook users, but a little harder for Mac Pro users.

It doesn't matter if your Mac is still under the original warranty or whether you have purchased AppleCare. You can make an appointment at the Genius Bar for any Mac product—Mac, iPod, iPhone, earbuds, iLife, iWork, displays, Apple TV, and so on.

If you are outside of your warranty or AppleCare period, and your computer needs repairs, you may have to pay. The genius will tell you what your options are.

> **NOTE**
>
> If you are having your Mac repaired by Apple or any other shop, be completely prepared to get it back with the hard drive completely wiped. Even if the problem is not related to the drive, the technician may do it as part of the process. So you should always back up your drive completely using Time Machine or some other method before you take it to the Apple Store.

Using the Genius Bar doesn't cost anything for the initial consultation. But you can pay $99 per year for Apple ProCare at http://www.apple.com/retail/procare/. This gets you faster service at the Genius Bar, faster repair services, and a few other benefits.

Apple Support from a Distance

What if there is no Apple Store near you or your Mac is broken?

One route is to look for other authorized retailers in your area that also offer Mac service. You can check your local phone books or look online. You can also look at http://www.apple.com/buy/locator/service/ and put your zip code into the search box. This gives you a list of official Apple service centers.

You can also try to hire an individual consultant to help you. Consultants are usually top-notch experts who can give you one-on-one service, but at a price. You can go to http://consultants.apple.com and see if there is a consultant near you that can help.

From online forums, to Apple geniuses, to independent shops and consultants, there are many options to choose from when you need help. In addition you can also go to http://macmost.com/contact to ask questions and make suggestions for future video podcast episodes and tutorials.

Index

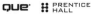

FREE Online Edition

Your purchase of **MacMost.com Guide to Switching to the Mac** includes access to a free online edition for 45 days through the Safari Books Online subscription service. Nearly every Que book is available online through Safari Books Online, along with more than 5,000 other technical books and videos from publishers such as Cisco Press, Exam Cram, IBM Press, O'Reilly, Prentice Hall, Addison-Wesley Professional, and Sams.

SAFARI BOOKS ONLINE allows you to search for a specific answer, cut and paste code, download chapters, and stay current with emerging technologies.

Activate your FREE Online Edition at www.informit.com/safarifree

> **STEP 1:**   Enter the coupon code: KBFHTZG.

> **STEP 2:**   New Safari users, complete the brief registration form.
>   Safari subscribers, just log in.

If you have difficulty registering on Safari or accessing the online edition, please e-mail customer-service@safaribooksonline.com